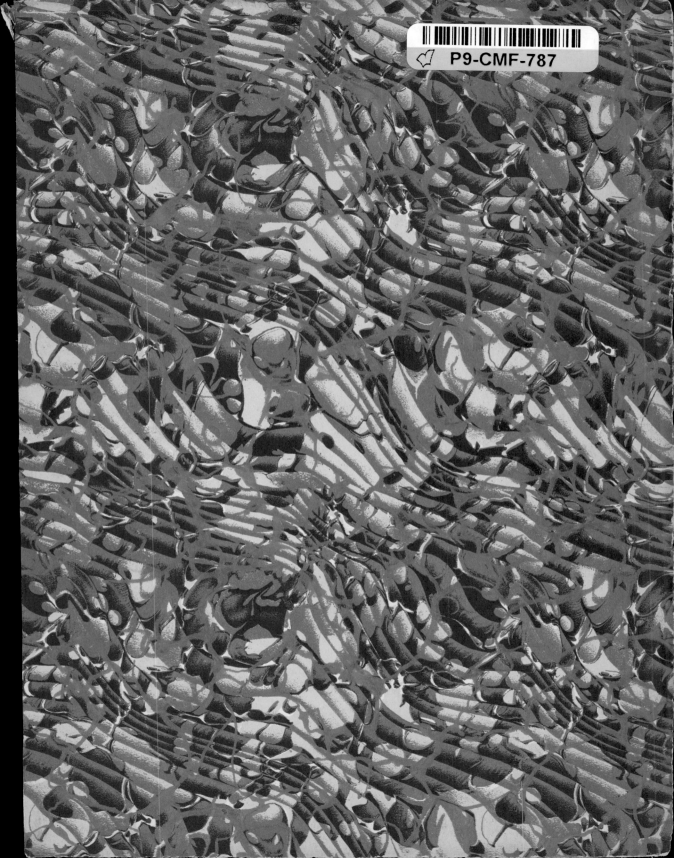
P9-CMF-787

For Mrs. B. F. Barr Pres.

Historic Gardens of Virginia

Compiled by The James River Garden Club
Member of The Garden Club of America

From The Women's Association
of American Nurserymen
1924 & 1925.

First Printing, July 14, 1923.
Second Printing, September 1, 1923.
Third Printing, November 15, 1923.
Fourth Printing, October 30, 1924.

"Castle Hill"

Double Box Hedges at Foot of Lawn, Running from Eighteen to Twenty-six Feet in Height, Painted by Pierre Troubetzkoy

Historic Gardens of Virginia

Compiled by

The James River Garden Club

edited by

Edith Tunis Sale

Committee

Edith Tunis Sale

Laura C. Martin Wheelright
Juanita Massie Patterson

Lila L. Williams
Caroline Coleman Duke

PUBLISHED BY
THE
WILLIAM BYRD
PRESS
INC.
RICHMOND
VA.

Lila L. Williams

DEDICATED

TO

Mrs. Malvern Courtney Patterson

FOUNDER AND FIRST PRESIDENT OF

THE JAMES RIVER GARDEN CLUB

FOREWORD

TO all who made the compilation of this book a possibility, the James River Garden Club is deeply grateful, for it has but taken the garden histories, which their owners generously unrolled that the public might see, and bound them into one volume, hoping that in the future it may prove an inspiration in garden lore.

The revival of interest in old-fashioned gardens, the enthusiasm which has recently developed for their restoration and preservation; the passion for the past which is in the air and is having a marked influence on landscape architecture, encouraged our Historic Committee to make a study of the old gardens of Virginia. This manifestation has led to our research with historical and horticultural intent.

Until now, the State possessing more colonial and early Republican gardens than any other has made no attempt to preserve their histories, though it must be remembered that the oldest were planned and planted before the corner-stone of America was firmly laid in Virginia soil. Their space was carved from the un-dated forest; their designs were borrowed from countries abroad and seeds for them journeyed from far overseas to bloom through the years as the multi-great-grandchildren of their original wealth of flowers. This is the only book which has undertaken to tell the stories which should possess deep significance for every American, as they have more than a mere local interest. And these stories have been collected by personal visits paid by the authors to the old gardens. Rare histories, valuable letters, garden records and personal reminiscences have been placed at our disposal with a gracious readiness, making of the task a sincere labor of love. The pilgrimage to each garden has been fraught with a pleasure which we hope, through these pages, to share with the reader.

A large part of this material has never before been made public. Many of the illustrations are entirely original and were made expressly for this book and all but four of the garden plans were drawn especially for it.

But the book makes no claim for literary merit. With the exception of the introduction, it is altogether the work of amateurs. Nor does it profess to tell *all* about Virginia's old gardens. It does not undertake to tabulate all their beauties and recite everything for which they are famed. It tells but little of the celebrated men and women who have trod their paths, for throughout the aim has been for historic accuracy rather than romantic interest or literary value.

The editor would record her grateful appreciation of the work of the Historic Garden Committee and all those who so kindly aided in the research. She acknowledges particularly the courtesy of the garden owners, the kindness of those who lent paintings, prints or photographs for reproduction and all who, personally, drew or had drawn, the plans which lend such interest and value to the book. Great thanks are due to Mr. William G. Stanard and Mr. Robert A. Lancaster, Jr., authorities on Virginia history.

It has been with a desire of lifting the latch of some of the old gates and, through the courtesy of their owners, inviting the reader to enter the gardens that the James River Garden Club has undertaken, before it is too late, to "gather up the fragments that remain."

EDITH DABNEY TUNIS SALE.

Tuckahoe, Virginia.
March, 1923.

[4]

TABLE OF CONTENTS

TABLE OF CONTENTS

TABLE OF ILLUSTRATIONS

COLOUR ENGRAVINGS

PLANS OF THE GARDENS

HALF-TONE ENGRAVINGS

TABLE OF ILLUSTRATIONS

[9]

TABLE OF ILLUSTRATIONS

INTRODUCTORY

"GOD ALMIGHTY," saith Bacon, "first planted a garden; and indeed it is the greatest refreshment to the spirits of man."

Let us add, "Of women also."

For—at least in Virginia—women and gardens go together. Perhaps it is so in those British Isles from which sprang Virginia. At any rate, dwell in memory or in imagination upon Virginia gardens and there arise women— in late seventeenth century dress, in eighteenth century dress, in nineteenth century, in twentieth century dress. Men also have planned, men also walk in these gardens, and there forever children sing and play. But women, young and in prime and old—it is chiefly women. They move among the box-bushes; they train the roses and tie the hollyhocks; they sow pansies and candytuft and snapdragon and mignonette; they cut the dead away, they gather for bowls and vases, gather from daffodil and lilac to the last marigold and mourning bride. They are there in the spring time, in the summer and the autumn.

For Virginia gardens are not, after all, affairs of huge expanse and expense, given over to gardeners, the owners' knees and fingers warned off. After all, they are simple—Virginia gardens—simple and sweet. We call them old. Many of them are old, even very old as our country goes. Others are not so old. But alike they are fragrant, alike they are dear. There is something—I do not know—they are poetic.

So it is fitting that this book—the book of the Historic Gardens of Virginia—should be a book thought of and largely written by women. Once they interchanged knowledge of one anothers' gardens through letters and long, leisurely visits. Nowadays they make Garden Associations. Such an one, the James River Garden

Club, mothers this volume. Again to women is owed garden pleasure—the whiff of box, of mignonette, of clove pinks and damask roses; the sense of sunny brick walls, of butterflies and bees and lovers and children in a world of blossom; an old, sweet wind of garden romance, garden poetry.

Gardens began early in Virginia. At Varina, in 1614, lived that wedded pair, John Rolfe and Pocahontas, daughter of Powhatan. Rolfe experimented with tobacco, and who shall say that in turn he did not show the young, wonderful Indian woman how they set flowering bushes, how they made beds of flowers, in Norfolk, in England? In 1625, on the banks of the James, George Sandys translated Ovid's Metamorphoses. Surely he had some planting of flowers about his door! In 1642, at Greenspring, Sir William Berkeley had a garden of extent and colour. When, a little later, the King's men, the cavaliers, fled with their families to Virginia from an England, no longer Stuart, there came with them garden ideas and garden seeds and slips and cuttings. Washington, Mason and Lee, Pendleton, Randolph, Cary, Madison, Monroe, Brodnax, Skipwith, and many others—these men and their wives and sisters and daughters soon had their sunlighted, their moonlighted gardens in Virginia. English squires, English and Scots merchants turned Virginia planters—near their houses of wood or of brick rise gardens with fruit trees, with old, fair shrubs, with low, formal beds of blossom, with paths winding or straight, with arbors and summer-houses. Jamestown is burned and Williamsburg arises, and there are gardens still in Williamsburg, gardens of lilac and daffodils, violets and roses.

In 1732, leaving his own garden at Westover, William Byrd travels to Germanna and with Governor Spotswood takes "a turn in the Garden. . . . Three terrace walks that fall in slopes one below another." The valley is settled, and gardens arise about the homes of Lewises and Campbells and McDowells and Gays and Prestons and Wilsons and Alexanders, and many another. And there is Greenway Court where the young surveyor, George Washington, walks and talks with Lord Fairfax. And in March, 1774, in Northumberland County, young Mr. Philip Fithian, the tutor at Nomini Hall, "has the honour of taking a walk with Mrs. Carter through the Garden. . . . We gathered cowslips in full bloom and as many violets. The English honeysuckle is all out in green and tender leaves." Presently he rides to Mount Airy, in Richmond County, and finds "a large, well-formed, beautiful garden, as fine in every respect as any I have seen in Virginia. In it stand four large, beautiful, marble statues."

Throughout the Revolutionary and the post-Revolutionary periods come whiffs of colour, song and perfume. There are flowers at Mount Vernon, and flowers at Red Hill where lives Patrick Henry, and John Marshall has his flowers in Richmond, and Jefferson at Monticello. Of Jefferson his granddaughter says, "Every day he rode through his plantation and walked in his garden . . . . I remember the planting of the first hyacinths and tulips. There was 'Marcus Aurelius' and 'The King of the Gold Mine,' the 'Roman Empress' and the 'Queen of the Amazons.' . . . . When the flowers were in bloom and we were in ecstacies over the rich purple and crimson, or pure white, or delicate lilac, or pale yellow of the blossoms, how he would sympathize with our admiration, or discuss with my mother and elder sister new group-ings and combinations and contrasts. Oh, these were happy moments for us and for him!"

The first sixty years of the nineteenth century was probably the heyday of gardens in Virginia. Then long and dread war, and houses burned and gardens trampled! Many old houses, many old gardens, have disappeared from Virginia. But many are left. And other gardens have been begun, are beginning, flourish now and will flourish more and more.

Those that are written of in this book are major gardens, old, well-known pleasaunces. But it were odd, thinking of Virginia, if the thousand, if the fifty thousand, little gardens did not come into mind, if the flowers in old towns, if the flowers in village yards,

[15]

if the flowers about farmhouses did not rise in beauty, in every hue, in fragrance! If the flowers around coloured folks' houses did not rise—the morning glories, the scarlet bean, the prince's feather and zinnias, the old pink roses, the tiger lilies. Close the eyes, let yesterday and tomorrow rise with today, and all Virginia is a garden! It smells of the rose, it smells of the locust blossom, it smells of the cedar.

So beautiful are the very names of homes and gardens in this volume! Flower de Hundred, Weyanoke, Mount Airy, Sabine Hall, Folly, Oatlands, Sweet Briar, Avenel, Chatham, Castle Hill, Shirley, Westover, Brandon, and Upper Brandon, Tuckahoe, Rosegill, Prestwould, Mirador, Morven, and many another! As beautiful as the old names of the old roses.

> "A garden is a lovesome thing (God wot!)
> Rose plot,
> Fringed pool,
> Ferned grot.
> The veriest school of Peace; and yet the fool
> contends that God is not!"

They who make and use and open to others a garden are servants of us all. So let us praise them who made Virginia gardens. And let us praise this book which opens for many the wicket gate.

MARY JOHNSTON.

The James River Plantation Belt

GARDENS OF WILLIAMSBURG

VEN the most skeptical person must admit that the narrow strip of land lying between the James and the York rivers is America's richest historical possession. Here are the tombs of those who risked their lives to build a nation. Here are old churches and courthouses standing as they stood in days long past and gone. This is the spot where Bacon planned his disastrous rebellion, and here is the college where Jefferson and Marshall first gained fame. Here, too, is the site of the famous Raleigh Tavern, where Jefferson danced with "Fair Belinda," and the Apollo, where many jovial feasts were held among the great men of the Colony.

The situation of Williamsburg, upon a ridge midway between the two rivers, was wisely chosen, and gave rise to the first name, "Middle Plantation." The town was impaled by Sir John Hervey, Governor of Virginia in 1632, and in 1699 succeeded Jamestown as the capital of Virginia.

Architecturally, the little city is white and rambling and dormer-windowed, and wandering dreamily through these aisles of history one revels in the romantic houses, the oldest all being built along the same lines, in accordance with a law which considered the number of stories in its taxation.

Williamsburg the quaint—so the old town has been called for years—is truly a place of many memories. On some of its streets there still stand aged trees that shaded Washington and Cornwallis, and about some of the houses the latter-day gardens are reminiscent of the time of the English Georges. One is prone to dream at the whispered name of Williamsburg, for it belongs to the picturesque Virginia of yesterday—the Virginia of feudal life and gallant living, of adventurous men and Watteau-like women;

of stage coaches and boxwood gardens. Its leafy streets and lanes have charmed travelers from many countries. One of these, the Marquis de Chastellux, wrote in his diary in 1780: "The chief magnificence of the Virginians consists in furniture, linen and plate; in which they resemble our ancestors who had neither cabinets nor wardrobes in their castles, but contented themselves with a well-stored cellar, and a handsome buffet. If they sometimes dissipate their fortunes it is by gaming, hunting and horse races; but the latter are of some utility, inasmuch as they encourage the breed of horses which are really very handsome in Virginia."

Standing in the spring sunlight in the Williamsburg of today and shutting our eyes to the growing city, what lover of history can not obtain glimpses of the panorama of the past. Through its old garden gates many historic figures pass—Colonial governors with lords and ladies from foreign shores; awkward Patrick Henry with his tongue of silver fire; John Marshall, Thomas Jefferson and Richard Henry Lee. Then Washington, LaFayette and Rochambeau; Cornwallis the conquered, and Tarleton, too. And in the days of the early Republic, Madison and James Monroe. Since their brave day nearly every president of the United States has, at some time, visited the picturesque town.

The most important thoroughfare, Duke of Gloucester Street, begins at William and Mary College, to end at the Palace Green. Using this as a central or starting point, a quiet ramble through the little town will repay one with interest and patriotic thrills, as each street has its particular story; around every corner, about each nook, is woven a web of historical associations that bring from the dustiest memory an answering appreciation. And, though some of its dwellers have modestly said, "There are no gardens in Williamsburg," this ramble along shady streets and about century-old houses will prove that in the springtime, at least, the whole of the town is one beautiful, old-fashioned garden.

The Palace Green, lying just on the east of old Bruton Church, has given way to a school building, which was constructed of the

From an Old Print

The Saunders' House—Governor's Office on the Right

Peyton Randolph House

Bassett Hall, Where Tom Moore Wrote "The Firefly"

bricks of the Governor's palace. The latter, which stood upon this spot until just after the Revolution, has been described as a "magnificent strcture built at the public expense, finished and beautified with gates, fine gardens, offices, walks, and a canal and orchard embracing in all three hundred and seventy acres, bordered with lindens brought from Scotland." Where the Governor's garden once bloomed so gayly, daffodils and buttercups now grow into flower. The last named plants—ranunculus acris—are said to be direct descendants of the first ever in this country, which were brought from "Merrie England" to adorn the palace grounds. Wild artichokes take up the golden note in autumn beneath the boughs of trees planted by loving hands as a memorial to the gallant sons of James City County who gave their lives in the great World War.

At the brown-stained Wythe house, which faces the Palace Green and adjoins Bruton churchyard, cherokee rose vines smilingly greet one before the gate is opened. The original garden laid off on formal, English lines, was, in its best days, hedged with boxwood, and lay at the rear of the house. A long walk between two flower-crowded borders was its dominant feature, and, though most of the old lines have been washed away by the rains of time, white and purple lilacs and pink crepe myrtle trees succeed the countless jonquils and narcissi that come up on the lawn each spring.

This house was the home of George Wythe, designer of Virginia's emblematic seal with the motto, *"Sic Semper Tyrannis,"* and teacher of Jefferson, Marshall and Monroe. The dwelling is rich in history—in traditionary lore, too—for it was in it that Washington lived at times during the Revolution and where members of LaFayette's suite were quartered. And legend tells of two ghostly visitors. One, the wraith of Lady Skipwith, a belle and beauty of colonial days, who restlessly trips through the ages on high-heeled, clicking shoes, to be known as the dainty dame of the tapping tread. The other tale tells of a young French officer who died in the house and returns punctiliously to prove the ghost lore well attested. The Wythe house is faithfully pictured by Ellen Glasgow, in "The Voice of the People," as the home of Judge Bassett.

On the same side of the street stands the white-columned dwelling where the Pages and Saunders lived in early times. The original garden at this place must have been among the most pretentious in Williamsburg, and even now the well-defined terraces compare favorably with those of newer design. The hospitable old house stands upon the topmost fall, where the broad lawn is graced by two large magnolia grandifloras and two gnarled crepe myrtle trees. Beneath the shade of an ancient mulberry tree and occasional clumps of Japanese pomegranate, snowdrops, jonquils and blue hyacinths rival each other for bloom. Most years the Star of Bethlehem blossoms so thickly along this fall that it looks as if a billowy bridal wreath had been thrown over and above it. Shade trees, locust and hackberry, grow on the second terrace; this gives way gently to the third, which ends at a picturesque stream. Beneath the old willow which shades this grassy, sloping bank, General Washington is said to have held important conferences while drinking spiced wine with officers of high command.

Across the Palace Green and opposite the Wythe and Saunders houses is the quaint little building once the home of Governor John Page. Near the old theatre, as it was in Colonial days, this little house passed from history into fiction as the home of the heroine of Mary Johnston's "Audrey," and now is known altogether as "Audrey's House." Though its paneled walls are interesting, the stories of its spirit world are more so, and the tragic words etched upon one of the old window panes quickens both pulse and fancy as does nothing else in all Williamsburg. Firmly outlined upon the glass are the words, "1796—Nov. 23—Ah, fatal day!" The story the few words tell must have been one of sorrow, of heartache and of love.

The prim walk up to the house on one side begins under old

locust and pecan trees, and is box hedged all of its length. Honeysuckle riots over the fence. Crepe myrtles and altheas grow on the lawn, and lilac bushes, with age written upon them in moss, show even now where the garden once was. And, gentle reminder of this sweet plot, the lily of the valley has massed so densely and spread so far afield that now it is securely naturalized.

Diagonally across from the church is the hospitable building where Judge St. George Tucker lived about 1779, and this, fortunately, is still in the possession of the same family. The old house was also the childhood home of John Randolph of Roanoke, and its charming old garden is still preserved much as it was when the little descendant of Pocahontas played in it. The flagstone walk and grassy falls are gay in spring with many violet blooms and a wealth of old-fashioned bulbs. The lilac bushes are as sweet as ever; the syringa or mock orange still bears gold-chaliced cups, while the Rose of Sharon and spiraea speak eloquently of the garden of yesterday. Roses in quantity and of many colors enliven the garden in June, and pink and white crepe myrtles lend their crisp freshness for a glory of midsummer bloom. When autumn comes, quantities of yellow fall crocus—crocus speciosus—remind one of jonquils next year. The following verses, "In a Garden of Dreams," by Elizabeth Eggleston, were inspired by what is now known as the Coleman garden:

> There's a garden of dreams where the crepe myrtle swings,
> And the roses are white in the gloaming;
> Where the hush of old beauty lies heavy and sweet,
> Scarce stirred by the winds that are roaming.
>
> There a tiny swing hangs from a gnarled old tree,
> There the larkspur's a blue-petaled glory;
> There the grey flagstones lead through a way that is dim,
> Like a thread to the heart of a story.
>
> There time holds its breath, there shrubs grow to trees,
> There beauty grows old in its questing;
> And the garden dreams on in its fragrance-hung calm
> Where even the shadows are resting.

[23]

Immediately next door, the original Coleman house will be found, in the midst of a charming old garden. Here, still more yellow crocus bloom in the fall, and narcissi and squills rise each spring upon each terrace.

Around the Garrett house on Capitol Street grow many old-fashioned shrubs—crepe myrtle, spiraea and mock orange. Bulbs, too, are here in plenty; the grape hyacinth's blue, and the daffodil's gold, painting a gay picture each spring. But the queen of this garden is the red amaryllis, which opens its petals in the fall.

Within a stone's throw is the home of Dr. Peachy, who played host to General LaFayette during the Revolution. Later, in 1824, when the Marquis was touring America, he was given a banquet at this same house when he visited Williamsburg. Stop for a bit—wander back over the years and gaze at the company who welcomed him. See the multitude of Virginia people thronging the highway, the doorways and roofs of near-by dwellings; the soldiers in their peace-time uniforms; stately Governor Pleasants on his prancing horse. Another moment—watch the crowd fall back. Grand old LaFayette, the hero of the hour, steps out upon the balcony—the multitude cheers—the General bows. When all this comes before one's mind it is easy to forget today.

The same bulb flowers bloom about this colonial house as are found all over Williamsburg, but a new note is struck when we see the anemone, Saint Brigid's kind, in a frail, petaled dress when it blooms.

At the east end of Francis Street, where there once was a beautiful old garden, stands the home of Burwell Bassett, friend and many times host of Washington. Bassett Hall, as the place is called, was later the town house of President John Tyler, and here, it is said, Tom Moore wrote "The Firefly," fresh from a visit to the great Dismal Swamp. The broad lawn, now cut by a long entrance lane, was once the scene of cavalry drills, but the only reminder of those stirring days is now found in the old-fashioned flowers. Violets, blue hyacinths and daffodils of many kinds—the

Home of George Wythe, Where the Once Beautiful Garden May be Traced

The Peachy Home, from the Balcony of Which LaFayette Spoke in 1824

The Tucker House, Where John Randolph of Roanoke Lived as a Boy

Tazewell Hall, Home of Sir John Randolph

Bruton Parish Church, Where a Pink Hawthorn Tree Blooms Above Masses of Violets and Narcissi

From an Old Print
*Maycox, on James River, Site of the First Attempt at
Horticulture in America*

*Carter's Grove, on Lower James, Where a Terraced Garden Once Led
Down to the River*

phoenix, the golden spur and Lady of Leeds in proper succession. No one knows just who it was who planted the multi-great-grand-parents of this present wealth of jonquils which mantle Bassett Hall in a robe of gold in April as year follows year.

So profligate have they become in number, so far-spreading have they gone, that the right has been given the Williamsburg Civic League to take from them enough bulbs to naturalize on the esplanade which extends along Duke of Gloucester Street.

Along the path which leads from the lane to the house, a chain of cowslips links the present to the past, and fragrant lilies stand together like angels in a dream. Bassett Hall is, in truth, the envied possessor of what many of us dream of, but few fortunates possess—"a lily avenue climbing to the doors."

Adjoining this lawn is the former home of Peyton Randolph, Speaker of the House of Burgesses and President of the Continental Congress. The acreage here has dwindled with the years and the garden has given way to modern needs of a town, but the same staunch bulbs return season after season. And in August, when the grass is brown and the leaves are withering, masses of tiny purple lilies hold up their crowns in loyalty to the first master of the home.

Just across the street is the Gault house, built just when, and by whom, no one knows, but rich in its historic lore and legend.

At the Thompson house, on Nicholson Street, Patrick Henry lived when he practiced law in Williamsburg. One of its tiny attic windows, the outlook from which is now so restful, was once the scene of frenzied watching against Indian depredations. There is, perhaps, more of a formal garden at this particular place than anywhere else in the little town. Box clumps are scattered here and there among lilacs and snowballs and the early flowering shrub yellow jessamine. Violets and narcissi; iris and jonquils; lilies—the pure Madonna and the tigerish Jamestown lily. The yellow Rose of Texas, known better as the Harrisonii, blooms above beds of bloodroot and hepatica brought from the woodland beyond.

[25]

The hardy bulbs, known to our grandmothers as butter and eggs, poet's narcissi and squills, are found in places where no house has stood for a century, loyal mementoes of cottage and farmstead leveled as progress marched into the town.

As a last word—let me beg you—when the cares of a restless existence are burdening too heavily the broad, though pessimistic, shoulders of today—throw them aside for a glimpse into Eden, and go to old Williamsburg when the daffodils that carpet each lawn and garden are bursting into the season's bloom, and the birds which share the old churchyard with the country's most illustrious dead are caroling the joy of living. Go where each flower face will tell you of the making of history, then dream in the sunshine of that romantic age. And when you leave the appealing little town you may repeat to yourself the words of one who has studied its past, played a part in its present and appreciated its beauties as can only those who call this little city home.

"Intangible, but real; invisible, but ever present, the spirit of the days of long ago haunts and hallows the ancient city and the homes of its honored dead; a spirit that stirs the memory and fires the imagination; a spirit that will, we trust, illumine the judgment of those who have entered upon the rich inheritance of the past and lead them to guard these ancient landmarks and resist the spirit of ruthless innovation which threatens to rob the city of its unique distinction and its charm."

EDITH DABNEY TUNIS SALE.

CLAREMONT MANOR

THE Claremont plantation, situated in Surry County, on the south side of the James River, about half way between Richmond and Norfolk, was bestowed upon Arthur Allen as an original grant from England.

The romantic legend, told along the river, is that two brothers, Allen and Eric Guelph, princes of the house of Hanover, were rivals for the love of a high-born English lady. Eric was successful in his suit, but on his wedding night was fatally stabbed by his brother, Arthur, who then fled from England. Taking refuge in America, he is said to have changed his name to Arthur Allen, in which name he held the large grant of land given him in 1649. Upon this plantation, a few years later, he built the house known as Claremont Manor, which today is an excellent example of the best architecture of the seventeenth century.

Built of bricks, said to have been brought from the mother country, this old house combines, as do other homes of the early Colonial period, the deep English basement and spacious high-ceiled rooms of the first floor, with the quaint dormer windows and high-pitched roof of the second story. As the colonial workmen were wont to build on the line of a letter of the alphabet, these three stories, each, conform to the shape of the letter "T."

The house is said to be an exact replica of Claremont Manor in Surrey County, England, which, during a long period, was a favorite royal residence. It was the property, at one time, of Lord Clive, then of Princess Charlotte and her husband, Leopold the First, King of the Belgians. It was the home, also, of the Duke of Kent, the father of Queen Victoria.

Claremont-on-the-James is massively and strategically built. It has its brick-walled underground passage to the river, which was

[27]

used in Indian days. It also has its secret room, the entrance to which was discovered during the War Between the States by a party of Federal soldiers. In this room the soldiers found a score or more half-gallon bottles of old brandy. To this day, one of these curious old decanters remains intact, and is highly prized by a family of Petersburg, Virginia. Cut deeply into the bottle is the name of William Allen, and the year 1753.

Each President of the United States prior to the time of the War Between the States is said to have been a guest at the old Allen house, and Edgar Allan Poe, whom tradition claims as a frequent visitor, is believed to have found inspiration for some of his beautiful poems while wandering in the historic gardens of old Claremont.

The Manor stands in a park of ten acres, where one sees an intermingling of beauty and age. The lofty and aged oaks, the glorious crepe myrtles, and the wide spreading boxwood hedges testify to a growth of centuries. The driveway approach to the old home, after passing between the huge, moss-covered gate piers, swings around in curve after curve in a friendly way. Converging from this driveway are the avenues of lindens and cedars.

Beauty in the park and its gardens was a tradition. Among the members of the Allen family, who continued to interest themselves in adding to the attractiveness of the grounds, were Arthur Allen, who, in 1688, became Speaker of the House of Burgesses; Colonel William Allen, who, one hundred years later, was a member of the convention of 1788; and his son, Colonel William Allen, Junior, who was a colonel in the War of 1812. Generation after generation, during two centuries and a quarter, continued the work thus early begun. Rare trees from foreign countries were later brought to Claremont. Today artistic groupings are seen, and charming color schemes changing with the seasons, but everywhere there is a quiet dignity and a gentle elegance.

The river approach to this old Queen Anne dwelling is by way of a wide avenue of linden trees, which extends from the river terrace to the driveway at the foot of the steep terrace upon which

[28]

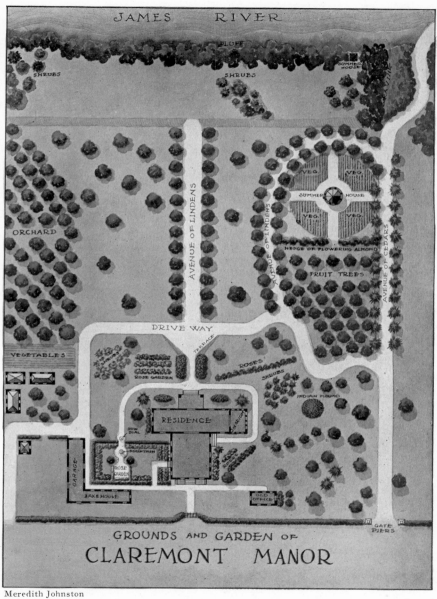

GROUNDS AND GARDEN OF
CLAREMONT MANOR

Meredith Johnston

The Little Garden at Claremont

Entrance to the "Old Mansion" at Claremont

the great double row of boxwood hedge, with shelled walk between, completes the approach to the steps of the mansion.

On each side of this box walk are the rose gardens, dotted and shaded with groups of shrubs and nature-planted trees. There are many varieties of roses—perpetuals, teas, simple old-fashioned bushes, the blossoms of every shade of pink, salmon and crimson and pure white, the rich odors of which, mingling with that of the box, lend an indescribable charm.

Contrasting with the age and dignity of the box walk and its rose gardens, is the warmly companionable little garden on the west side of the mansion, offspring of an ancient one. Here a fern-bordered, rose-covered pergola, surrounded by tall privet with under-borders of heliotrope, snapdragon, sweet william, bachelor's button and phlox, is enclosed by the walls of colonial outbuildings. Within the privacy of this small garden a figured fountain plays, and an ancient sun-dial lends charm.

There is one mood, one picture in which the physiognomy of the gardens of Claremont may be ideally contemplated. That is when the twilight falls and you walk under the magnolias on the terrace, through the rose-gardens and down the great avenue of lindens to the space where the crepe myrtles bank their layers of rich, heavy shadow. Behind these rise twin birches in virgin white and frail translucent green and just beyond a giant pecan thrusts up boldly against the wide expanse of river.

Between mimosa trees may be had a glimpse of the flowering almond hedge and ivy-covered summer-house. Then, let your eye follow the avenue of cedars, checkered with shadow, into the old garden through the gate of the cedars. Here, white, oval-shaped stones light up the half-hidden parterres that still bear a tangle of fern, honeysuckle, lilies, hollyhocks, peonies and other old-fashioned blooms. On through the faintly fragrant paths in a half-circle, until the lichen-covered summer-house that crowns the great bluff of the river, and stands like a period at the end of the dim lines, is reached. Close in here are columnar aisles of mock-orange standing like a row of pawns upon a chess-board. Bisecting with every shade of green, from blackest fir to brightest emerald, the great cucumber trees, English walnuts, chestnuts, hickories and slender gingkos, stand in close array.

MEREDITH ARMISTEAD JOHNSTON.

TEDINGTON

ANDY POINT, or Tedington, named for the English village on the Thames, is one of the most fertile of the many famous plantations lying along the banks of the lower James River. The place was originally known as the Indian town of Paspahegh. In 1700, when it became the property of Captain Phillip Lightfoot, the first of the name in Virginia, it contained about five thousand acres. Captain Lightfoot was a man of prominence and wealth in his day, a member of the Council of Virginia, a lieutenant-colonel and justice of the peace. Beneath an armorial tomb he now sleeps in the family burying-ground at Tedington.

For many generations the estate remained in the Lightfoot family and, according to old chronicles, they lived there in "great splendor." They drove a coach-and-four and dispensed royal hospitality to friends and relatives. The old house was built in the year about 1717, and is a fine type of the frame dwellings of that period. It contains ten rooms, with a high pillared front porch, and stands about forty yards from the river in a beautiful shaded lawn that slopes gradually to the low, sandy beach.

The interior of the dwelling is very attractive. Most of the rooms are large and high pitched with wainscoated walls. A huge chimney, which is nine feet thick and solid brick, runs through the center of the house.

The flower garden and borders at Tedington are noted for their beauty. The old box-hedge, on the north side of the garden, is at least twenty feet high.

Though the original lines of a formal garden have been obliterated by time, quantities of shrubbery and tangles of roses still charm the visitor to the historical spot. The chief interest of this garden, however, centers about the tree-box, which in quantity and quality, ranks with the finest in the south.

When the grounds for the Jamestown Exposition were being laid off, in 1906, the owner of Tedington was offered four thousand dollars for the boxwood, but the trees had fastened their hold on their latter-day master, and the offer was declined. Today these trees and lines of boxwood rear their heads as proudly as of yore.

The widow of William Howell Lightfoot married John Minge, Esquire, and their daughter, Sarah Melville, married Robert Bolling, of Petersburg, Virginia.

An interesting description of a Christmas at Tedington, by Charles Campbell, the Virginia historian, presents to the reader of today a vivid picture of the season of gifts on an old James River plantation in ante-bellum days. The letter is dated Tedington, Christmas, 1841, and reads, in part, as follows:

"Rainy Sunday. In the drawing-room at Tedington, three sisters, descendants of Pocahontas [evidently the Misses Bolling], Alice, Virginia and Rosalina; Miranda from an Italian city famous for its pictures and palaces. Five darkies put off in a rowboat to meet the river boat. Ten more ladies join the party, afterwards breakfast.

"Breakfast: Buttermilk rolls, Sally Lund, hominy. Prenala and Miranda ride with two gentlemen, Farrel and Racket. Ground half frozen. The cows stand close together in cowpen, stoically chewing their cuds; several little mules are huddled up in their shed eating their fodder; flocks of wild geese are flying over the broad wheat fields, reiterating their 'cohonk,' 'cohonk,' as they disappear from sight. Later, the ladies are firing 'poppees,' in the dining-room.

"Dinner: Ham of bacon—in Virginia, sine qua non. Without it we cannot organize or take any parliamentary action. Ham of mutton (Napoleon's favorite), a venison with jelly, oysters (Back River), stewed and baked, a huge round of beef, potatoes, Hibernians and sweet, salsify, hominy, celery, and cauliflower.

Tedington, Home of the Lightfoots

Brandon

Original Seat of the Harrison Family

For dessert, pound cake, mince pie, lemon pudding, raspberry puffs, jelly, amber-colored and purple with sylabubs, blanc mange, one couleur de rose, like the light of Aurora's cheek, the other typical of innocence and in Russia of morning, snow white. Champagne, sparkling like wit, in cranelike glasses. A contemplative mind will observe light, volatile particles ascending with accelerative velocity. Ambitious, evanescent aspirants, they hasten to the top only to expire. Madeira and Malaga also revolve in their proper orbits; cloth removed.

"Third course: Apples, red and green—the red grow at Tedington. Almonds, raisins, olives (de gustibus non disputandum), sweetmeats, brandy peaches, and cheese (old English).

"The sun now sinking in the west, it grows dim crepuscular; candles are lit, healths drunk, easy slipshod dialogues, an occasional cross-fire of puns and concerts, 'a moment there and gone forever,' interspersed with diagonal glances across the table, a sweet, surreptitious meeting of the eyes."

A pretty picture of those good old days!

In 1852, Tedington again changed hands, becoming the property of Colonel Richard Baylor, of Essex County. About this time the plantation was considered one of the very finest on James River, and contained about its original five thousand acres of land with a river front of nearly three miles. Hundreds of slaves tilled the broad, fertile fields. It is said that during harvest nearly three hundred men would be at work in the wheat fields. A hundred or more dusky "cradlers" cut a swath of yellow, heavy-headed, breast-high wheat. A binder followed each "cradler," gathering up the wheat into sheaves, a crowd of young darkies stacked the wheat, and were followed by a long line of the older men (shockers) who gathered the heavy, golden sheaves, and built them into substantial shocks, in straight lines across the fields. The overseer rode along, giving orders, or speaking words of encouragement to the harvest gang. The plantation owner was on horseback or in the carriage, perhaps, with some visitor or, maybe, some

[33]

ladies of the household, looking on at the animated scene. These were familiar sights at Tedington during the old-time harvests.

Today all of this is changed. Almost every one of the former slaves have passed into the great beyond, and Tedington has been divided up to consist of five farms of one thousand acres each. In the harvest fields the metallic click of the reaper is heard instead of the swish of the old-time cradles. But many of the older inhabitants around the neighborhood recall the days when the former owners of Tedington lived like kings.

At that time the walls of the old house were decorated with portraits painted by English masters; the polished dining-room table shone with silver and cut glass; the great wheat crop was loaded aboard vessels by means of an elevator, said to be the first in the country, and the owners of the old plantation ruled a little principality.

J. M. BELL.

BRANDON

THE garden of gardens in Virginia is that of Lower Brandon, situated on the broad waters of the James River. One can hardly put into words the beauty of a garden so saturated with intangible charm. It has no rare blossoms, nor shrubs brought from foreign lands, no delicately-planned parterres so loved by our English grandmothers, but just the same old-fashioned flowers we have known from childhood. We meet them again at Brandon in such health and wealth of beauty, and such dignity of surroundings, that it is hard to believe the feeble attempts in our own gardens belong to the same family.

The Brandon garden is not merely one enclosure, where we may enter through a gate and, when we have closed it, feel a delightful sense of seclusion. No, it is different from any other garden in Virginia. The masses of blossom, the ample grounds, the greens, the groves, and the wide spread of the peaceful James, are so closely blended with the house, the home and the people, that there is a unique charm of landscape and atmosphere mellowed through eight generations. If you want to let your imagination run hand in hand with poetry and romance; if you want to skip and dance and make merry with childhood, laugh with youth, meditate with the wise, and dream with sweet, placid old age, then go to Lower Brandon, and stroll at sunset down the long grass walk that leads to the river.

Brandon was first called Martin's Brandon, as it was granted to John Martin, who came over from England with John Smith. John Martin was a member of His Majesty's first Council in Virginia. In 1635 it was granted to John Sadler and Richard Quiney, merchants, and William Barbour, mariner. Richard Quiney married Judith, the daughter of William Shakespeare. He left his share of the property to his great-nephew, Robert Richardson, who sold it, in 1720, to Nathaniel Harrison (1677-1727), of Wakefield, Surry County.

Brandon was next inherited by Nathaniel Harrison II, and the present house, or its original part, was built by him in 1735, and subsequently grew, with its various generations and needs, until it spread its wings almost across the lawn. Some of the most distinguished Virginians were born within its walls, and many more have been sheltered under its hospitable roof.

A wide space of open green is left just in front of the door, and from the steps of the porch there stretches a double line of box across the front of the house on both sides. The double line continues down each side of the front grounds for about four hundred feet, where it joins enormous bowers and hedges of lilac which lead out from the main grounds to more secluded arbors and garden houses. These ancient box-hedges have grown far past all expectations of the original planter, and have assumed queer shapes, gnarled and twisted, each more beautiful than the other, and they have furnished days of endless pleasure for the many little children who have played "house" on the velvety brown carpet under their soft green boughs. The grass walk, about fifteen feet in width, leads down to the river, the vista of which is one of the most beautiful on the James.

It is wild and wide, and takes one back to the days when the Indians fled in their canoes from the white settlers. Though Jamestown was a thriving settlement, with a House of Burgesses in session in 1619, the Indians still held for themselves the kingdom of James River. We feel this historic fact at Brandon today.

On either side of the garden walk from the open green to the river, a distance of some two hundred yards, there is a continuation of fine old specimens of spiraea, syringa, weigela, calycanthus, crepe myrtle, forsythia, japonica, lilac, corchrous, or rock rose, and snow-

June in the Garden at Brandon

Lila L. Williams

ball, known to our grandmothers as guelder rose. There are openings at intervals, on both sides, leading into various kinds of rose gardens, and perennial borders, also large squares of iris, lilies, and every variety of spring bulb.

The narrow walks, which lead in and out of the small gardens, are edged with little yellow primroses or cowslips and sweet violets, both white and blue. There are evidences still left of great hedges of fig and dogwood; but the latter being short-lived, it is hard to determine just when and how they were planted. The enormous grove on the land front of the house is as rich with magnificent trees as the river front. Tulip poplars, oaks, lindens, ash, sycamores, junipers and a pecan tree that is said to be one of the finest in the world.

My first visit to Brandon is a beautiful memory. It was in May, 1902. We had been on a pilgrimage to Jamestown and stopped at Brandon just after a thunderstorm. It was in the late afternoon, and a great burst of golden sunlight had just come out of the grey clouds and touched every glistening raindrop on every blade of grass, while the dripping foliage was made golden against the solemn black trunks of the trees.

There seemed to be hundreds of wood robins, mocking birds and cardinals singing their fullest notes for that last bit of day. I followed many of the little cowslip paths that led me into masses of roses in full bloom; Marechal Neil, damask, and every variety of tea rose, each holding the raindrops. Enormous wild grapevines festooned some of the trees, and they, too, were in full bloom, all filling the air with a wonderful fragrance, added to that delicious scent of box, so essential to old gardens. Many of the borders were heavily shaded, and in these columbines, forget-me-nots and bleeding heart were blooming.

The charm of that garden will live always; and one who is fortunate enough to visit Brandon in May will feel an awakening of all the poetic in his soul. Almost unconsciously he will repeat the old childhood's rhyme:

[37]

"What care we though life be short,
We'll dream a fine dream, and think a fine thought.
We'd grow fine feathers, sing fine songs, too,
If we lived in a garden as the cardinals do."

A certain romantic incident is a matter of history at Brandon. There hangs closely tied in one of the chandeliers in the drawing-room, a small gold wedding ring.

Each generation seems to have known and reverenced the ring; but no one knows when or why it was hung there. Whether some bride had cast it off because of the secret love in her heart for another, or whether it was the dying request of some dear old grandmother, who wished to leave the sign of her happy union in the room where she was married, is still a mystery at Brandon.

Every old place has at least one particular ghost; and here it may be the bride who returns to guard her wedding ring and wish a blessing on her descendants. We'll call her the patron saint of brides; and I feel sure that this little saint draped in the silver-white robes of moonlight, with a wedding veil of mist, still frequents some of the enchanted paths in the garden at Brandon.

CAROLINE COLEMAN DUKE.

Vista of the James River in the Garden at Brandon

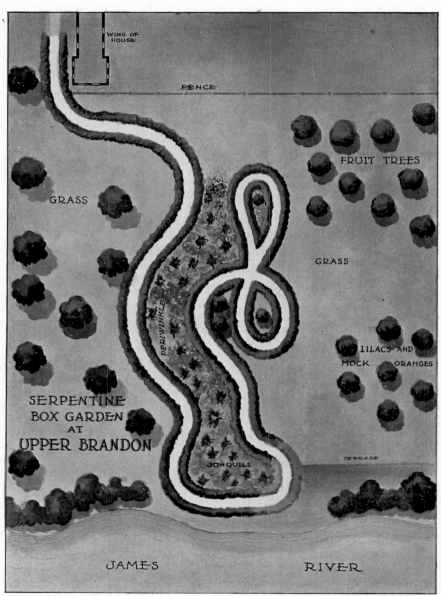

WING OF HOUSE

FENCE

FRUIT TREES

GRASS

GRASS

PERIWINKLE

LILACS AND
MOCK   ORANGES

SERPENTINE
BOX GARDEN
AT
UPPER BRANDON

JONQUILS

TERRACE

JAMES   RIVER

Lila L. Williams

UPPER BRANDON

PPER BRANDON, so called in contradistinction to the older plantation of which it was once a part, lies also on the south side of James River. The three miles of roadway leading to it from Brandon, family seat of the Harrisons, is very lovely, winding at times along the brink of the river, and again through woodland dense in shade and greenery.

Although several generations junior to its venerable sisters, Brandon, Shirley and Westover, a hundred years have come and gone since the spacious foundations for the house at Upper Brandon were laid on the fertile slope, one hundred and fifty yards back from the river.

Built by William Byrd Harrison, son of Benjamin Harrison, of Brandon, its general plan is somewhat like that of the older place, though the lines are a trifle more massive, and the wings have two stories. The situation of the dwelling commands one of the best river sites, and the park which surrounds it is heavily shaded by many trees. Conspicuous among the latter are the willow oaks, which have made such prodigious growth that now they rear their tall tops above the highest gables. Still other trees upon the lawn are beech, poplar and magnolia.

Box lines the walks leading from the front of the house to the old terraced garden, where they end in a serpentine, now somewhat difficult to trace. This design, the only one of the kind in America, is said to be one of the oldest and rarest to be found in England. Within many of its sinuous curves jonquils and grape hyacinths are naturalized, giving in spring an effect both beautiful and interesting. This dwarf boxwood found a genial home in the soil of Upper Brandon and, during the past centuries, has made such notable growth that now it is the glory of the place.

The garden itself, which suffered greatly from 1862 to 1865, has never been completely restored, though many old shrubs were left to define certain spots—japonica, althea, lilac, and syringa. Not in any special or ordered form, but scattered about the lawn and garden are roses—new and old. Boxwood and roses—that is what one remembers from a June visit to Upper Brandon today. An old poem, written about the two Brandons, gives an idea of what this garden was many years ago:

> A garden full of roses—
>   Red, yellow, white and pink,
> And many other posies
>   Grow near the river's brink.
> Along the walks are cowslips
>   Of many colors bright,
> Some red as a young maid's lips,
>   Some full of yellow light;
> The daffodils and jonquils,
>   The box and the snowballs
> The hyacinth the air fills
>   With perfume which enthralls;
> There are some dear old flowers
>   In this quaint garden spot,
> And rose leaves fall in showers
>   Whene'er the wind blows hot.

Like many another stately Virginia home, Upper Brandon had its part to play in history. During the War Between the States four of its stalwart sons crossed its fair threshold to battle for their State and country. One of these now sleeps forever on the field of Malvern Hill.

Federal troops made their home from time to time in the old house during this period. Today all that is left to recall those stirring days are the sabre cuts in the old balustrade and the liberal sprinkling of bullet holes in the paneled walls.

After the death of William Byrd Harrison, Upper Brandon became the property of George Harrison Byrd, whose son, Francis Otway Byrd, now makes it his home.

F. OTWAY BYRD.

Upper Brandon

The Garden at Upper Brandon

James River, Near Upper Brandon

Weyanoke

WEYANOKE

THE estate of Weyanoke, the name of which was borrowed from the Indians, lies on the north shore of James River and is mentioned in history as early as 1607. When John Smith and Christopher Newport made their adventurous voyage up the James, they found seated here the Weyanoke Indians. This tribe, though in reality under Powhatan, was nominally governed by a queen to whom the early colonists often referred as the "Queen of the Wayanokes." Unfortunately, no other name seems to have been bestowed upon her.

When Sir George Yeardley was Governor of the Colony of Virginia, he acquired an estate at this point, but this he sold later to Abraham Piersey. Towards the end of the seventeenth century, the place passed into the possession of the Harwood family. Though there had been an earlier house on the property, in 1740 William Harwood built the present large frame house at Weyanoke. Some years later the estate was inherited by the daughter of Samuel Harwood, who married Fielding Lewis of Warner Hall, Gloucester County, Virginia. The portrait of the latter now hangs in the Virginia State Library as that of an early scientific planter. Through the marriage of a daughter to Robert Douthat that part of the plantation known as Lower Weyanoke became the property of the family who own it today.

In 1854, Mary Willis Marshall, granddaughter of the Chief Justice, a slip of a girl, came to Upper Weyanoke as the bride of Fielding Lewis Douthat and there began with her husband's assistance the making of a garden.

Near by is Lower Weyanoke, where the mother-in-law lived and where flourished what was said to be one of the most beautiful gardens in Virginia. The mistress of the older place gladly gave to her young daughter and son from her overflowing garden all that they needed in the way of plants and shrubs. Her knowledge and experience which was lovingly given to the young couple was of great value and a very extensive garden was laid out.

Broad alleys were laid off to run between borders of flowers and shrubs. These alleys or walks ran lengthwise and across the garden with plots of vegetables between.

After the War Between the States the changed conditions and a different mode of cultivation made it necessary to do away with the cross-walks and borders in order that the cultivators could have room to move more freely in working the vegetables.

As the garden now is one sees a long walk fifteen feet wide bordered on each side with evergreen shrubs and all the old garden favorites. In February begins the season of bloom, with the long succession of daffodils and narcissi; next comes the breath of spring and winter heliotrope, which mingles with the old world fragrance of bloom and boxwood as do also the cowslips edging the borders.

The gate of the entrance is covered with yellow jessamine or, as it is called in England, woodbine. Surely dull care is driven away when spring comes upon the James and our many beautiful birds begin nesting in the old gardens. One's senses are bewildered trying to tell from which comes that divine scent—calycanthus, lilac, jessamine, or what not—when it is a combination of all.

In the midst of this calm beauty came the horrors of war. To Weyanoke marched a part of Sheridan's army after a recent defeat at Cold Harbor. We can imagine the weary and wounded soldiers who found rest in this garden. Under a rose bush the young mistress found one who had there given up his life and gone, we hope, to where flowers bloom eternally.

In the years that have passed since then changes have come not only in material things. For in this garden where once all the bitter feelings called forth by war held sway, here come many charming and cultured friends from that one-time land of the enemy, and beneath the shade cast by the old shrubs here have partaken of tea.

CATHERINE DOUTHAT.

[42]

Flower de Hundred

GARDEN AT
FLOWER DE HUNDRED

N. P. Dunn

FLOWER DE HUNDRED

N Tindall's "Charter of Virginia" (a map preserved in the British Museum), under date of 1608, we find the clear outline of what was to become Flower de Hundred plantation, with the Indian village of Wynagh, or Weyanoke, indicated on its bold cape-like projection into James River. Here General Grant landed his forces from his pontoon bridge on his way to Petersburg on a then far-off, undreamed-of day.

The place was patented by Sir George Yeardley, 1618, and named—as we now know—for his wife's family, Flowerdew. This fact was early lost sight of. Certainly, by 1671 the name was written Flower de Hundred, and something in the corruption in the spelling has attracted interest and piqued curiosity until now, I imagine, the maiden name of Lady Temperance Flowerdew will never come into its own. She, by the way, later became the wife of Governor West, and moves, a stately figure, in several records of her day and times.

In 1619, Flower de Hundred was represented in the first Assembly by Lady Yeardley's nephew and John Jefferson. The place was sold to Abraham Peirsey in 1624, and the deed, said to be the oldest in North America, mentions the "windmill and the messuages." We know from a State paper that the windmill, which gives its name to the Point, was built in 1621, and that it was the first in the country. Now the word "messuages" includes the idea of a homestead, "house, outbuildings, yard, garden, etc.," but these were, no doubt, down by the windmill where, tradition has it, that a brick house was long since burned—so regretful we admit to ourselves that the garden of today is probably not the garden of my lady Temperance.

Peirsey left the plantation to his daughter, Elizabeth Stevens, and we have the old paper of 1636, in which it is repatented to her by Governor John West. She later became Lady Harvey. Its next owner was the picturesque William Barker, mariner, who sailed the seas in the *Merchant's Hope,* and was one of a company to found the old plantation, courthouse and church of that name, along with one Quiney, whose brother, Thomas, married Judith Shakespeare—not uninteresting are these links with Old England.

Barker's descendants divided the land into three parts, and one of these corresponds to the site of the present house. It was described in 1673 as the share falling to his daughter, Sarah Lucy, "with houseing, fenceing, buildings and all other profits, vantages and priveledges whatsoever to the same belonging"— surely this includes a garden!

Joshua Poythress I bought Flower de Hundred in 1725 and 1732 from the various heirs of John Taylor, and it is still the property of his direct descendants of the seventh and eighth generations, that part on which the house and garden stand being owned by Dr. William Willcox Dunn, of Richmond, Virginia.

The Poythress house is thought to have been on a bluff near the river, close to the burying ground. Certain it is, that here one still finds old brick and clumps of blue flags and traces of other garden flowers. This brick house was burned and its site abandoned. Susannah Peachy Poythress, only daughter and sole heiress of Joshua Poythress III, was born at Flower de Hundred in 1785 and was buried there in 1815. She married John Vaughan Willcox, of Charles City County and Petersburg, in 1804, at which time they built the present house—a white wooden structure—on a rolling bit of ground, back from the river and, as has been said, doubtless already an old site and homestead.

It was never their home, but was often visited; the plantation was under full cultivation, and she must have known and loved the present garden. Later, her son came to live here and added wings to either end of the house. His children, in turn, built other wings. His wife was the moving spirit in making the garden a

Westover, the Home of William Byrd

Garden Walk at Westover

glory and a joy to her generation, and it is as she maintained it that I shall try to describe it now. If not, strictly speaking, a colonial garden, it at least preserves an old-world air—a sense of rest and permanence pervades its scented walks, in spite of present neglect and almost abandonment.

The house stands in a large yard—hardly a lawn—where magnificent trees have within the last few years gone down before successive storms. A large box circle, four or five feet high, occupied the center. Formal beds of tulips were dotted here and there, while a border of peonies lined the fence. A walk passed the front porch and led to the rose arbour which sheltered the garden gate, and four box-trees guarded this walk—only one of which survives. The garden covered a large area, some of which was later taken into the orchard, leaving about an acre and a half in flowers, vegetables and small fruits. A plan accompanies this description. Center, a magnolia tree. Around this, a circular box-hedge, and in the space between, lilies of the valley. Intersecting walks—wide enough for a cart to drive along—that fertilizers might the better be handled and spread—passed through the garden, with flower borders on either hand. These borders also ran along walks following the line of fence. In the center of each square were vegetables, strawberries or ornamental fruit and nut-trees. Trellises held grapes, and there were two rose-covered arbours. At intervals rosebushes stood, and still stand, for that matter, seven and eight feet tall, a riot of bloom in May and early June. In the autumn they bloom again with surpassing beauty. Huge syringas stand at the angles, with spiraea and calycanthus. The borders were edged with violets and spice-pinks. Back of these are remembered among other plants snowdrops, tulips, butter-and-eggs, hyacinths, night shade, lavender, bay, Poet's laurel, Madonna lilies, yellow day lilies, citronella, star-jessamine and peonies. Behind these, lilacs, pyrus japonica, golden honeysuckle, flowering almond and, always, roses, and again—roses.

Formal scarlet geraniums came out of their cold-frames at

proper times and made a glory of color in their appointed beds, back of one of the grape trellises. Three gardeners were kept busy ordering all this beauty. The soil is of a wonderful richness and the English bulbs—a sturdy stock surely—come up year after year. One can still fill the house with bloom at most seasons, and in its decay the old garden has not forgotten to be lovely.

N. P. DUNN.

WESTOVER

IKE an exquisite emerald clasp upon the golden, chain-like river, lies the green lawn of Westover. Upward from the winding James the sward, studded with great, gnarled tulip-poplars, sweeps smoothly to the stately and magnificent old homestead of the Byrds. Nearly two hundred years ago some of these trees are said to have been planted, and now they stand like giant guards upon the ancient lawn. On each side brick walls descend to the edge of the river bank.

Westover goes back almost to the beginning of the English in America. In the year 1688, William Byrd, the first of his name in Virginia, who had come with his young wife, Mary, to the Colony in 1674, and settled at the falls of the James, purchased the plantation from Theodorick Bland. About 1735 his son, the second William Byrd, built the beautiful home, which still stands, surrounded by the lovely emerald lawn, the flag-pathed courtyard, and the gracious old garden in which his dust reposes.

The house, of red brick mellowed to a warm old-rose, without porch or ornament, is considered one of the most perfect examples of Georgian architecture in America. It has a high, steep roof, set with dormer windows and flanked by lofty chimneys. Before the door gray-stone steps rise in a pyramid to a beautiful doorway, which many a builder has copied.

The main entrance to the grounds is upon the side opposite the river and is through wonderful gates of wrought-iron, which often have been described. Nowhere in America, unless it is in ancient and historic Charleston, which has so many lovely gateways, is there a finer example of the iron-master's art—a double grill, ten feet high, surmounted by the monogram of William Evelyn Byrd, and swung between two massive, square brick pillars which bear leaden

[47]

eagles with wings spread proudly as if for flight. It is a curious thought to recall that these eagles, symbols of our country, were set there long before our country was even a dream. From this great gate a graceful iron fence slopes to each side, divided into sections by square pillars, each capped with a different emblem of stone.

Here, in the wilderness, Byrd set a bit of England. It was in the English blood to make and to love a garden. Even now, this overgrown old garden, with its formal box-hedged squares and old-fashioned flowers, reminds one of the lanes and hedge-rows of England. The sweet-smelling box recalls the old fragrance of forgotten memories—rosemary and rue—lace laid away in lavender—the spicy scent of sandalwood.

Quaint sweet williams bloom in company with the pale forget-me-not; foxgloves, purple and white, grow beside iris, white and purple; clove-pinks, the progenitors of all our regal carnations, vie with peonies, shaded like the inside of a flushed shell; lilies of serene and virginal white look chastely upon their gaudy, flaunting cousins, tiger-striped and voluptuous; timid violets peep out from beneath bold hollyhocks; and everywhere are roses, some of which, the legend says, will bloom in no other ground.

Flowering shrubs are there—the modest bridal wreath spirea, syringa, or mock-orange. Crepe-myrtle bushes grown almost into trees and calycanthus with deep red-brown flowers verging upon purple. In this rich, moist soil the vines have grown with almost tropic luxuriance. Rambler roses and trumpet vines riot through and over the old hedges, which, untrimmed in spots, have grown into tree-like proportions, and wistaria has woven and twisted itself into tangled thickets of verdure, which in season are masses of purple bloom.

But the greatest charm of this rare old garden lies neither in the sweet box-hedges, the beautiful beds of old-time flowers, the graceful shrubbery, nor the clambering vines. Nor in the countless birds that make the enclosure melodious with their song. It is found in the thoughts, redolent with romance, that this

Tomb of William Byrd II at Westover

River Wall at Westover

sequestered spot recalls. What a procession has passed through the Westover garden! The visitor who loves to dwell upon the past may close his eyes and see pass before him all that has gone to make Virginia picturesque and great.

There stands the tomb of William Byrd the second, who was called "The Black Swan." His epitaph upon the stone informs us that, not only born to ample fortune, he was of brilliant mind, courageous spirit, and kindly disposition. It is related of him that he was handsome, graceful and fascinating; educated and traveled; the most elegant of gentlemen and the best of good fellows. In him the most solid qualities of mind and character were united to all the courtly graces and accomplishments of his time.

How delightful to picture William Byrd and his companions as they strolled through this garden two centuries ago! Courtly and sophisticated gentlemen they were, in brilliant coats and flowing ruffles and satin small-clothes. How the sun must have flashed from their silver buckles and their golden sword-hilts as, in leisurely fashion, they offered each other their jeweled snuff-boxes! With what stately courtesy they addressed the beauties who, with powdered hair and fans and patches, in gowns of flowered silk, walked with them here when the garden was young!

These gravelled paths must have known, too, the soft tread of the moccasined Indian, bronzed and painted, stern of face and guttural of tongue.

Then would come the runners of the woods, the hardy frontiersmen (pressing ever westward up the river in canoes), swarthy as the Indians, fur-capped, shirted in fringed leather, their flint-lock rifles on their knees, alert and keen eyed, grateful for a moment's rest and the hospitality of Westover.

William Byrd the third, an officer in the Colonial troops, must have passed through those gates in his scarlet regimentals, gold-laced, well-horsed, his sabre by his side, on his way to the French and Indian wars. And up to these same gates rolled the lordly

Byrd coach-and-six with the liveried outriders, when the Colonel and his ladies would go a-visiting to Shirley or Brandon or to Buckland.

Then came the Revolution. Burgesses from Williamsburg and the first men of the colony, perhaps, sat on those benches and through the smoke of their long-stemmed clay pipes discussed the peril of the times. Officers of the Continental line, in buff and blue, strode the paths in shining jack-boots, or made love beneath the arbors to the beautiful Byrd girls.

Westover knew Red Coats again, too, for Arnold, the renegade, stopped there in 1781, and a few months later Cornwallis crossed the river there, bound for Yorktown and his doom.

To the gay French officers who took part in that siege, the fair chatelaine of Westover and her beautiful daughters were magnets, and their bright uniforms must have made even the roses pale. The Marquis de Chastellux claimed in his memoirs that Westover was the most beautiful place in America.

The clouds of war passed and the only scarlet coats seen at Westover were those of fox hunters. Quiet fell again upon the garden, and how pleasant it is to recall the children who romped along the paths in charge of their old negro mammies! The garden rang with laughter and there was no thought of the darker days that were yet to come.

Westover was no longer in the wilderness. The Indians had vanished; the river had become a highway of commerce. Broad fields around smiled with rich crops and in the garden all was peace and happiness.

Yet war was to come again and in more frightful guise. McClellan, on his retreat from Richmond, used the house for his headquarters, and the garden resounded to the clatter of arms. The fences were torn down, the flower beds trampled, the hedge-rows broken; but McClellan passed, as Arnold and Cornwallis and the Indians had passed, and the garden remained to spring into new beauty.

[50]

Among all these pictures of memory, the one that most affects the tender heart is the vision of lovely Evelyn Byrd, the eldest daughter of the second William, whose gentle spirit seems to haunt the garden yet. Her charm and beauty captivated not only the colony, but England; at eighteen she was presented at court and became the toast of the nobility. Tradition tells that she was wooed and won by Charles Mordaunt, Lord Peterborough, but her father broke off the match and brought her home to pine and die.

One thinks of her in slender, slowly-fading loveliness, wandering through the box-bordered paths in her flowered gown and high-heeled silken shoes, and wonders if her thoughts were those that Amy Lowell has so poignantly expressed in "Patterns":

> "I walk down the garden paths
> And all the daffodils
> Are blowing, and the bright blue squills.
> I walk down the garden paths
> In my stiff brocaded gown.
> With my powdered hair and jeweled fan
> I, too, am a rare pattern. As I wander down
> The garden paths.
> My dress is richly figured
> And my train
> Makes a pink and silver stain
> On the gravel and the thrift
> Of the borders.
> Just a plate of current fashion,
> Tripping by in high-heeled, ribboned shoes,
> Not a softness anywhere about me.
> Only whalebone and brocade.
> And I sink on a seat in the shade
> Of a lime tree. For my passion
> Wars against the stiff brocade.
> The daffodils and squills
> Flutter in the breeze
> As they please
> And I weep . . . . .

So the beautiful Evelyn must have thought, one can fancy, as she walked in her fading beauty and her elegant apparel, and wept, until she died.

Not far from the house the ashes of the beautiful Evelyn Byrd lie, near those of her grandfather, William Byrd the first, in the yard of old Westover Church, which, if we may liken Westover itself to an emerald clasp upon the necklace of the golden James, we might call a pendant.

The first Westover Church, which was built in the early part of the seventeenth century, stood on the shore of the river, still nearer Westover. The present church, which was erected about 1740, is somewhat back from the James, upon Herring Creek, a lazy, brown stream, bordered near the river by marshes, which give way to banks crowned with pines and cedars, sycamore, holly, and beech trees.

It is a plain, low, rectangular structure of red brick, dwarfed by the great trees by which it is surrounded. The little church has passed through many vicissitudes. For many years the Byrds worshipped there, but early in the nineteenth century, when the Byrds had passed away and the Episcopal Church suffered its great depression in Virginia, its sacred offices were almost forgotten and it was used as a barn. Later still, during the War Between the States the graveyard wall was thrown down, the tombs broken, and McClellan's troopers stabled their horses within the venerable walls of the edifice.

After the war, the building was restored by James Hamlin Willcox, and is now again used as a church.

A gentleman relates that, as a boy, his negro mammy carried him to service in this church. On weekdays he was allowed to go barefoot, but on Sundays his reluctant feet were forced into shoes. Safely ensconced in the pew, he would slyly wiggle his feet out of confinement and then wriggle his toes in the sand between the stone slabs of the floor. Through the old diamond-paned windows he would watch the bees clustering upon the roses that clambered about the embrasure, and, at last, to their drowsy hum, that blended

Westover

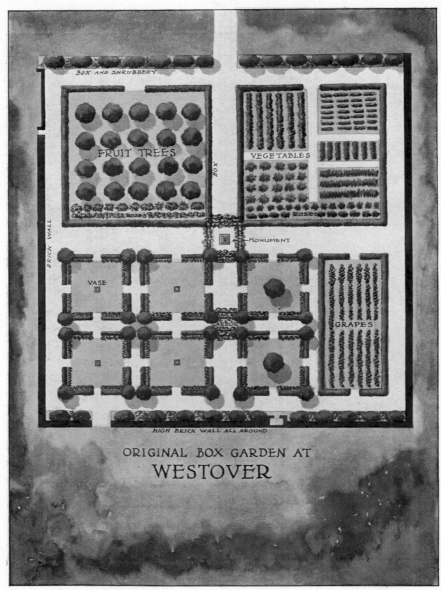

ORIGINAL BOX GARDEN AT
WESTOVER

Lila L. Williams

with the monotone of the minister, he would drift away upon the wings of sleep.

In this old church, as in the garden, one's thoughts go back into the storied past and recall the days when the great land-owners worshipped there. Some rolled up in great six-horsed coaches with servants and outriders; others came from up and down the river in pirogue or pinnace or sloop; the more humble yeomen rode up on horseback, their dames upon pillions behind. The plain little church must have been gay with bright silks and satins, plumed headgear and jeweled fans, brilliantly-flowered waistcoats and pompous wigs.

Many of the old gentry sleep under the mouldering slabs in the graveyard. The earliest date is that of 1637, in which year the first church was erected. The tomb of Evelyn Byrd is kept from disintegration by iron bands. Yet the church yard is no place of gloom; it is more like a garden than a cemetery.

All that man could select, all that Nature can give, has contributed to make the Westover garden a bower of fragrant beauty. But it is neither the flowers, nor the trees, nor the shrubs that most touch the heart which is tuned to ancient memories. To dream of these, there is no more fitting place, where, as the old verse, so often used on sun-dials in England, has it:

> "With the song of the birds for pardon,
>   And the joy of the flowers for mirth,
> One is nearer God's heart in a garden
>   Than anywhere else on earth!"

SHERRARD WILLCOX POLLARD.

[53]

APPOMATTOX

ROM Richmond, crossing the James through old Manchester, we follow the Petersburg Turnpike on our way to Appomattox. The soldiers of all our armies have trod this road and fought for a stand on nearly every foot of ground between Petersburg and Richmond; for this part of Virginia has been rightly called "the spanking spot" of the nation.

At beautiful Falling Creek, in Chesterfield County, we come to the site of the first iron works in America, established by John Berkeley in 1619 and abandoned in 1622 when the Indians fell upon and massacred Berkeley and all his men.

During the Revolutionary War the British Red Coats traveled on this pike, and Tarleton with his troopers destroyed the iron works completely; but the falls over the dam and the double-arched stone bridge still remain to make a charming scene. To the left of the bridge is the entrance to Ampthill, the home of the Cary's, built in 1732. From the site of the formal garden, which once graced this hilltop, a broad view of the lowlands and a commanding prospect of the river may be had. Washington and the famous men and women of his day enjoyed frequently the hospitality of this charming Colonial home.

A little farther on at Kingsland Creek may be seen remains of the old fort built during the War Between the States to guard the road to Richmond. Mule teams and dusky drivers are today robbing both fort and hillside of gravel to mend the scars on the old roadway. The Tavern, or "Halfway House," at Proctor's Creek, claims to have refreshed the great Generals Washington and LaFayette on their march up this road, and one would have to pause but a few moments to have the cheery present owner tell of the hundreds of watermelons and cantaloupes he hospitably dispensed from his "gyarden" to the khaki boys of Camp Lee as they came and went over the pike while training for overseas service.

Just before Petersburg is a stone marker put up by the Daughters of the Confederacy. This marks the headquarters of General Robert E. Lee from June to September, 1864, at Violet Banks, the old estate of John Shore. The plantation has gone and a modern subdivision has taken its place, but a quaint facade of the interesting old house still remains, the rear portion of sixteen rooms having been shot away. It will well repay the tourist to detour a bit and see the remains of the house and the beautiful trees which enframe it.

John Shore, it is said, had a passion for all ornamental plants. He used shrubs and flowering trees in great variety for the embellishment of his grounds. Years after, the grounds and garden supplied family and friends with specimens for ornamenting their new driveways and gardens in many parts of Virginia—flowering locusts, mimosa, horse-chestnut, hawthorns, crepe-myrtle, magnolias (grandiflora, glauca, acuminata), acacia (yellow, pink and white), and every variety of fruit tree then obtainable. Two torch-like hollys stand on either side of the house.

It is said that a suitor came a courting one of the Mistresses Shore; from far away he came on horseback with a switch from a tree in his hand as a whip. This switch he stuck in the ground and it grew and grew into a tremendous magnolia acuminata. Under its spreading branches General Lee had his tent, and a little child brought him each day baskets of fresh vegetables from her mother's garden. She remembers yet his lifting her in his arms to gather one of the pale yellow blossoms of this great tree.

Following a road, still flanked with marvelous old oaks, down the hillside and around the river banks studded in spring with millions of violets, we cross the Pocahontas bridge, which leads over the Appomattox to Petersburg. We go through the town to Camp Lee, now silent, shabby and dilapidated, but so recently the scene of bugle calls and intense activity; thence to Hopewell, the city of paper houses and war munitions, now transformed to stable peace-time industries; to City Point, whose newly-laid-off streets and building lots for World War developments were acquired from the acreage of the Eppes Farm. Turning into a picturesque avenue of century-old cedars, and passing old St. John's Church whose steeple was used as a signal tower in wartime, and on through the splendid trees which surround it, we catch our first glimpse of Appomattox Manor. Just beyond sparkle the waters of the James and the Appomattox. We are at once reminded that the first of the family of Eppes approached this matchless site for a home from the water, travelling by boat or canoe on the river, the natural highway in those early roadless days.

Seals attached to old deeds in possession of the late Dr. Richard Eppes of City Point bore the arms ascribed by English heraldic writers to Epes or Eppes of Canterbury, Kent, England. The records of Prince George County which would have thrown most light on this family history were burned by Federal Troops during the War Between the States, and but few family letters and other personal records survive the burning and sacking of two great wars.

Of this we are assured: the family embarked from "Merrie England" not as men in political disfavor and threatened with disaster, nor yet as cavaliers with dreams of fame and fortune, but as colonists and settlers to found a home in a new world of peaceful employment and productive enterprise, to till the soil and plant and reap.

To Francis Eppes, a member of His Majesty's Council, was granted in 1635 broad acres of land, which included estates on both sides of the James and the Appomattox, and an island laved by the waters of both rivers, called "Eppes' Island," still owned by the family.

On a most beautiful and commanding eminence, jutting out into a broad expanse of water at the confluence of the two rivers, Francis Eppes built his frame dwelling. The place is still the home of his descendants, and represents a tenure of nearly three hundred

A Gateway at Westover

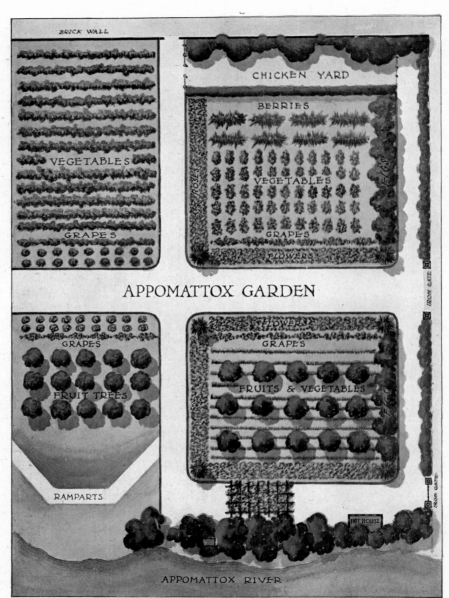

APPOMATTOX GARDEN

Lila L. Williams

Appomattox—Founded by Francis Eppes in 1635

Cucumber Tree at Violet Banks, the Shore Estate Near Appomattox, with Spread of One Hundred Feet
General Lee Camped in Its Shade During the Campaign of 1864

years. He sent back to Jamestown for his slaves, and direct descendants of these same servants are in the employ of the Eppes family to this day—a circumstance exceedingly rare in the annals of any American family.

The first house, which stood nearer the river, was torn down and the present one built from the materials of the original in 1751. This second dwelling was set on fire by the British during the Revolution, but the fire was fortunately put out by faithful slaves. There is a feeling of home and contentment in the cozy charm of the quaint, low, rambling frame building, with its dormer windows and many broad porches. Its latticed columns are hugged by climbing roses—William Allen Richardson, Douglas, Lady Ashton, Banksia, Marie Henriette, Dr. Van Fleet and other modern introductions which replace the old-time festoons of Virgins' Bower (Clematis Virginiana).

The house is pierced with bullet holes, and without doubt a more lordly mansion of brick and stone would have fallen before the onslaughts of musket and cannon. During the War Between the States the place was used as a hospital, and General Grant had built between sixty and sixty-five cabins as wards for wounded soldiers. One of these cabins was sold and may be seen in Fairmont Park, Philadelphia. The last of those remaining was torn down at the time of the World War. An old print of the place as it was at the time of General Grant's occupancy may be seen in the dining-room. There are also cuts in the framework of one window made for the passages of telegraph wires, and from here were sent and received messages affecting the movements of the vast Federal army. Passing from the front around the south side of the house and over flagstones brought from the site of Sir Thomas Dale's settlement at Bermuda Hundred, we come to the original colonial outhouses with their huge old chimneys—the kitchen, laundry and quarters.

The original garden was to the south of the house, where is now the apiary of dozens of hives. Though probably not laid off by one trained in landscape design, it must have combined much of the aesthetic with the practical, because a knowledge of plants and a skill in growing them was a family trait.

Thomas Jefferson, an intimate friend, said he considered Colonel Eppes of Eppington, kinsman of John Eppes of Appomattox, the first horticulturist in America.

This pre-revolutionary garden was completely destroyed, as far as it is possible to destroy a garden, for to this day, each spring, blue hyacinths and golden jonquils pierce the green sward under the spreading trees to mark the place of old-time flower beds and fill the air with a perfume suggestive of the beauty in the garden of long ago.

About 1845, Dr. Eppes returned from extensive travels in Europe and the Holy Land, bringing many seeds and cuttings back with him—ivy from Kenilworth Castle and other things for memory's sake. About this time he planted a great variety of trees and shrubs at Appomattox: acacias, locusts, willows, magnolias, elms, copper beech, pines, spruce, yews, plane-trees, lindens, oaks and Murillo cherries. Many of these were destroyed during the War Between the States, but many survive, and as they are approaching the century mark, now appear majestic and dignified. These splendid trees edge the driveway and are grouped on the sides of the lawn. The pecan tree is especially at home here, and one given by Colonel Eppes to his butler, which was planted over a well in front of a driveway, has attained immense size and height and is a landmark on the way to wharf. Scions and cuttings from this vigorous tree have been used extensively for propagating and marketed under the name of "Appomattox."

On Dr. Eppes' return home after the war, about 1865, he planned and planted the present livable and lovable garden; he walled it in on the front by a honeysuckle hedge growing over an iron fence and on two sides by an embankment of earth planted in trees after the fashion of many gardens in Devonshire, England. The trees on such an embankment make a charming background for garden shrubbery. Included in the garden boundaries are the remains of the old Confederate rampart. Fruit trees, flowers and vegetables mingle and blend in friendly harmony. Straight and direct paths are bordered with roses and perennials which look happy and luxuriant.

On the day of our visit, a border of fig trees was profligately laden with fruit. The mistress of the garden told us she had been preserving figs all day and the supply seemed undiminished. This is the way of the happy fig tree. One of the visitors from a northern clime was enraptured to be invited to gather as many ripe figs as she wished. "I have never seen anything like it," she said. "Of course, I have seen fig trees when I was in New Orleans covered with bloom, but I never saw them in full fruit before." We smilingly told her that these fig trees had never bloomed, and that no other fig tree anywhere would be guilty of so flaunting and daring a thing as bursting into full bloom, unless, perhaps, that rare variety she had seen in New Orleans.

On the outskirts of the garden, near the little iron entrance gate, is a clump of poet's laurel, Semele Androgyna, a daughter plant of "Laurel of Westover." The glossy evergreen leaves and red berries made this a favorite evergreen of old-time gardens. The steep river bank, which slopes from the lawn, is covered with tartarian honeysuckle, crepe myrtle and clumps of evergreens; among these and around the summit is a clump of Scotch broom brought over from Scotland in 1790 by a friend, Mr. Robertson.

Following the rim of the bluff we come to the rustic cedar summer-house at the head of the steps that lead down to the boat landing. A straight, arbored pathway, bordered with shrubs, leads from here back to the house, and around the corner we catch a glimpse of a tall pear tree, planted more than one hundred years ago and still bearing generously. It nods to us in the breeze; we feel friendly and at home. Let us tarry a while in the summer arbor, listen to the sweet sounds of birds, watch a strange insect outline Japanesque tracery underneath the bark of the cedar post, hear the lapping of the water against the boathouse below, enjoy the cool breeze and smell the new-mown hay. We may catch something of the spirit of these early planters and home-makers who builded with a permanent purpose for children and grandchildren and great-grandchildren; for reposeful visits of leisure, not modern calls of haste and hurry, a permanence which has survived the ruthless battles of time and war, and which still holds the peaceful spirit of the times of long ago.

LAURA C. MARTIN WHEELWRIGHT.

A Garden Walk at Shirley

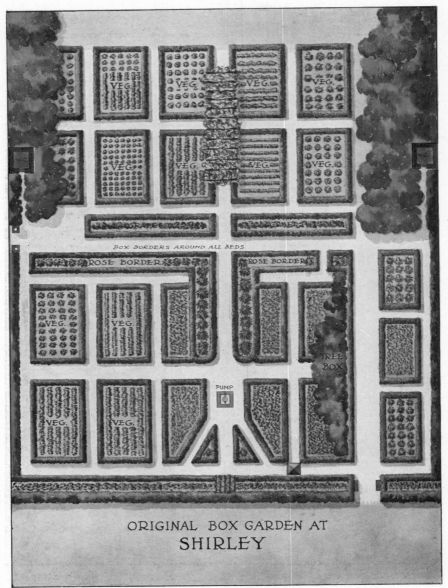

ORIGINAL BOX GARDEN AT
SHIRLEY

Lila L. Williams

SHIRLEY

GO ALONE on a day in June into the old garden at Shirley. As you step from the semi-circular, gravel drive which passes the land front of the house on to a grass walk, thence down to the small gray wooden gate set in a tall box-hedge which overtops it, pass through and close the gate, I pray you, and stop a moment to inhale the fragrance and to let the magic of the green things growing enfold you.

The garden has stood witness to the passing of many generations since its squares were laid out; since its walks were strewed with gravel yielded by the river shore, and its box-hedges and trees were set out. You may pass on, now the magic has its hold upon you, down the main walk where great box-trees flank your left—trees in whose shady hollows little children used to play the drama of home and family.

On your right there is a large rectangular plot about one hundred feet by twenty-five, which bears within its generous dimensions fragrance and beauty enough for one garden. Roses, Fortune's New Yellow, Gold-of-Ophir, the York and Lancaster which is sometimes a white rose streaked and spotted with red, or a red rose streaked and spotted with white, columbines, fox-glove, Chinese honeysuckle and hydrangeas are there, with the old-fashioned corchorus which spelling is probably incorrect, though it sounds like that, but which is not a rose at all, only a tall flowering shrub covered with richly petaled yellow flowers, beautiful to behold. Then there are lilacs, violets, sweet-shrubs, winter honeysuckle, forsythia and more of other fragrant beauties whose names I would be glad to give but that the spelling is somewhat involved and I am not courageous in that line.

At the end of this main walk one comes to a parting of the ways, to the right the transverse walk is sheltered in box-trees and to the left it continues between walls of box and borders of roses, roses, roses on one side and on the other the squares laid out for vegetable and fruits. Among the latter a huge frame-work bears the heavy branches of an ancient Vitis Vulpina, known to us as the scuppernong grape. The transverse walk continues quite to the other side of the great garden and is again sheltered by large box-trees up to which it is still bordered with roses. Turning to the left, to follow an equally broad walk, parallel to the main walk, you pass a large garden square the left half of which is filled with jonquils, daffodils and narcissi. All the rest is roses, save close to the box border where there are shrubs of all varieties and a wonderful ash-tree which, on this day in June, is laden with its bloom of white fringe.

Now you are under an arbour covered with a shower of pink roses and, if you do not swoon with the emotion caused by all the beauty you will in a few steps come to the soul of this garden—a well, everlastingly old and everlastingly preserved, covered with a pump without whose homely bounty beauty would perish. Nearby, there is triangular bed bordered with box which bears within its limits so much linked sweetness, so much refreshment and joy that one is loath to leave it. Heliotrope, lilies, mignonette, rose-geraniums, tea-roses, blue phlox, myosotis and the resurrection lilies. As to this last, plant the bulbs in the fall and watch their spring growth, green and promising, then let your hope die, for the growth withers and decays to nothingness and you think you will plant some other thing to comfort you, when in August there springs to life a leafless stalk—many of them—and in a few days your heart is gladdened by a vision of clusters of exquisite pink lilies, than which there can be nothing more lovely.

Just beyond the well stands an immense pecan tree planted by John Randolph, of Roanoke, when on a visit to his relatives, the Carters. It has borne for many years. In a square, to the right of the tree, there is a large bed of Cynara Scolymus, the burr arti-choke of ordinary parlance. Its gray-green leaves, its dilated, imbricated and prickly involucre is composed of numerous oval scales whose fleshy bases are much esteemed as an article of food, so plentiful in California and so rare with us in the east.

Now you turn and pass along another transverse walk parallel with the former. On your left is the pit which in winter holds the Marechal Neil rose, the lemon and gardenia, begonias and all those plants and shrubs that can not be left out to the blight of winter. On your right there is another border leading to the gate and continuing beyond it to the garden fence. This border merges into another border at right angles which continues along the fence up to the transverse walkway. Every border is surrounded by box-hedges of ancient growth. The last border mentioned encompasses a wealth of bloom and fragrance—irises, Madonna lilies, nasturtiums, petunias, cosmos, gladioli and chrysanthemums, delphiniums, as well as shrubs of many kinds. Fortunately the hedges are sufficiently low to allow one to step over into squares and small plots and here, with gloves, basket and scissors, one can cull to one's heart's content and joy.

The vegetable squares, as before said, are towards the upper end of the garden, as are also the small fruits, currants, gooseberries and raspberries. Just beyond the artichoke bed behold the strawberry bed! Push away the straw and pick the glorious crimson globes and thank God that you are alive. One feels like a ravager of shrines, but there is strawberry cream for dinner and strawberry jam all the winter!

Fruit trees bloom at distant points about the garden and give additional beauty, while the vegetables vie with one another, turnips and radishes near the gray-green cabbages; peas, beans and potatoes stand in neighbourly proximity to tomato plants.

In the early morning, in the long noonday, in the cool of the evening, the garden is a place of refuge, solace and happiness; the atmosphere is laden with the fragrance of boxwood; birds, bees and butterflies are there, their confidence in the Infinite provision

[63]

is exemplified as though their Creator had spoken. To us humans
the call is distinct:

> "Come into thy garden,
> From root to crowning petal it is thine.
> Thine from where the seeds are sown
> Up to the sky, enclosed with all its showers."

LANDON RANDOLPH DASHIELL.

Shirley, Original Home of the Carters

Falling Creek, Site of the First Iron Furnace in America

AMPTHILL

AR up the winding river named in honor of King James, there stands upon the southern bank an old brick house. With flanking outbuildings once used as ballroom and kitchen, with a garden once terraced and a brick-walled graveyard, it is a type of the stately bygones of Virginia's ancient aristocracy. This is Ampthill, ancestral home of the Cary family, but famed before that as the site of the first iron furnace ever operated in America.

Known in colonial days as Falling Creek, The London Company, at a cost of four thousand pounds sterling, in the year 1619 erected on this estate a forge to be used for smelting iron and lead. John Berkeley, son of Sir John Berkeley, was placed in charge of the works, and the iron made here was said to be as good as any in the world. When the crushing year of 1622 came, with its fateful tidings of the Indian massacre, only two of the twenty-four settlers at Falling Creek were spared.

For many years the works were abandoned, but, April 20, 1687, William Byrd was granted eighteen hundred acres of land, which included the ill-fated iron furnace. On October 29, 1690, he secured an additional grant of fifty-six hundred and forty-four acres, the reason given for the latter being that, "there having been iron works at Falling Creek in the time of the company, and Colonel Byrd having an intention to carry them on, and foreseeing that abundance of wood might be necessary for so great a work, he took up a large tract."

In 1733, the second William Byrd, on one of his adventurous rides, bribed an Indian to drop secretly a tomahawk on the spot where the mine was supposed to be. In his "History of the Dividing Line," Byrd tells the story: "We sent for an old Indian called Shacco Will, living about 7 miles off who reckoned himself 78 years Old. This fellow pretended he could conduct us to a Silver Mine, that lies either upon Eno River or a Creek of it, not far from where the Tuscaruros once lived. But by some Circumstances in his Story, it seems to be rather a Lead than a Silver Mine. However such as it is he promised to go and shew it to me whenever I pleased. To comfort his heart I gave him a Bottle of Rum with which he made himself very happy."

Prior to the Revolution the estate, which up to this time had been known only as Falling Creek, became the property of Archibald Cary, who changed the name to Ampthill, and for the third time the iron works were put in operation. Though Colonel Cary abandoned the old forge and used its pond for a grist mill, he built new works on the original spot in 1760.

Known as "Old Iron," Colonel Cary was chairman of the Virginia Committee which drafted the first Declaration of Rights and State Constitution in 1776, so it was not surprising that his iron works were destroyed by Tarleton during the Revolution. The square brick structure, now faded to a warm old rose, which was built by him, has four rooms on each floor, with a long hall cutting between. Distinction is found in the heavy paneling and interior carving; in the inside blinds, and the gracefully designed windows with deeply embrasured seats.

Flanking the dwelling, about sixty feet to the west, is a smaller building of one story and a half, built also of brick laid in Flemish bond. This was the colonial kitchen, its massive iron crane and ample fireplace giving testimony of the lavish food once prepared there.

Balancing the kitchen upon the east, a similar building stands. But this house is paneled from the floor to its conical ceiling and was used as a formal ballroom. Though now bare and cheerless— even forbidding—its rich oak walls have responded to the tune of harpsichord and flute, as they reflected against their polished sides the frills of the dancers of the colonial minuet.

[66]

On his way to Petersburg from Richmond in 1781, the Marquis de Chastellux lost his way, but he says, "We had no reason to regret our error, as it was only two miles about, and we skirted James River to a charming place called Warwick where a group of handsome houses form a sort of village, and there are some superb ones in the neighborhood; among others, that of Colonel Cary, on the right bank of the river." The town to which the Marquis referred was established in the second year of the reign of George III. At the time of the Revolution it boasted mills, ware and storehouses, rope-walks and a shipbuilding yard. Unfortunately, everything was destroyed by the British in 1781. Up to this time, however, fortune smiled upon the Cary family and burnished their rooftree with a golden horn. It was to this James River country seat that Archibald Cary brought his beautiful bride, Mary Randolph, from Curles Neck, across the river. At that time jewels, laces and brocades were brought in their own vessels, to land on the Ampthill shores. There were coaches and fine horses, rare wines to stock the now empty cellar—in short, everything connected with this splendid old home was the very finest to be found in Virginia.

The road which leads from the Petersburg highway to Ampthill is rich in trees and native shrubbery. Dogwood, birch and oak trees shade a narrow, drowsy brook which flows from a spring near by to supply the old mill pond. Scattered throughout—along the roadside and through the woodland—are quantities of Scotch broom, or gorse. This seems to point to some British encampment as, since Revolutionary days, gorse has come down to Americans under the name of "Cornwallis hay." The story goes that the seeds were brought over in the hay used to feed the horses of the British army. One can easily fancy a red-coated trooper, disconsolate, and wandering beneath the dogwood trees, singing the words of the old Scotch ballad, "Kissin's out of fashion when the broom is out of bloom."

The entrance road turns sharply onto the lawn which surrounds the house and is shaded by locust and walnut trees. The garden, which lies immediately in front on a broad terrace, though without consistent care for many years, is still rich in old-time shrubs—lilacs, crepe myrtles and mock orange—which stand inconsequentially within its boundaries. Althea—white, rosy and purple; lilies—white, tawny and yellow; yuccas—"our Lord's candles," as they are called in Mexico, lift high their torches to light up the romantic spot. Scattering box bushes, gnarled and scant of leaf, show the outlines of ancient walks of romance, their pungent odor bringing a breath of days long past and dead. The outlines left prove that in its early days this garden was one of pretense, but time and changed conditions have had their play at Ampthill, and now the garden follows no certain, formal lines.

At its best this garden was, in many ways, like its sisters across the sea; it had the same knots of flowers in the shape of diamonds, crescents or squares, all bound by the shrub dear to us and the hearts of our ancestors—the gallant, cheerful boxwood.

It was a typical Colonial garden that lay on the banks of James River, and it is still a garden to wander in, to sit in, to dream in. All is very quiet here; happily, the bustling world seems very far away. Some of the old-fashioned flowers still stand where they were set out in the old-fashioned way. The outlines of the prim circles and squares may still be hunted out by the remnants of their stiff and straggly box borders; but for so many years have shrub and plant and vine lived together that all of this formality has been done away with, and across old lines new bloom now mingles with new bloom.

A snowdrop now brings the memory of a bride long gone; later in the springtime, jonquils and narcissi dance gayly in the breeze. The winsome, profligate bulbs no longer confine themselves to the garden proper, and they blend deliciously with the delicate blue hyacinths, which are very abundant and much in evidence here. This wealth of pale spring flowers has scattered over the lawn on both fronts of the house and raced down the terrace

Ampthill, Home of Colonel Archibald Cary

Old Stone Bridge Over Falling Creek

to end its pilgrimage at the high brick wall which secludes from idle gaze the Temple burying-ground.

This six-foot wall, covered with the grays and golds of age and topped with crescent bricks, is in such good repair that the only break in it was made when it was built, and this was to permit the entrance way. Roses and periwinkle here live together as kindred in a spot as peaceful as the imagination can picture. A wistaria of patriarchal age, with gnarled and knotted stem, with ivy of ancient lineage, drape the walls and festoon the tombs, the oldest of which dates back to 1800. To the south and the east and the north of the graveyard the apple orchard of about fifteen acres extends.

In April, the rosy-red bud unfolds its blossoms near this garden. In May, a dogwood pitches its tent within its borders. In June, the frail mimosas call to the humming-birds, which fly to it from the acacias that overshadow it from the lawn. With September, the hickory and walnut trees give warning of autumn's onslaught. Then comes the glory of flaming maples, which lose their leaves only in time to give way to the blue and red berries of cedar and holly which brighten old Ampthill till spring.

And it is in the spring that the old place is at its loveliest, for then the apple trees are in full bloom. At this season no one walks in the garden or stands on the lawn, but is told some tale of haunted chambers or of water sprites seen on calm May nights dancing in the lowlands. For, when the gorse throws out its gold banners and the apple trees pitch their pink tents, Colonel Cary walks once more in his garden to see if all goes well with his place.

This old garden in its calm repose means—ah, so much! Memories come to the least romantic and fancy slips back over the bridge of two hundred years to recall what Ampthill stood for in the days of the English Georges. But, the thing of all others that appeals to us of this later and much changed day, is the human interest the old garden awakens. It is this very quality that lends to the semi-neglected spot its elusive, haunting charm.

[69]

The Ampthill of today is very different from the Ampthill that Archibald Cary knew. Its spacious rooms have been used as a tavern, and it has been otherwise desecrated. The sweeping lawn, which once led to the river, has been cut into fields, and time and the hand of man have felled many of the aged trees which once guarded the place like a corps of faithful sentinels. How sad to think that it should have passed from the possession of the family who made it famous! But that seems to be the fate of most old homesteads. They are doomed to linger on in poverty and neglect long after their original owners are sleeping. In poverty, because they must starve in their old age for the sound of familiar and much-loved voices; and in neglect, because new owners seldom seek them with a feeling of pride in possession. They have nothing left but their memories and traditions—a few bright flowers grown among too many tears.

EDITH DABNEY TUNIS SALE.

Richmond and Vicinity

The Garden at the Adams House, in Richmond

Original Home of Richard Adams, Built About 1760, One of the Oldest Houses in Richmond

View Through the Garden from the Portico of the Adams House

(Signed) Mrs. W. Chase Morton   *Carrington House on Church Hill*

CHURCH HILL

IN Mordecai's "Richmond in By-Gone Days" he speaks of the Adams family as original proprietors of the eastern portion of the city. Certainly this statement is true if we may judge by their once stately homes and ornamental gardens.

Colonel Richard Adams, son of Ebenezer Adams and Tabitha Cocke, was born in 1723 and became a man of wealth and influence, being a member of the House of Burgesses, also a member of the famous Convention of 1775. Colonel Adams had three sons, each of whom were prominent men of that day and whose homes were the rendezvous of many distinguished Virginians.

By some strange trick of fortune, the oldest of these homes, built by the first Colonel Adams in 1760, is the only one which has withstood the onward march of progress, and today is standing almost unchanged after a period of one hundred and sixty-three years. Built in the shadow of old St. John's Church, it has shared alike its joys and sorrows and many of its traditions.

We are indebted to Mrs. Edmund Randolph Williams, the fifth in descent from Colonel Adams, for the photograph of this interesting old home.

Tucked away behind the high walls of the Roman Catholic Convent of Monte Maria it stands, far from the "weariness, the fever and the fret" of the busy world; mellowed by the sunshine of years, gently touched by the hand of Time. From its lofty height it has watched a "scattered village growing into a city, far out on the landscape seen the iron roads bringing commerce to its merchants, heard the multitudinous sounds of a great city."

The Sister who showed us through the house and grounds told us, with much pride, that portions of the ceiling had never been repaired. The plaster walls with their delicate tracery, and the floors of wide boards and hand-wrought nails brought over from England, are still intact. The house is entirely hidden from sight, and if one should go to the very bottom of the steep hill and peer up with all their eyes, only the tops of the dormer windows would be their reward.

Unlike the house, the grounds had a very different tale to tell. Nothing was left of the spacious lawn with its many shade trees and flowering shrubs, though here and there a few lilacs and crepe myrtles bloom bravely on. Remnants of the formal garden could still be seen, with its oblong plots, edged with box to keep the unruly little plants off those neat gravel paths. But the avenue of lindens, which bordered the brick walk leading to the house, had long since been cut down, one lone tree standing guard near the doorway.

At the south of the house, and overlooking the river, are five terraces covered with old-fashioned flags, which must be a marvel of beauty in the spring. Fig bushes bask in the southern sun, while at the east of the house a few gnarled fruit trees and a quaint old grape arbor stand. The pit on the slope of one of the terraces, still used by the Sisters, is filled with bloom.

Benedict Arnold, in his brief raid on Richmond, used this house, as well as St. John's Church, as barracks for his British soldiers.

Thomas Jefferson was an intimate friend and frequent guest of Colonel Adams, and we can picture the two on that memorable March day of 1775, their breasts filled with apprehension, hurrying over to St. John's Church, where Patrick Henry was so soon to sway that illustrious body of men, and where then and there George Washington determined on his definite policy of war.

HOME OF DR. JOHN ADAMS

Dr. John Adams, the third son of Colonel Richard Adams, built on the corner of Twenty-fourth and Grace Streets that stately mansion which, up to a few years ago, was such an ornament to the eastern part of the city. It stood on one of the highest of Richmond's seven hills, its dignified appearance, as seen from the street, hardly preparing one for the exquisite beauty of the rear. A large columned porch extended across the entire back of the house, and from this porch marvelous mosaics of beauty were glimpsed through the great trees, whose spreading branches swept the lawn; in the distance the peaceful river, beyond the fields bathed in sunshine.

Like the paternal home, terraces edged with box broke the steep descent to the river, while at the foot of each terrace blossomed the peonies and roses, the columbines, and sweet william. A fernery flourished in a shady corner, and here masses of lily of the valley sent their fragrance out on the summer air. A broad graveled path, bordered on either side by masses of shrubs and evergreens, led down to the summer-house, smothered in roses.

Many distinguished men were entertained in this home, notably LaFayette, when he visited Richmond in 1824. Edmund Randolph, aide-de-camp to General Washington, Secretary of State, and Governor of Virginia, was also a frequent caller at this house. It was here, that after visiting his wife's grave, as was his daily custom, he was stricken with paralysis, though his death did not occur until three years later. It is an interesting coincidence that Edmund Randolph Williams, fifth in descent from Edmund Randolph, should have married the fifth in descent from Dr. Adams.

In later years, this house was much in the public mind, on account of its being the home of Miss Van Lew, a noted Federal spy during the period of the Confederacy. A secret passage way led from the house to the river, and this Miss Van Lew is said to have used in aiding Federal prisoners to escape. Nothing remains of this once lovely home. Down at the very bottom of the grounds we found a few fragments of the old brick wall, which at one time had encircled the entire place.

THE CARRINGTON HOUSE

Facing Libby Hill, and with an uninterrupted view of the surrounding country, stood the residence of Colonel George Mayo

Carrington. He married first, Margaret, the widow of Colonel Charles Pickett and daughter of Dr. John Adams. His second wife was Susan Grymes Braxton, the third in descent from Carter Braxton, signer of the Declaration of Independence. His land on the east sloped down to that historic spot known as Bloody Run, where Bacon, in 1676, had such a fierce battle with the Indians that the little stream at the foot of the hill literally ran with blood.

Just as the stirring days of Revolutionary history hang around those other homes, so memories of 1861-65 come crowding over one as we recall how the sick, the wounded and dying of the Confederate army were nursed and tenderly cared for by the inmates of this house, one poor fellow being buried in the garden while Richmond was under fire.

In the "Diary of a Southern Refugee," Mrs. McGuire speaks of this house "as a picture of comfort and hospitality, the wealth being used at this troublous time for the comfort of others." So freely was this wealth used that Mrs. Carrington found herself after the war not only widowed, but like so many gentlewomen of the South, obliged to part with some of her land. Year by year portions of the grounds were sold. The first to go was the vegetable garden in the rear of the house. A white paling fence, hidden by a hedge of bridal wreath and single and double hollyhocks, enclosed this part of the garden, where, in large square beds, many varieties of vegetables were planted, and strawberries and raspberries grew in abundance: and what garden of that time could fail to have its sage and rue, sweet marjoram and silver thyme? Grape vines covered the long arbor which separated the vegetable garden from the orchard, with its cherry and pear trees, mulberry, apricot, apple, and peach. At the extreme end of the ground was the old carriage house and stable, which was standing long after the house had gone. In a brick courtyard the servants' quarters and old smokehouse stood.

Ruskin has said that "Flowers only flourish rightly in the garden of some one who loves them." If this is true, there were many

[76]

The Archer House, in Richmond

The Garden of the Archer House

which bore mute testimony to the love of the owner, for never have shrubs and flowers reached such perfection. Lilacs and snow-balls, mock oranges, crepe myrtles, white and yellow jessamines, calycanthus bushes, winter honeysuckle—all blooming in profusion. Roses, a perfect riot of roses—tea roses, moss roses, Giant of Battle, York and Lancaster, Seven Sisters—roses everywhere, clambering over fences, up the old pear tree, anywhere, everywhere! The hyacinths and daffodils, snowdrops and tulips, white and purple violets peeping through the snow. The tiny "lady iris," with its faint elusive odor, which mammy said "nobody but 'ristocrats could smell." Summer-houses, covered with roses and carpeted with periwinkle, were on either side of the moss-grown brick walk leading to the gate, while magnolia trees, with their wax-like flowers, were a delight to the eye.

A large evergreen, called the "Tree of Heaven," grew on one side of the porch near the greenhouse, its branches hanging gracefully down. On the other side was a most beautiful double-flowering crab-apple tree. I have seen old-time "hack drivers" point this out to tourists on their sight-seeing expeditions.

Much of the beauty and charm of this garden was still there when, in later years, my father was called to the rectorship of St. John's Church, and this house was used as a rectory, and as the shadows lengthened around the old home, the laughter of children and the song of birds were once more heard in the evening air.

PENELOPE WRIGHT WEDDELL ANDERSON.

THE ARCHER HOUSE

THE Archer house stands at the corner of Sixth and Franklin Streets, and was built in 1815, by Edward Cunningham, an Irish gentleman.

It was designed by the well-known London architect, R. A. Mills, who also drew the plans for Monumental Church, the Wickham house, now the Valentine Museum, and the Marx house, all of Richmond.

The general plan of the Archer house, with its parapet walls, has often been copied by architects from other places. In the early twenties the house was bought from Mr. Cunningham by Dr. George Watson, of Ionia, Louisa County, Virginia, and it has been occupied continuously by the same family for a century. The present owners are Misses Anne and Virginia Archer and Mrs. Andrew H. Christian, daughters of Mrs. Robert S. Archer, who was the youngest daughter of Dr. George Watson.

The large, square, stuccoed mansion, with its Ionic portico and small brass door bell, the first to supplant the knocker in Richmond, is surrounded by one of the few walled gardens left in Richmond. The high brick wall is covered with English ivy, which falls over the top and sways gracefully before the eyes of the stranger, who looks with wonder at such dignity and seclusion in the heart of a city teeming with life and twentieth-century progress.

Perhaps the most interesting view of the garden is the one from the steps which lead into it from the long portico at the rear of the house. Here one sees the old gray urns and the Italian marble seat, well beaten by time and suggestive of old world gardens. Serpentine gravel walks wind out from an ivy-covered circle in the centre, where a tall and noble magnolia tree stands. In the most secluded corner is hidden the brick pit greenhouse, where the pink camellias and fruit-laden lemon and orange trees, brought forth on great occasions to decorate the house, once flourished. To the left of the greenhouse are two large box-trees.

There was a custom among the ladies of the earlier period to exchange flower slips and seed. In this way friendships and memories were renewed each year as the plants blossomed. So the Watson or Archer garden gave out the fragrance of Westover, Shirley and Brandon; Barboursville and Castle Hill. In return, the Byrds, Carters and Harrisons; the Barbours and Rives, received their slips from the chatelaine of this house. All the old-fashioned flowers grew here—lilacs and snowballs; cydonia japonica, syringa, calycanthus, and yellow roses. There were others, and many rows of hyacinths and jonquils; tulips and daffodils.

A brick courtyard adjoins the garden and a low gateway leads into it. On the right of this gate are several stone steps with foot-scrapers, and here one passes under an arch of roses into the kitchen-garden.

Opening onto this court are several brick buildings, a smoke-house, a large kitchen building with servants' quarters, a green-house, and numerous wood and coal houses.

At the end of a long, straight walk in the garden is the stable, with a high and heavy gate, through which the family carriage was driven.

For a hundred years a picturesque sycamore tree stood in the middle of the pavement outside the garden wall. This tree measured fourteen feet and three inches in circumference, and the oldest inhabitant cannot remember when it was not there. Of primeval growth, it had boldly taken possession of the street, and it was only removed by the city authorities when pedestrians demanded it. Its silvery branches furnished material for several of our best and most beloved writers. The late Thomas Nelson Page likened the pallor of a dying man to the bark of this tree, in one of his short stories, and both the tree and the Archer house are described in Ellen Glasgow's "The Romance of a Plain Man." It was planted by Samuel Dobie who, as early as 1782, occupied the stuccoed building which stands on the northeast side of the residence. Samuel Dobie was the architect of the roof, the steps and the interior of the Virginia State Capitol, the plan of the exterior, a reproduction of the Maison Carrée at Nismes, France, having been brought to America by Thomas Jefferson.

In the year 1847 Daniel Webster was invited to Richmond by the citizens and a public banquet was given for him. This distinguished statesman was entertained in the Archer home at a notable dinner. Many other interesting men have been within its walls— Henry Clay, Chief Justice Marshall, the Virginia Ambassadors to England and France—James Barbour and William C. Rives; and greatest and most beloved of all, General Robert E. Lee. The late Dr. S. Weir Mitchell was a kinsman of the family and visited there when a boy and again in later years, after he became one of America's eminent men in medicine and letters.

FRANCES ARCHER CHRISTIAN.

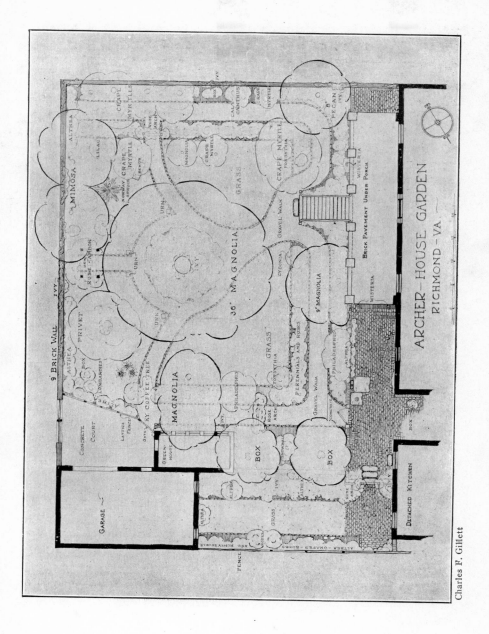

ARCHER-HOUSE GARDEN
RICHMOND-VA.

Charles F. Gillett

Garden at the Valentine Museum, in Richmond

VALENTINE MUSEUM

N old Clay Street, in Richmond, there still remain many beautiful houses, reminiscent of the prominent families who played their part in the life of the city in the early years of the nineteenth century. At the far end, on a hill-top, overlooking Shockoe Valley, is the White House of the Confederacy with its majestic and imposing columns. As the Confederate Museum, it harbors today invaluable records and relics of the times of its palmy days.

Just one block above is the Valentine Museum, built by the gifted architect, Robert Mills, in 1812 for John Wickham, Esq., who was the leading counsel in the defense of Aaron Burr in 1807. It is said that it was largely through his eloquence that Burr was acquitted. Chief Justice Marshall and Aaron Burr dined together with Mr. Wickham at his home. The Chief Justice was very much criticized for this by the opponents of Burr and he replied to them, saying if Mr. Wickham did him the honor of inviting him to dine at his home, he could but do him the courtesy of accepting.

During the Civil War the Honorable C. G. Memminger, Secretary of the Treasury of the Confederate States, resided here. More recently it was the home of Mr. Mann S. Valentine, who founded the Museum, and through whose bounty and love for the beautiful, this Treasure House has been preserved for the people of Richmond.

From the street the house presents a plain and dignified, but imposing, appearance, with its thick brick stuccoed walls, and a square porch with rounded columns and broad steps leading from the street. But it is not until after we have sounded the knocker and passed through the vestibule into the most beautiful circular hall that we feel we are in a house planned by an artist as a dwelling for people of taste and distinction.

The splendid winding stair ascends to the hallway above, terminating in a gallery the shape of an artist's palette. The banisters of the stairway are of rich mahogany, while on its base board is carved a festoon of magnolia buds and blossoms. An ornate chandelier of bronze suspended in the center of the spiral stairway has gas jets of exquisitely wrought design on each landing, so arranged as to light both upper and lower halls, replacing the original chandelier of prisms and candles. Square and gracefully-arched doorways lead from the hall into the spacious rooms on the first floor, and the doors are of solid mahogany with silver knobs and hinges. One of these is of a very unusual curved design. The rooms are of beautiful proportion, giving a sense of stateliness and elegance, and contain now many handsome carved mantels of Florentine marble, which take the place of the originals of carved wood.

First, one enters a small library, thence into a large drawing-room, through the center music-room into a spacious and imposing dining-room. Running along these three rooms, the outer wall of which makes a sweeping curve at the back of the house, is a beautiful pillared veranda, which opens out onto the old garden.

It is, indeed, an unique surprise when visiting this treasure house of *objet d' art* and relics of ancient days, to step from the drawing-room onto the portico and find oneself in the midst of a garden. It is true, the small strip of ground on the street front of the house boasting of old evergreens, yews, euonymus, yuccas, on each side of the porch, would suggest plant lovers here as well as builders; nevertheless, one experiences a thrilling surprise on descending the steps at the back into the terraced garden of a century ago, which originally occupied a city block. An archway in the wall enclosing the flower garden led into a paved court where were the outbuildings, thence into the fruit and vegetable garden. Splendid hollys, elms and other trees can still be seen beyond the wall. It is a pity its confines have ever been restricted an inch.

The outlines of the terraces repeat the lines and curves of the house and portico, making it, indeed, a living extension of the house itself. This was the place of the confidential talks, the intimate unrestrained life—the out-door living room.

Old-fashioned brick walls invitingly lead one under rose-arched pathways to a refreshing pool and fountain in the center, which is guarded on three sides by marble forms of the goddesses of Beauty, Flowers and the Harvest. From these radiate paths around parterres filled with every old-fashioned flower which can now be coaxed into bloom by the skillful hands of its present loving caretaker, who says she receives each season plants and seeds from numberless appreciative guests who have visited the house and loved the garden. All do not thrive, alas! For the trees have grown since the days the builder first planted them there and the garden is now one of shade and sifted sunlight.

We find an amazing variety of plants for so small a space and of course among them the "vine and fig tree," indispensable, it seems, to "ye olde time garden." In the far corner a tall, magnificent magnolia grandiflora planted in 1807 looks like a giant candelabra shining and shimmering when it carries its full load of pure white blooms from base to top; then fragrance and perfume spread like incense all through the garden.

The garden seems to recall the life of a hundred years ago even more vividly than does the beautiful house, and to speak even more eloquently of the charm and elegance of the ladies and gentlemen who then enjoyed it. The fragrance of flowers, the ripple of water, the witchery of half-concealed marble forms, the romance of moonlight, the poetry of the past are still there.

No better model can be had to this day for a city garden. The ivy-covered brick walls, the arched gateway to the side, the curved and straight paths, a hedge here, a clump of shrubs there, an archway or vine-clad column yonder! The trick is turned, exclusion in the midst of crowds, complete!

LAURA C. MARTIN WHEELWRIGHT.

[83]

AN OLD RICHMOND GARDEN

IN the good old days of Richmond there stood on the square bounded by Franklin, Adams, Jefferson and Main Streets, two large stucco houses surrounded by gardens. That nearest Adams Street was owned by Dr. Robert Archer, and the other by his son-in-law, General Joseph R. Anderson, C. S. A. Dr. Archer's house, somewhat changed, became later the property of his grandson, Colonel Archer Anderson, whose wife and children still own it.

Just half of the old garden remains, with its primeval trees; its old brick walls covered with ivy, honeysuckle and Madeira vine. There, every spring, come up afresh the lilies of the valley from the garden of Edgar Allan Poe's foster mother. There the cowslips and peonies and Harrison roses bloom today as they did when "old miss" (as Mrs. Harrison of Brandon was called by her intimates) sent them with her own hands to my mother so many years ago! There still are the circular benches around the enormous trees; and there, too, bloom the honeysuckle, microphylla roses, mimosa tree and so many shrubs from the beautiful old garden at Fortsville, the John Y. Mason country home.

Fortsville, an estate of one thousand acres lying in Southampton and Sussex Counties, came to Judge Mason through his wife, Miss Fort (de Fort). The oldest part of the house was built of original timbers which were pegged together by wooden pins—having been constructed before iron nails were used. The garden, too, was old and unique. A centre mound, on which was a small maze of large box bushes and "grey man's beard"—I always likened it to Rosamond's Bower—dominated the garden, which went from it like the spokes of a wheel, in green sunken alleys and masses of flowers.

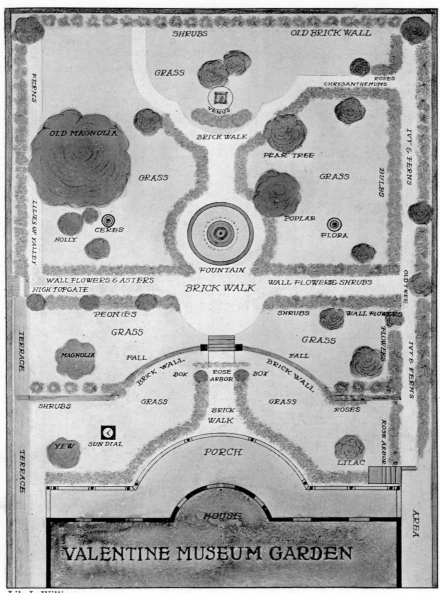

VALENTINE MUSEUM GARDEN

Lila L. Williams

South Front of Home and Garden of General Joseph R. Anderson, Now the Site of the Jefferson Hotel

There were snowdrops, followed by the grape hyacinths and a varied assemblage of old favorites. The roses were notable, even in those days, when there were so many to "tend" these old gardens that they flourished like the proverbial green bay tree; the yellow jasmine twining in among the microphylla roses, the thousand leaf, the musk cluster, the Cherokee, the damask, and, above all, the great favorite—the moss rose. Who that ever grew up in a Virginia garden but knows the prick of a moss rose?

On her return from her residence in Paris, Mrs. Mason, whose husband had died in his second term as Minister Plenipotentiary and Envoy Extraordinary from the United States of America to the Court of Napoleon III, would wander through her beloved garden, gloved and veiled, giving orders and instructions to her train of ebony gardeners, whose greatest joy was to carry out her beautiful taste in the garden that had been planted by her great-grandmother.

The house and garden of General Anderson have been swept away by the growth of Richmond, and on their site stands today the Jefferson Hotel. I have always understood that it was the plan of the designers of that hotel to leave some of the lawn and trees on Franklin Street and the beautiful row of horse chestnuts which bordered the pavement; but the engineer, not calculating on the great drop of the land, drew the plans so that the hotel had to be put on the line of the street. A pang shot through every child of two generations when they saw not only their playground, the garden, but even the horse chestnuts go, for General Anderson's pavement was the roller-skating-rink for the neighborhood for squares around. The delicious odor of the horse chestnut bloom brings to many an adult mind of today the happy skating there in the springtime of the long ago. And with the thought of the odor of the horse chestnuts, mingled with the fragrance of the paulownias in the garden, comes, too, the wafted fragrance of another bit of the old South, for this home, its owner and the garden were the truest exponents of the Virginia, the Richmond of those

[85]

days. That was "Aunt" Elinor and her room—where every skater was privileged to go to repair skates or, in colder weather, to get warm. She was Mrs. Anderson's sempstress, a fine example of the best of the colored race, dying from a broken heart a few weeks after the death of her mistress.

A pretty story has always been told of the courtship of General Anderson and his first wife, Sally Archer, the daughter of Dr. Robert Archer, surgeon in the "old army," as the United States Army has always been spoken of by those who were in it before 1861, and who left it then or before. His home was in Norfolk; his summer home, Olivera, was where the town of Phoebus now is, but he was stationed at Fortress Monroe. He had several daughters. Coming into his home one day he announced that a handsome young lieutenant, who had just graduated second in his class, engineers, at West Point, had been detailed there to build a fort on the Rip Raps, and that whoever guessed his first name might have him. Sally, not quite seventeen, said, in her gentle, soft voice, "Joseph"; and, in reality, in a few months she became the wife of this young lieutenant, was the mother of his children and his devoted companion for forty-four years!

But, to the garden and house! The latter was a typical Colonial house of grey stucco, the spacious front porch with its Corinthian columns surmounted by the Greek pediment. Through the porch passed not only the best of the town, but also "the stranger within its gates"—for this home was known during its whole existence for its unbounded hospitality, here and abroad. General Lee's frequent visits there during the War Between the States brought happiness to all, the children included. His love for, and recognition of them, was ever present. One of the daughters of the house tells how he always drew her, a little girl, to his side on the sofa in the family sitting-room, raised her hand and kissed it with the affection of a father, the deference of a gallant!

On their return from Europe in September, 1871, Mr. and Mrs. Jefferson Davis and their family came directly here, and Mrs.

[86]

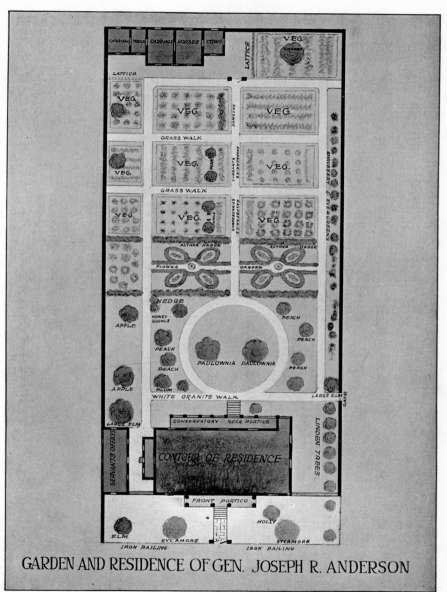

GARDEN AND RESIDENCE OF GEN. JOSEPH R. ANDERSON

Joseph R. Anderson, Jr.

The Home of General Joseph R. Anderson

Davis, Winnie and Mrs. Hayes felt it was their home when they made their visits to Richmond after Mr. Davis' death.

There Mr. Matthew Arnold visited, and a long list of "worthies," never ending.

My mother, the wife of the oldest son, lived in the wing room toward Jefferson Street, whilst her husband, a colonel in the Confederate Army, was at the front. In the dead of night, the rest of the family being in the second story, she often heard a disaffected slave passing coal and provisions out of the basement door under her room to the Northern sympathizers.

But let us go through the house on to another old-fashioned porch, the east end of which was a charming greenhouse, and thence to the garden. In the writer's memory it was the more formal terraced garden, at the end of which was a long line of maple trees, back of which a grape arbor extended the whole width of the garden, thus screening from the view of the house the stables, yards, etc., which opened on Main Street—on a much lower level than the garden. But to the child, that stable guarded so closely by old "Uncle" Sam, the coachman, held delights as interesting as the garden. The tuberoses, mignonette, heliotrope and, O, such tea roses! were beautiful, but the glamour of the big old landau, the victoria, the glittering silver-mounted harness, the spirited horses! To penetrate there spelled heaven to the childish mind.

The accompanying picture only gives a poor view of one of the four terraces which formed the garden, and no idea of the long side lawn extending from Franklin to Main Street. But it does show some of the trees of the original garden—the lindens and the paulownias. This view was taken after the death of General Anderson and when the property had been sold to give way to the Jefferson Hotel. And the borders, etc., look in it little as they had under the care of my grandmother. One hears much now of the "Newport Pink" and such "novelties" of these days. There used to be always planted there thick masses of geranium, just the same shade as Newport Pink, with corresponding masses of heliotrope. The English gardener and his greenhouses at the lower end of the garden were both our fear and our delight. A lattice, weighted down with clematis and Madeira vines, was between the mansion and the servants' quarters, smokehouse, the kitchen, those busy hives of industry, for the entertaining was unceasing.

But let us speak of the real garden—the garden of my father's childhood—"the enchanted garden," the garden that refreshed the heroes of the Confederacy, from the generals to the privates, who would come for a brief visit to the family, the recuperating officers who were being restored to the Confederate Army by devoted care; the garden that could tell of many a courtship and many a heart pang at parting, with the insistent booming cannon of the Seven Days' Battles around Richmond calling, calling through the sylvan peace of this old-fashioned Virginia garden! In the happier days, the children and grandchildren and all the neighborhood held here their "Queen of May" and "Sleeping Beauty" and such old English delights, while the garden for all time was the playground for many generations of children and their friends. The plan of this garden is given here. As I have already said, it adjoined the residence and garden of my great-grandfather, afterwards my father's. It was, therefore, more than half of a city square. The garden was in four divisions. First, you entered it from the back porch by steps to a gravel walk running parallel with the house. The main arteries of the garden were of gravel, the walks or paths around the flower beds, bordered each side with box bushes, and through the vegetable plots, were of grass. The upper part of the garden was given over to grass. Here was the lawn dotted with peach, apple, plum grafted with apricot, and cherry, holly and elm trees, while a gravel walk cut out of this lawn a circle of grass where the beautiful paulownias, whose purple blooms exhaling such fragrance, one of the glories of the springtime, stood in sovereign majesty. Then came the hedge, four feet wide, six feet high, of coral honeysuckle and hawthorn (that "oped in the month of

May") separating this lawn from the flower garden. To the east were the rosebushes, with a famous old microphylla known far and wide, the flowering shrubs, pyrus japonica, calycanthus, crepe myrtle, bridal wreath and mock orange, lilac and snowball, then the bowknots of flowers as they came in season—tulips, hyacinths, lilies of the valley, pinks, heartsease (the name pansy was not the name in those days for these old favorites), ageratum, verbenas, geraniums, heliotrope, mignonette, etc.—flowers, old-fashioned, simple, true, like everything else here.

In the centre of each knot, stood a stately evergreen, the box-edged grass walks radiating from it; each flower border, too, having a narrow grass walk around it, bordered each side by the box.

The rare cactus, lemon trees, cape jessamine, japonicas or camelias of such waxen beauty, from the greenhouses, were massed around the porches of the house in summer; but in the garden itself there were no forced flowers or shrubs—none not indigenous to the place, and consequently everything grew luxuriantly. Then another hedge, six feet high, four feet wide—but this was of althea—often said in old Virginia to be the "Rose of Sharon." Beyond this hedge were the vegetable plots, grass walks running across, gravel walks running lengthwise, bordered with currants, gooseberries and raspberries, with stately apple and damson trees marching along. To the east wall of the garden grew the ravishing fig bushes—the delight of all, young and old. As Main Street was neared, a part of the garden was latticed off for the stable, yards, etc., while the fruit trees and vegetables held sway on one side full to the street. If to live in the memory of our friends is not to die, then the gracious owners of this home live on—for their personality, their delightful hospitality, the dignified simple luxury of their home and garden, will never be forgotten by any who knew them.

Inter folias fructus.

MARY MASON ANDERSON WILLIAMS.

[89]

BROOK HILL

COMPARED with Brook Hill house, the main Brook Hill garden—"the Big Garden" as it is called—is a very recent affair. Originally, the vegetable garden lay just north of the house on a large, level lawn. Within the last few years, the pear trees that used to be in this garden were still producing fruit, and the almost imperishable jonquil bulbs—in spite of browsing cows and ruthless lawn mowers—fought their way along for twenty-five years after the garden was moved.

Before 1850 this garden was transferred to a location of extraordinary beauty. It now lies on the crest of a sharply sloping hill with a charming view across trees and meadows to the north. To the south and east, at some small distance, lie "the woods," which have never been slaughtered for fuel, and in whose keeping stand beeches of immemorial age.

The site of the garden, in truth, should have been the site of the house itself. Yet so beautifully is it located that one is apt to forget in its contemplation that this particular site could have been used for any other purpose. Entering by a gateway cut through an arching hedge, the grass-edged walk runs straight for a hundred and fifty yards or more. On either side are deep beds of flowers, so designed that each season, from the earliest

> "Daffodils
> That come before the swallows dare and take
> The winds of March with beauty,"

to the last Michaelmas daisy, has each its own peculiar gonfalon of flowers.

Perhaps the most gorgeous period is when the Harrisonii roses are in bloom. Then it seems as if a field of the cloth-of-gold itself were spread in waving welcome.

The Brook Hill Garden

Entrance to the Park at Brook Hill in Winter

Behind the flowers stand grape trellises, and then the useful, but not decorative, plots where grow beets, radishes, celery, asparagus, and that celebrated tuber which has been so justly called "the unostentatious po-ta-to."

There was a day when damsons were in this garden; now only the apricot, peach and pear trees survive. The apple trees of fifty years ago no longer furnish even practice grounds for sapsuckers. But the intimate violet, in its ever-enlarging beds, has thriven and multiplied, while the great trees died.

The garden itself is a rough oval traversed by two walks on different levels, one of grass and the other, gravel. Across these at right angles, under a rose arbor, runs a transverse allée. Around the whole garden, just inside the hedge, is another walk that is purely utilitarian. In this garden are "the new hothouses" as they were called—sixty years ago—the old hothouses stand much nearer to the house itself in the "Little Garden."

The date of the latter is unknown, but a colossal magnolia, glorious in its symmetry, has spread, from generation to generation, its great trailing limbs, and speaks of an age that really surpasses mere dates. The "little garden" is just for roses, and three great magnolias; true, there are two immense willow oaks on its south border, and flowering almonds, which look very modern in the presence of the old trees, stand on the edge of the central grass plot. This garden is a rough circle. On the side nearest the mansion is an iron fence, now arbored with trailing roses; within the fence are rosebeds, then comes a narrow walk that runs around the whole. Within this walk stand two great magnolias, and one magnolia grandiflora; there are rosebeds in this grass plot, too.

On the north side of the garden are three hothouses, one of which has been there for seventy-five or eighty years; the other two are forty years old.

Just east of the garden stands a group of magnificent evergreens, under whose peaceful keeping lie the bodies of the ancestors of the present owners of Brook Hill. The whole effect, in its tranquility and detachment, reminds one strongly of Von Boeck-lein's "Sanctuary by the Sea." There are no fountains, and there is no glint of water, but the grass waves of a wide lawn roll to the very verge of the garden where stand, like protecting sentinels, the great trees planted in other days by those who had faith in the power of gardens.

JOHN STEWART BRYAN.

Hickory Hill

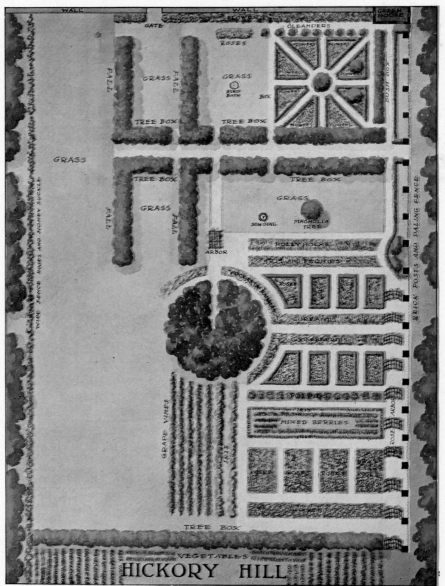

HICKORY HILL

Lila L. Williams

HICKORY HILL

HE plantation known as Hickory Hill, home of the late Williams Carter Wickham, Brigadier-General of Cavalry, C. S. A., is situated in the County of Hanover, twenty miles north of Richmond. It came into the possession of the Carter family the 2nd of March, 1734, and was long an appendage to Shirley on the James.

The house was built and the garden begun in 1820, when William Fanning Wickham, son of John Wickham, of Richmond, and his wife, Ann Carter, of Shirley, made their home on her share of the estate inherited from her father, Robert (after whom General Lee was named), son of Charles, son of John, son of Robert Carter, of Corotoman, known as the "King." The house was destroyed by fire in 1875 and the present dwelling then erected.

The grounds surrounding the house were laid out in 1820 on broad and long lines by Mr. and Mrs. William F. Wickham. The avenues of cedar trees, cedar hedges and boxwood hedges, as originally planned, are still standing and have excited the admiration of many. The feature of the home is the old pleasaunce with its tall, stately trees—its roses and violets, its arbors, avenues and terraces—the emerald of its broad stretches of grass and its matchless boxtrees now more than one hundred years old.

The pleasure garden is a rectangular plot of ground, three hundred and fifty-five feet by four hundred and forty feet, containing approximately four acres, to which adjoins the vegetable garden of approximately two acres. Its central glory is "the box-walk"—an avenue of the Sempervirens boxwood—the trees varying from thirty to forty feet in height, extending a distance of three hundred and seven feet in double line from the entrance gate and forming a perfect arch above the fifteen-foot walkway. At every season, at every hour and in every weather there is beauty—majestic beauty. The legend is that the small bushes were passed through the hands of General Wickham, then an infant, by his mother, the creator of the flower garden. It recalls the dim stretches of a cathedral aisle. Some prefer the sunlight percolating through the arched branches and the feeling of uplift and inspiration. Those who have not seen it in a light snow can scarcely grasp its fairy-like beauty, and by moonlight there is romance indeed.

The members of the Philadelphia Garden Club standing at the entrance were moved to silence, and one of them sent the following lines in memory of their visit:

HICKORY HILL

A Retrospect

"A dream it was, a dream of fairy trees,
  Great Box trees, bending o'er our lifted heads
As we gazed skyward, through their bending green,
Or looked through their long vistas, ere we trod
The path beneath them. 'Twas a path oft trod
By courteous and by gentle men and dames
This hundred years which have so changed our world.
Its Season-changing beauty, new to us,
Yet dear from just one seeing, is to them
A heart-close tie, to tie and bind them fast
In deeper love and bond to that dear home,
Where even those who serve, both serve and love.
Nine times has dusky father left to son,
And he to son or grandson of his line,
Duty of service to this blood and place;
Nor could war break nor freedom's call could win
These from their loyal service, gladly given."

The most recent poetic effusion inspired by the box-walk comes from a charming young woman, who looks more as if she belonged to Watteau's landscapes than to Washington Square and Greenwich Village. This came with a New Year greeting:

"I love your Box Trees! taller than Pope Leo's in the Vatican!
His garden as a wonder shown no Box Tree has like these you own.
And this I think is quite a pity because his garden is so pretty."

Another tribute, dated May 10, 1920, is from the graceful pen of one of the most charming writers in Virginia, the author of the "Commuter's Diary":

"I have just seen for the many hundredth time the most wonderful of gardens. It would take more than the length of this paper to describe it properly. It has a century and more behind it—the roses in one border are the same, which were originally planted there when the grandparents of the family, as a young married couple, established themselves and made a home for themselves and their posterity. There, flowers appear in all due seasons and a well-kept greenhouse carries the winter plants and shrubs too tender to stand the cold of the open borders. Walks, fringed with lilies and violets, gladioli and pansies; trellises covered with climbing rose-bushes; rows of grapevines, now budding into leaf, abound on all sides.

"The most striking thing, however, about it is the noble 'box walk' formed by the double line of great box-trees, beginning at the entrance and extending away to the far side of the garden, where a green bank, bathed in sunshine, gleams in the distance, through an arcade whose graceful curve reminds one of the arch of the Natural Bridge.

"An examination of the individuals composing the group now bordering on the century-mark brightens one's admiration. Interlacing branches form the beautiful arch within, while without, the massed effect of the rich-green alignment mounting heavenward is most effective—each tree in its

[95]

severalty looking as if it might be a Titan among evergreens."

To the right of the entrance gate is a broad walk one hundred feet in length (leading to the greenhouse), flanked on each side by lines of suffruticosa box, beyond which extend on each side formal flower-beds edged with dwarf-box. Here are some of the original roses brought by Anne Carter from Shirley in 1820: the Noisettes, Champney's Blush Cluster, Seven Sisters, La Tourtrelle and the ever-blooming Pink Daily. To the left extends a small maze of box, with beds of lilies of the valley and hardy begonia, at the foot of tall magnolia trees. The inner circle of the maze contains, carefully cherished, LaReine, Dr. Marx, Baron Provost, Rivers', George IV, White Rose of Provence, and other old-fashioned remontant roses, planted by Mrs. W. C. Wickham when she came as a bride in 1848.

To the left of the entrance gate a gravel walk extends, three hundred and forty feet in length, the first one hundred feet being flanked with formal rose-beds edged with dwarf-box. Beyond this is a series of rustic arches covered by climbing roses.

At intervals, and on both sides of the box avenue, other broad walks extend through the garden, some at right angles and some parallel. Along some of these, rows of raspberries, gooseberries and currants extend. Others are bordered by peonies, phlox, and iris, while scattered here and there are tall crepe myrtles, calycanthus, and pyrus-japonica shrubs.

On the two terraces or falls (as they are preferably called), at the lower end of the garden, box-trees, still higher, cast their cool shadows on the thirty-foot stretch of grass and fragrant shrubbery. These are closed in by fences covered with climbing roses, yellow jasmine and honeysuckle, at the bottom of which nestle long stretches of iris, syringas, jonquils and periwinkle.

Turning to the left, at the end of the rose-covered arches, a broad grass walk marks the southern limit of the flower garden,

Box Walk at Hickory Hill

Formal Garden at Hickory Hill

edged by a new box-hedge recently planted to screen the vegetable garden.

To the right of the walk, we come to four plots filled with pink, white, red and yellow roses (called "Credilla's roses"), with charming narrow grass walks between and around them. To the north of this, we find eight other large beds of white American Beauty, Paul Neyron, Hugh Dickson and Soleil d'Or roses. Beyond the roses we see a curved walk around the "boscage," or thicket, formed by a mass of shrubbery—an old-fashioned tangle of lilacs, syringas, yuccas and evergreens, which crown the garden with joy at all seasons.

The War Between the States caused desolation in the garden, but General and Mrs. Wickham strove to keep it up, the General after his arduous day's toil standing on a chair and clipping the box to keep the walks open. It is today recognized as one of the most characteristic and representative gardens of the Old South.

No account of the garden would be complete without a reference to the escape on the 23rd of June, 1863, of General Lee's youngest son, Robert, during a raid of the Northern troops. When General William Henry Fitzhugh Lee, at the time desperately wounded, was taken prisoner and removed from the office in the yard, as it is called, so graphically told in Rob Lee's "Recollections and Letters of General R. E. Lee," a clump of box-trees afforded a safe place for concealment.

Twice each year during the last three years of the war the contending armies swept over Hickory Hill, its garden, its grounds, and its plantation. Innumerable raids occurred, and once the Confederate skirmish line fell back in disorder through the yard and garden, followed by the enemy.

Two incidents especially stand out connected with General J. E. B. Stuart—the first on the night of the 12th of June, 1862, when he left the head of his column in the famous "raid around McClellan" and, accompanied by Colonel William Henry Fitzhugh Lee, came in to grasp the hand and cheer a desperately

[97]

wounded soldier, then a paroled prisoner within the Northern lines, and to say to him how much he regretted he could not have that soldier with him to share in the glory which he felt would crown his efforts.

The other incident was on the 12th of May, 1864, when General Stuart received his mortal wound at the battle of Yellow Tavern, a few miles south of Hickory Hill. The soldier above referred to led General Stuart's right wing on that fatal day. When the battle opened, the wife of the soldier brought a chair, placed it between two pillars of the south marble porch and sat all day listening to the volleys of musketry and the sound of cannon. When evening fell, she knew by the approaching sounds of the conflict that the day had gone against the Confederates.

In the dusk she saw approaching the body-servant, whose duty was to carry the fresh horse in when it was needed, and she recognized him as well as the horse he was leading. She ran to the fence and upbraided him, asking where his master was. The reply was, "Miss Lucy, I don' know; the white mens all runned and I runned too." It is due to the memory of this faithful servant, however, to say that he did not tarry, but, endeavoring to ascertain where the Confederate troops had rallied, duly reported under fire with the fresh horse, though it must be admitted rather late.

Many gallant gentlemen and gentle ladies have graced many a glad and happy hour in this glorious old garden. Many boys and girls have shared their joys and sorrows in it in the past, and it is fondly hoped many more will in the future bring to it the sunshine of their charming presence and merry laughter.

HENRY TAYLOR WICKHAM.

Box Trees Shading the Lowest Fall at Hickory Hill

An Arch of Boxwood at Williamsville

Williamsville, Hanover County

WILLIAMSVILLE

NOT far from Studley, in Hanover County, the birth-place of Patrick Henry, there stands, just fourteen miles from Richmond, an old homestead named Williamsville. It is worthy to take its place in the Virginia collection of noted homes because of its beauty of location, its family associations, and its historic setting.

A recent visitor to this place stood on its lawn, now luxuriant with the shrubbery planted by hands of long ago, and looked across the hills to counties far away, so high is the elevation above the surrounding country. The view reminded her of that from the lawn of Monticello, the home of Jefferson. Then down in the glen, just outside the yard gate, may be seen traces of landscape-gardening rarely equaled by any garden in old plantation days. To the rear of the house is a rustic view. Here, the boxwood has grown into trees and forms an archway which, with the spontaneous shrubbery around, makes a picture of rare beauty.

One day, nearly sixty years ago, during the sad days of the War Between the States, two men stood on the back porch of Williamsville overlooking this very spot. One of them was General Winfield Scott Hancock, of the Federal Army; the other was Dr. George William Pollard, the master of the house and plantation, which had been so cruelly devastated by the exigencies of the war. Here had been the camping ground of the enemy, and here and roundabout had been the battle ground of many a hard-fought struggle to keep the enemy from the Capital of the Confederacy.

"General, will you not give orders that the most sacred spot of our home be spared? I have pleaded with your subordinates that they do not build their breastworks over our family burying-ground. They have destroyed our garden, the pride of our home and the

[99]

joy of our family life. Will you not see that this last resting place of our loved ones is left untouched and unviolated?"

General Hancock, afterwards nominee for President of the United States, looked out upon the violated beauty of the rose-beds, the tulip-borders and boxwood walkways of the garden. A wave of tender feeling passed over his sympathetic countenance. He said, "Dr. Pollard, it shall be as you request." He then gave orders that the plan of the breastworks, originally meant to go over the graves, should be changed to go around, and not through, the burial-ground.

Today may be seen at this spot, where the breastworks are still in evidence, a reminder of General Hancock's kindly spirit in sparing to posterity this hallowed ground untouched.

But what of the garden of other days? In looking from this same porch at Williamsville, one may see through the boxwood trees and the shrubbery near the house, the remains of the garden-acre where beautiful flowers once blossomed in profusion.

In these days of the renaissance of the gardening art in Virginia, many would be interested to know from whose bounty and from whose taste these signs of beautiful home-making came. Who did it? Who was the builder of the house, and who were the mistresses who made this home one of the show places in the Old Dominion of generations long gone?

To tell the story of Williamsville, one must go back one hundred and twenty years, for in the bricks over the front door we may read the date 1803. The name was given the place by its builder, William Pollard, who owned it until his death, in 1840. He was the clerk of Hanover County from 1781 to 1824, and succeeded his father, William Pollard, the first, who lived at Buckeye, just a few miles distant. It was William Pollard, of Buckeye (according to William Wirt's *Life of Patrick Henry*), who acted as secretary of a meeting of the citizens of Hanover County, called to pass resolutions instructing Patrick Henry, delegate to the Virginia Convention of 1774, to vote for the independence of the

Colonies. A section from the resolutions reads, "We are free men; we have a right to be so. . . . Let it suffice, to say once for all, we will never be taxed but by our own representatives. . . . We will heartily join in such measures as the majority of our countrymen shall adopt for securing the public liberty."

William Pollard, the second, was born in 1760 at Buckeye, and at the age of twenty-one took up the duties of clerk, having been in the office with his father since his eighteenth year. He grew to be a man of such accurate business methods in his work that he was called "Billy Particular." His farm at Williamsville of over one thousand acres, was so well managed that he became one of the richest farmers in Virginia for the time in which he lived.

William Pollard was a revolutionist in mind, heart, and soul. Tradition says that many a patriot of those early days of the republic enjoyed his hospitable roof. Here were entertained Edmund Pendleton, first judge of the Court of Appeals of Virginia, who had married Sarah Pollard; and also Edmund Pendleton, the second, colonel in the Revolutionary Army, who had married Mildred Pollard. Both were kinswomen of the owner of Williamsville. John Taylor, of Caroline County, who was United States Senator, was his first cousin, being the son of Anne Pollard, his father's sister. These were all members of the family group who gathered at Williamsville to talk of political affairs when the nation was in its infancy.

From this family of Pollards are descended Senator Underwood, of Alabama; John Garland Pollard, former Attorney-General of Virginia, and Henry R. Pollard, attorney for the city of Richmond for many years.

During these history-making days, Williamsville had two mistresses—not simultaneously, of course, but consecutively—for William Pollard was married twice. His first wife was Elizabeth Dabney, widow of Isaac Dabney, and formerly Elizabeth Smelt, whom he married in 1786.

The second wife of William Pollard was Elizabeth Shackle-

[101]

ford, widow of Lyne Shackleford, and formerly Elizabeth Dabney. The Dabney records say of her: "Elizabeth Dabney Pollard was a very lovely woman, both in person and character." She was the daughter of George and Elizabeth Price Dabney, and had a brother, Chiswell Dabney, who was the grandfather of Chiswell Dabney Langhorne; she had also a sister, Nancy Dabney, who married Judge Alexander Stuart, and was great-grandmother of Henry Carter Stuart, former Governor of Virginia. When Elizabeth Dabney Shackleford married William Pollard she had one daughter, Louise Shackleford, who married Colonel Edmund Fontaine, of Hanover County. The only child of this second marriage was George William Pollard, who inherited Williamsville, and lived there all his life.

About 1840, Mary Peachy Todd, of King and Queen County, became the bride of George William Pollard. She brought with her much wealth and many accomplishments, for she was artist, musician and lover of the beautiful. She found at Williamsville, the inherited home of her husband, a situation and landscape which could lend themselves to one of the most charming gardens in Virginia. The lane leading from the house had a double row of shade trees for a quarter of a mile, and was a joy to the eye as a landscape feature. There was a lake just outside the yard, with an island in it, and a bridge stretching from it to the mainland. This was surrounded by luxuriant shade trees and shrubbery.

At the back of the house Mistress Pollard set apart an acre of ground and, with the help of her slaves, she planned and laid out a garden of rare beauty in design. Flowering plants of all kinds she planted, regardless of expense. Boxwood lined the walkways which were laid with white gravel and kept in as perfect order as in a city park. Summer-houses added picturesqueness. These were built with large white pillars, upon which vines and roses climbed in profusion. Inside, were floors of white rocks, and seats to invite visitors to stop and hold sweet converse in these surroundings. The sons and daughters of this beautiful and hospitable home cherished this spot as a precious playground in their childhood, and later in their youth, as a trysting place of many a happy friendship. Who knows but that here was made many a pledge of troth between happy lovers?

Tradition says nowhere was hospitality more abundant or more cordially extended. In this home were entertained the Pendletons, Taylors, Prices, Fontaines, and Dabneys, of Hanover County, and later, the Todds, Garnetts, and Fauntleroys, of King and Queen.

These were the days of romance and beauty in Virginia, when plantation life was happy, luxurious, and artistic. The master, George William Pollard, was a physician and, also, a man of literary ability. His war poetry was especially favored in the days of the internecine strife, for Williamsville was, at one time, the tenting-ground of the enemy. Generals Grant, Hooker, and Meade took up headquarters in the house, ate in the dining-room, and drove the family to the second floor until the Federal army left the house and the farm.

One of the sons of Williamsville, Bernard Chiswell Pollard, gave his life to the Confederacy, at Spotsylvania Courthouse. His sister, Ellen, grieved so for her favorite brother, that she became a fierce "rebel." On one occasion a Federal officer tried to get from her some information concerning the movements of the Confederate troops. She refused with such defiance that he pointed his pistol at her to compel compliance with his order. She replied, "I will die first." This same officer returned next year on a raid and, in passing her front door, lifted his hat. As Miss Pollard did not return the salutation, he remarked, "You do not seem to recognize me." She answered, "I have no acquaintances in the Yankee army." In 1866, this daughter of the Confederacy married Rev. F. B. Converse, editor of *The Christian Observer,* of Louisville.

The present owner of Williamsville is Harry Todd Pollard, of Louisville, but it is occupied and cultivated by George William Pollard, the second, who has reared there a delightful family of

[103]

boys and girls, the youngest of whom, Mildred, presides over the home, since the death of her mother, with the grace and hospitality of her forbears.

MARY POLLARD CLARKE.

A Corner in the Airwell Garden

Airwell, Hanover County

Claremont, in Surry County

Edgewood, One of the Berkeley Homes, in Hanover County

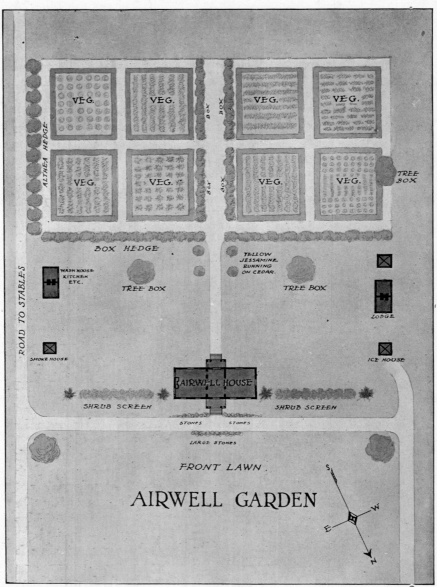

VEG.   VEG.   VEG.   VEG.

VEG.   VEG.   VEG.   VEG.

ALTHEA HEDGE

BOX

BOX

BOX

TREE BOX

BOX HEDGE

YELLOW JESSAMINE. RUNNING ON CEDAR.

ROAD TO STABLES

WASH HOUSE KITCHEN ETC.

TREE BOX

TREE BOX

LODGE

SMOKE HOUSE

ICE HOUSE

AIRWELL HOUSE

SHRUB SCREEN   SHRUB SCREEN

STONES   STONES

LARGE STONES

FRONT LAWN.

AIRWELL GARDEN

William C. Noland

AIRWELL

I N the upper part of the County of Hanover stands the old estate of Airwell, an original grant from the English Crown to Thomas Nelson. His grandson, Nelson Berkeley, of Middlesex, built the house and moved thither about the year 1760. It is interesting to note that his direct descendants still own and occupy the place.

It has been said that the bricks used in building the house were brought from England. That, however, seems improbable. Not only is the house too far from Tidewater for the transportation to have been practicable, but it was the custom for plantations to have their own brick-kilns. However, the Flemish bonding, the ample thickness of the walls and the general lines and proportions of the severely plain exterior, give the dwelling the unmistakable stamp of its early period.

When Tarleton with his English dragoons rode through the neighborhood, on his raid from Williamsburg to Charlottesville, he is said to have visited Airwell. It is certain that Lady Berkeley (who before her marriage was Elizabeth Wormely Carter, of Sabine Hall), is credited with having refused to give up to the new county commissioners the church communion silver, which was in her keeping and which they wished to confiscate as being English government property.

This silver, which is used when service is held in old "Fork" Church, is still kept at Airwell by the descendants of Mrs. Berkeley, to whom Bishop Meade referred as a "lady of dignity, firmness and authority."

On an ample lawn, surrounded by trees, Airwell house stands today, a monument to the past. In 1836, it was seriously damaged by fire, but in 1845 complete repairs were made. About twenty-five yards from the rear porch lies the garden, with its box-hedge on the north, and the long central walk bordered on either side with box, syringa and pink and red cydonia japonica (pyrus japonica), with an intermingling of roses, jonquils and violets. In winter, when the snow falls, the box-bushes look like huge frosted cakes, and in summer the syringas, with their graceful sweeping sprays of lovely white bloom, remind one of beautiful brides.

The plan of this apparently simple old garden is found to be quite symmetrical and satisfactory, especially if considered as it was originally and in its relation to the "Great House" and other buildings, as well as to the general layout of the place.

The garden formed a part of a well-considered plan of the grounds in the rear of the house, and there were flanking clumps of tree-box between the house and the garden hedge. The garden contained full half an acre and was, and is, divided in half by the box-bordered main walk. Originally each half was sub-divided by cross-walks into four equal squares. The cultivation of these squares was done with spading forks. It was only after the War Between the States that a plow was allowed to enter. That marked the end of the sod walks, which, by the way, stalled the plow, until the grubbing hoe was used to loosen the matted grass-roots. Formerly, a hedge of althea marked and helped to form the eastern boundary, but it has now been supplanted by severely practical wire mesh.

On this side is the grape trellis, extending the full length of the garden. Then come the red raspberries, strawberries, and, in their order, vegetables for all seasons; for this delightful old garden is a charming combination of utility and beauty. On the south side of the boxwood hedge, and protected by it, are the hot-beds and cold-frames for lettuce, tomatoes, and all early vegetables.

In the asparagus bed of this garden, during the War Between the States, some of the family silver was buried and successfully preserved from the temptation of "the enemy," and is still in daily use in the old house.

On the west is a group of gnarled and twisted box trees, presumably as old as the house. The paling-fence, on the same side, is bordered with masses of red lilies and purple iris. Looking farther to the west, one sees the family burying-ground where many generations of Berkeleys rest from their labors.

Less than a mile from Airwell, and plainly visible from the garden, is another old home of the Berkeleys, Edgewood, which stands in a grove of magnificent oaks and poplars. Here may be found some large single red roses with wide yellow centers, which are known in the neighborhood as "Offley roses."

These roses and their local name come from Offley, another house that once stood not far away on a part of this same Nelson grant. There the widow of General Nelson took refuge from Yorktown during the Revolution and made her home for some years thereafter, and there she doubtless gave tender care to the very roses from which these come.

With this in mind, one naturally feels that their parent rose in all probability was brought from Yorktown by their mistress, and cherished by her as a reminder of the fine old home she had left down by the York.

Many thoughts of bygone owners and their pleasure in these old gardens haunt us as we wander through them, and that is the reason they are so treasured by their descendants.

LUCY LANDON NOLAND.

OAKLAND

THE THOMAS NELSON PAGE HOME

THE land on which the Oakland garden was built was granted by George I to the ancestors of the present owners in 1718. Famous Old Fork Church, within the walls of which Patrick Henry and Dolly Madison both worshipped before the Revolution, was built about 1704, just beyond the eastern boundary of this Nelson grant of ten thousand acres.

The garden, however, did not come into existence until 1812, when it was laid off by General Nelson's youngest daughter, Judith, the year the house was built. The latter married her cousin, Captain Thomas Nelson, for many years Collector of the Port of Richmond, and with him came to live at Oakland.

The grounds of this historic estate slope gently from the house in all directions and are bounded on the east and west by flowing streams. On the outer side of the western line, in a grove of noble trees, is one of the far-famed springs of this section of Virginia.

In olden times, the Oakland yard and garden contained about four acres in all, surrounded by a substantial fence of cedar posts and square oak bars placed edgewise, with ends let into mortised posts, which were capped with squares of oak. Inside of this, a paling fence outlined the garden. This fence was flanked on the inner side by the pyr-acanthus whose thorns were a terror to barefoot boys, but whose radiant coral berries delighted all admirers of bright color. Among the berries, cardinals and thrushes, the latter then called "sandy mockings," delighted to disport themselves.

The garden was in front of the house and occupied the southern slope as it declined gently until it reached the slightly rising ground about two hundred yards away. It was elliptical in shape, with the broad side facing the house some hundred feet away. The entrance was through a gate which always brought to the boy's mind the wicket gate in "Pilgrim's Progress." Pyrus or cydonia japonicas, with their rich calico colors, grew on either side of this gate, and almost met overhead. Walks, leading lengthwise through the center and across, gave access to different parts of the garden, while borders for annuals and squares for tender plants abounded, convenient for the mistress or her daughter to plant or tend, when they chose to infringe upon the domain of Nat, the gardener.

As the fiery acanthus glowed along the far side of the garden, the rose bushes shone as the most noted things within it. They were everywhere in almost wild profusion—George the Fourth, Giant of Battles, Hermosa, York, and Lancaster, damask and tea roses, and even the Hundred Leaf and Microphylla. This one came from Shirley, that from Cousin Anne at Hickory Hill, another from York, and that from Aunt Nelson at Long Branch, or from Cousin Thomasia at Mountain View. Cherished above them all, were the Offley roses—only wild roses which still bloom on the tenth day of each June. These came from the place of that name, five miles away, so charmingly described by the Marquis de Chastellux.

Lilacs, syringa, forsythia, bridal wreath, and spiraea ushered in the spring with all their wealth of flowers, while violets, in cold frames and borders, with hyacinths, delighted the eye. Jonquils popping up in all directions gave the impression that the latter must enjoy some special privilege to be thus breaking out of bounds.

A little later came the snow-balls, and then the poppies, after the peonies had gone. Sweet williams and wall-flowers; nasturtium and alyssum; phlox and pinks—not then called carnations—all had their place, while off in a moist quarter were gladioli and lilies of the valley, about which Philip Pendleton Cooke wrote in "Florence Vane."

The fall flowers were not equal to what we now have, though many roses lasted until frost. There was plenty of shrubbery of all sorts—sweet-shrubs, and honeysuckle, white and coral; yellow jessamine, clematis, and even two or three fine grapevines which the mistress of Oakland had planted. The grapevines belonged more properly to a corner in the vegetable garden, west of the house, and out of sight. This was back of the interesting small buildings known as the "wash-house," "Aunt Suckey Brown's house," "the other house," the old kitchen, the smoke-house, and "Uncle Bulla's house."

Time has forced this old garden to give way to trees and lawn, but many of the shrubs survive to define its former locality still so accurately remembered by some who walked amid its bowers and enjoyed its beauty and fragrance.

It was at Oakland that Thomas Nelson Page did his first writing. It was from his old home that he found the inspiration for "Marse Chan" and other stories. It was here that he lived with the originals of "Two Little Confederates," and it was in this garden that he dug and chopped as a boy. It was back to it that his memories ever reverted. Just in reach of its confines, while interested in its restoration, and transplanting with his own hands one of the old shrubs, he rested from his earthly labors and joined those, who, like himself, had found so much delight in this old garden.

ROSEWELL PAGE.

Thomas Nelson Page in the Oakland Garden

Oakland, the Birthplace of Thomas Nelson Page, in Hanover County

The Box "Maze" at Tuckahoe, Goochland County

The Upper James

North Front at Tuckahoe When the Daffodils Bloom

The Tuckahoe Garden in June

TUCKAHOE

TEN miles west of Richmond, on the highway known as the River Road, an abrupt turn to the south brings one to a cedar-lined lane which leads into the plantation of Tuckahoe.

For one mile this double line of cedars stretches, and, though serious gaps have been made in the broad avenue by time and weather, the continuity of the evergreen trees, through successive plantations, is now unbroken. The oldest of these trees in their lusty age extend arms farther afield than in their youth, their naked trunks standing stiff and upright, so like the pipes of some cathedral organ that one would not start at the sound of deep, reverential tones coming along the lane. It is most impressive.

Down the lofty nave of this forest cathedral gleams, at the end, under the open sky, the old, white gateway which bars the lane from the lawn. And straight ahead in the distance, upon a little rise of ground, the old house stands like some fading seventeenth-century picture shut away in its immediate world. Approaching it through the old gateway, one will never forget the picture, especially if the season be spring. Hoary-headed elm trees and clouds of golden daffodils literally surround it. Goldfinches and mocking-birds twitter a welcome, and, girdling all, James River in the distance. The daffodils bend and sway, seeming to beckon one nearer, and the hospitable face of the old house wears the same warm welcome it wore in colonial days.

Tuckahoe, which is today one of the best examples of the colonial plantation left in America, was founded in 1674 by William Randolph, of Turkey Island, for his second son, Thomas. The acreage contained originally in the estate has been placed as high as twenty-five thousand, and it is said to have extended for twelve miles along James River. The place name was, as it sounds, borrowed from the Indians, and it may prove interesting to trace its origin.

Purchas, that observant historian of 1626, states that among edible roots known to the aborigines was one called "Tockawaugh growing like a flagge, of the greatness and taste of a potatoe, which passeth a fiery purgation before they may eate it being poison while it is raw." Botanically, the plant belongs to the arum, or lily, family, and is classified as wake-robin, jack-in-the-pulpit, and Indian turnip. The word Tuckahoe is found in dictionaries, and it was from the great quantity of these plants growing along the streams of the estate that its name was gained.

But the name is not the only reminder of the Indians, for, on a narrow arm of the little creek, which flows through the plantation, may be found the well-preserved remains of a stone basin used by the red men to pound their corn into meal.

A distinct character is given to the lawn at Tuckahoe by the many fine old trees that shade it—elm, honey locust, or gleditschia; willow-oak, catalpa, holly and dogwood. Some one has truly said "The man who plants even a single tree does a good work and an unselfish one; he plants for posterity, not for himself; he is laying up a store of perennial beauty for a world yet unborn." This comes vividly before us at the old plantation, and sincere thanks go out from our hearts to the early owners who, from a background of more than two hundred years, have added so much to the joy of present-day life and living.

At the very heart of the plantation stands the frame house of two wings, double stories and a great hall. It boasts no pretension to grandeur, but has claimed every right for hospitality since its beginning. The date of the building has been placed anywhere from 1674 to 1725, but, judging from the character of the carving upon the interior woodwork, the dwelling should belong to the seventeenth century.

[114]

The house has distinction. This comes partly from its paneled walls, witnessing to the good taste and knowledge of the builders—long since dead—who placed them there. The two wings, each a complete house, are held together by the long, wide hall originally intended as the ballroom. This hall is one of the features of the house, which, with its exits upon both ends and sides, may properly be called four-fronted. The interior, with its large, square rooms, engaged the attention of the first artisans of the country; the mantels and hand-carved stairway are particularly interesting.

All over the house the woodwork is elaborate and exceedingly good. The paneled rooms show refined cornices, while the graceful north stair is of particular note, along with the beautiful treatment of the newel post at its foot. Black walnut, mahogany and heart pine are the woods used.

The splendid paneled dining-room still speaks of the presence of century-dead masters. The sunbeams that steal in through the opalescent window panes light up the names and dates thereon as far back as 1779. The H and L-H hinges; the heavy brass locks and huge door keys; the iron locks showing the English coat-of-arms in brass; the personal reminders of Thomas Jefferson who lived here as a boy—these are among the many things that make this house as interesting as any in America.

Straight through the hall—from river to road—a vista ends down the cedar-bound lane and stretches its length into the house and out over flights of well-worn stone steps. These steps now present almost a dilapidated appearance, and suggest an indifference on the part of the owners, but they are really carefully left that way in respect to their great age. And, as if in a like appreciation of this same age, wherever possible, the mossy crevices are filled with violets and ferns.

The exterior of the house is unique. Begun, apparently, as a brick building, the south wing has both ends well laid in Flemish bond, as if the change to a frame construction came after these were built. The north wing is all frame.

From old papers and documents we learn that the Randolph family lived a life of cultured leisure at Tuckahoe for nearly two hundred years. William Byrd, that eighteenth-century author, wit and aristocrat, in his "History of the Dividing Line," speaks of the place: "I parted with my Intendant and pursued my journey to Mr. Randolph's at Tuckahoe, without meeting with any adventure by the way. The heir of the Family did not come home until late in the evening. He is a Pretty Young Man but had the misfortune to become his own Master too soon. This puts young fellows upon wrong pursuits, before they have sence to judge rightly for themselves. I was sorry in the morning to find myself stopped in my Career by bad weather." After a visit of three or four days, he writes: "The clouds continued to drive from the N-Est and to menace us with more rain. Therefore after fortifying myself with two capacious Dishes of Coffee and making my Compliments to the Ladyes, I mounted and Mr. Randolph was so kind as to be my guide."

In 1782, the Marquis de Chastellux wrote of his visit to the estate, describing it as, "Tuckahoe, on James River, the seat of Mr. Randolph a rich planter of Virginia." Chastellux further tells us that "The Virginians have the reputation, and with reason, of living nobly in their houses, and of being hospitable; they give strangers not only a willing, but a liberal, reception."

And Thomas Anbury, in his "Travels Through the Interior Parts of North America," published in 1789, says, "I spent a few days at Colonel Randolph's at Tuckahoe, at whose house the usual hospitality of the country prevailed." He then adds a description of the house, saying that it "seems to be built solely to answer the purpose of hospitality, being constructed in a different manner than in most other countries."

But the old home has had its adverse criticism, too. Not many years ago, Professor Edward Channing, in an address before the Massachusetts Historical Society, said "the house was interesting on account of its architectural features," but that "on the whole,

E. L. Coolidge   *The House at Tuckahoe from the Box Garden—Jefferson School House in the Foreground*

W. J. Wallace

Plan of the Tuckahoe Garden Showing Formal Box Maze on the Right

Tuckahoe only reinforced the impression . . . that Virginia writers, through ignorance, probably, have greatly exaggerated the social splendors of the 'Old Dominion.' "

And yet, William Ellery Channing, who was a tutor at Tuckahoe for two years, speaks with pride of the Virginians: "I blush for my own people," he says, "when I compare the selfish prudence of a Yankee with the generous confidence of a Virginian. . . . There is one single trait which attaches me to the people I live with more than all the virtues of New England. They *love money less* than we do. Their patriotism is not tied to their purse strings."

An interesting feature of Tuckahoe is found in the three-foot brick walk, which encircles the house and leads to the outside kitchen, over one hundred feet away, and still in use. The architecture of the house permits courtyards upon the east and west fronts, and, upon either side of these, clumps of boxwood grow as they did years ago, though unrelated as to family and newer as to age. Over the west entrance a gnarled catalpa leans to uphold a crimson rose vine, which makes it look "all rose-tree." Honeysuckle is banked against the brick foundation on the north side; lilies—Hemerocallis fulva—against the south. And to this wing, climbing vigorously to the second-floor windows, cling multiflora, microphylla and pink rambler roses. Nestling against the south steps, an old, red rambler reaches up to the paneled ceiling, which marks this portico as one of the most interesting in the country.

The present kitchen was, in plantation days, the Master's office, the original kitchen being the small brick building in the rear; and this still has its swinging crane and old Dutch oven. The quarters are still at Tuckahoe, and in excellent preservation. The smokehouse and toolhouse remain as they were, but the icehouse and the weaving-room have gone.

Flanking the office upon the east is the inconspicuous little building where Thomas Jefferson went to school. Peter Jefferson, father of the third president, in compliance with the dying request of Colonel Randolph, his wife's kinsman, moved to Tuckahoe in

1745 and undertook the guardianship of young Thomas Mann Randolph and the management of his estate.

Below the schoolhouse, jonquils have spread into a veritable Cloth-of-Gold field, flinging high their April trumpets above a mass of periwinkle blue as the sky. These signals of spring that dance so joyously leave the memory of their beauty throughout the garden year. And there are so many varieties of daffodils and narcissi at this charming old place. Beginning with the short-stemmed Obvallaris the beautiful Stellas follow in profusion. These bulbs were planted long before the days of the Olympia as the Golden Spur and the double sorts—Orange and Golden Phoenix, familiarly known as Butter and Eggs and Eggs and Bacon—will attest. But, daintiest of all the daffodil family which blooms at Tuckahoe, is the delicate, old-fashioned, little white flower known as "The Lady of Leeds."

Scattered about the garden, and all over the lawn, are four varieties of narcissi—the Polyanthus, which, though in the minority, compensates in its bright yellow flowers; the white Biflorus, and, most pleasing of all, Ornatus and Poeticus.

Beyond the schoolhouse comes the garden—the real feature of Tuckahoe. A magnificent elm throws out its arms protectingly over the garden entrance. A simple wood gate, between box-hedged violet beds, leads between this elm tree and two splendid specimens of sempervirens boxwood which rise on the other side. Through the opening, looking east, there is a charming vista down a turfed alley lined with old-fashioned or suffruticosa box and called the Ghost Walk. Shadowing the south side, a row of sempervirens interlines the dwarf hedge rows, and stands as a wind-break for the flowers. Below this lies the formal garden, cut up into fifty-seven "knots" or beds, a decorative arrangement, with paths of grass intervening. These paths are so narrow that only one person can walk there at a time, and they are separated from the flower beds by dwarf-box hedging.

Known as the "maze," this labyrinth of flower squares and

ovals, covering about one acre, proves upon investigation to be perfectly symmetrical, with direct exits leading from a central bed. Bordering each of the fifty-seven beds, as well as enclosing the garden plot, are hedges of suffruticosa, which average in height from two to four feet, with a girth of sometimes five. Only tall flowers, like phlox and hollyhocks and larkspur, can lift their heads high enough to show to advantage, but, for the pleasure of such glorious box, one is willing to forego many flowers, which, after all, can be had elsewhere. There is probably more of the old-fashioned dwarf or suffruticosa boxwood at Tuckahoe than anywhere else in America. By actual measurement, if lined off, it would extend about eight thousand feet, or more than one and one-half miles.

The beauty of this box garden's unlost configuration is retained with its early and remote contours. The invincible green of the box, darkling amid and above the flowers, takes from and gives to them the cheer which neither could have found without the contrast. It is like some garden of sleep, and here one finds rest that seldom comes in this world of unfortunate change. The spot is lovely enough by day; but at night————! With evening there comes into the Virginia air a soft, intangible, poetical dreaminess—a dreaminess that, with the fragrant boxwood, lets the Tuckahoe garden smile, even in winter, without any abatement to the effects of summer that would lessen the total of a year of joy.

Roses grow in the central or key bed of this formal garden and again in the first four long beds around it. The center ovals, also four, show in sequence, tulips—slate blue and yellow; cornflowers in contrast to lilies; sweet rocket, and last—phlox drummondi.

The ovals, which radiate from the central bed, begin with the Darwins, ranging from pale pink to purple. Larkspur follows— the old-fashioned kind—and, when it blooms, its purplish mist seems to envelop all the garden. Then come the asters. The general plan shows every plot of the same shape to contain the same flowers. Another group has iris, peonies and chrysanthemums, poppies, delphiniums and phlox. Digitalis grows around lilac clumps; these, with crepe myrtle and spiraea—with a cedar here, a euonymus there—appear to have been planted to point up the garden.

While the box maze is by far the most interesting, it is by no means the whole garden. Beyond it, on the east, is a vegetable acre, separated by a line of forsythia suspensa and bridal wreath. A slight fall drops above this, bordered by a scattering line of briar roses, where the half acre allotted to iris begins and the box-bordered Ghost Walk ends. On the north of this lies the rest of the vegetable garden, bisected by iris-bound grass walks, beginning beneath the shade of peach trees, to end in the shadow of plums.

Leaving the Ghost Walk at abrupt right angles, the path broadens to let the eye follow a second walk up to the old brick-walled burying-ground of the Randolphs. Opposite the graveyard, extending the entire length of the turfed walk, is the perennial border, where a chain of golden cowslips ushers in the spring. At the back of this flowery border, serving as a screen for the kitchen garden, are irregular lines of flowering almond, lilac, cydonia japonica, calycanthus, dogwood, forsythia, holly and Scotch broom.

In line with the boxwood at the garden entrance stand peach trees. Scattered among these, above the honeysuckle hedge, the ailanthus, or Tree of Heaven, with its fern-like foliage, gives an effect of almost tropical luxuriance. One receives, upon entering this garden, and one carries away, an impression of sunshine, even on gloomy days. And down below, upon a terraced bit of woodland, montbretias or blackberry lilies grow naturalized.

From an old farm record we learn how the land at Tuckahoe was tilled, and the contents of the orchards. We read with interest that in 1850 it took between seven and eight hundred pounds of bacon and one hundred and fifty-six barrels of corn to begin to feed the plantation force each year. At that time the estate was the property of Joseph Allen, and he it was who kept the farm

The River Terraces at Wilton, the Randolph Home on the Lower James, Where Jonquils
Taken from Tuckahoe are Lavishly Naturalized

The Cedar Lane at Tuckahoe

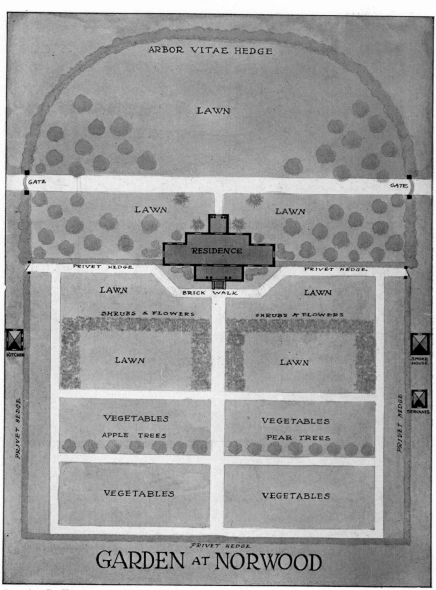

GARDEN at NORWOOD

Beverley R. Kennon

Norwood, the Kennon Home, in Powhatan County

journal and planted the well-stocked orchards with peaches, apples, cherries, apricots, plums and nectarines. The plantation book shows the plan of planting and lists all the fruits by name.

The account of liming operations; of sub-soiling; of fallowing the various fields, is given for the years from 1850 to 1860, and proves that the plantation was operated upon our so-called modern lines.

Every old house has, or should have, its ghost story, or its respectability might be impugned. And Tuckahoe has two. There is one tale of a youthful bride, in wedding veil and satin gown, wringing unhappy hands as she rushes along the Ghost Walk away from the husband three times her age. Then, there is the story of the dainty Little Grey Lady who, when the midnight hour has come, steps gently out from a cupboard in the lovely old "Burnt Room" to mingle with the mortals for a time. This tale tells, further, that it was through a dream of this fragile wraith that one of Tuckahoe's most loved chatelaines was brought to preside in the home.

Happily, the family still controlling the numerous acres of this estate is by direct descent the same which, in the person of William Randolph, established itself here in 1674. These owners—Joseph Randolph Coolidge, John Gardner Coolidge, Archibald Cary Coolidge and Harold Jefferson Coolidge—are grandsons in the eighth generation of the seventeenth-century builder of the house.

The place is full of gentle memories, and here one finds a restful permanence in an otherwise restless age. In the quiet old garden the flower faces that look up to cheer us are the same that have given heart and comfort to generations so remote that they lie half forgotten beneath grey, crumbling stones. Tuckahoe has lived through the centuries to stand today a precious relic of Virginia in the olden time.

EDITH DABNEY TUNIS SALE.

NORWOOD

ORWOOD, the home of the Randolph and Kennon families, is in Powhatan County about seventeen miles above Richmond. Its two thousand and sixty-five acres lie on the south bank of the James River for about three miles. It was originally bought by John Heth, the great-great-grandfather of the present owner, Mr. Charles Randolph Kennon, in 1813 from one John Harris. In those days the present home site was called "Greenyard," possibly because of the lovely grove which surrounds the house.

An extensive addition was made to the original residence in 1835 by Beverley Randolph, who then made it his home, he having acquired it through his wife, Lavinia, who was the daughter of John Heth.

The estate remains practically unchanged to the present time, the succeeding generations keeping up its old traditions; Beverley Randolph leaving it at his death to his son, Charles, who, dying unmarried, left it to his sister, Nancy Kennon, and now the Kennon name has owned it in direct line for three generations.

In the olden days it was a most lovely place, with its imposing grove and beautiful gardens in the rear of the house. The back was separated from the front by a privet hedge, which also surrounded the garden.

In front of the house was a large park containing some fifteen acres, enclosed by an osage orange hedge. The approach was by a long, curved driveway following this hedge. The front lawn, with its beautiful trees and grass, was separated from the park by a semi-circular arbor-vitae hedge.

In the rear of the house about three acres was enclosed by a privet hedge, and was laid out in flower beds which it was the pride of the old Scotch gardener and his six slave assistants to keep blooming with all the loveliest flowers; his peonies, lilacs, roses and many others too numerous to mention made of it a riot of colour through the seasons. The lower part was devoted to fruits, there being grapes, raspberries, gooseberries and other small fruits in profusion. The apples, cherries, pears and quinces kept the table supplied, and in summer the slaves were kept busy preserving them for winter use.

Though the ancient glories of the garden have departed, the trees and shrubs have increased in beauty through the years, there being at present some thirty varieties of trees surrounding the house.

In the winter the many shrubs and evergreens make of the place a veritable "greenyard"; the holly trees, of which there are twenty-three, being especially beautiful with their green foliage and red berries.

Though the arbor-vitae hedge has long since gone, many feathery cedars still drape the lawn with their graceful forms.

Through the years the old plantation has kept its grace and dignity as one of the best of the old "before-the-war" homes.

BEVERLEY RANDOLPH KENNON.

ROCK CASTLE

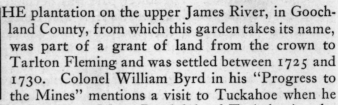

THE plantation on the upper James River, in Goochland County, from which this garden takes its name, was part of a grant of land from the crown to Tarlton Fleming and was settled between 1725 and 1730. Colonel William Byrd in his "Progress to the Mines" mentions a visit to Tuckahoe when he met Mistress Fleming (born Mary Randolph of Tuckahoe), who was about to join her husband at Rock Castle, "thirty miles farther up the river, in a part of the country little settled and but lately redeemed from the wilderness."

The original dwelling was an English cottage of weatherboarding, high brick foundations, enormous brick chimneys and a dormer roof, copied from the south wing of Tuckahoe, the Randolph home built about 1689 or 1700. Scottish names were given to several of the plantations in this vicinity, such as Dungeness, Snowdon, and Ben Lomond, but Rock Castle seems to have been chosen on account of the extraordinary conformation of the rocks and cliffs which form the sides of the very high hill that Mr. Fleming selected for his home.

The James River makes a bend at this point and can be seen from three sides of the grounds; on a clear day towards the western horizon stretches a long range of outlying peaks of the Blue Ridge, presumably forty miles away. From the south lawn the grounds slope quite precipitately towards the river, and there one finds a grove of handsome trees, huge boulders of rock and a natural cavern. Many generations of children and of older folk have enjoyed its cool shade within the sound of the rushing water of James River near by. The grounds on the north and west are very extensive, part rolling and part a handsome plateau planted in English elms principally, but with tulip and Lombardy poplars;

A Garden Entrance at Rock Castle

Rock Castle, the Rutherfoord Home, in Goochland County

wild cherry, very handsome holly trees and formerly (before their destruction by lightning) two magnificent spruces.

To the east of the house is the garden. In its far corner a giant elm rears its stately head and near by were laid the remains of Tarlton Fleming, the first owner. As years passed by, the Flemings built a larger house more centrally situated to their possessions and disposed of the Rock Castle portion. It was at this time that Mrs. Fleming, accompanied by some faithful slaves, drove down at night and had the body of her husband removed to an enclosed burying ground at Mannsville, their new home. Colonel David Bullock, whose handsome house and grounds are now the site of the Commonwealth Club of Richmond, was the next owner of Rock Castle, and used it as a fishing and shooting box. In spring and autumn many of Virginia's notables were his guests. After the death of Colonel Bullock the place changed hands several times, the Binfords of Richmond holding it longest and then, in the forties, it was purchased by Governor John Rutherfoord, familiarly known as "Colonel John," as a summer home. His only son, John Coles Rutherfoord, was so delighted with it that, deserting Richmond, the place of his birth, he made Rock Castle his permanent home and added a new front to the dwelling. He had traveled extensively in Europe and was a keen observer of architecture and of landscape gardening. The latter had not at that time been much cultivated in Virginia and it was under his supervision that the Rock Castle garden was laid out and many trees and shrubs planted in the grounds.

The garden was very large, with squares for vegetables divided by broad walks, and every sort of small fruit, of berries, of herbs and spices that could be grown in our climate were planted, as well as flowers. As you entered under an arbor covered with roses, honeysuckle and star jessamine, a broad walk opened before you, bordered on either hand with blooming shrubs and flowers. Inside of the old-fashioned white picket fence, and extending on either hand, were other broad walks with borders of shrubs and flowers, and the two squares next the entrance were laid out in formal gardens.

As the walks extended to the north and south the borders were planted with fig bushes for some distance. Then followed borders of raspberries, currants and gooseberries. Farther on there were quinces, apricots, nectarines and cherries, and there were two squares planted with rare peach trees. From north to south across the garden ran the pear-tree walk, a heavy green sward border on either side, out of which grew the carefully nurtured dwarf pears. Then there was the long grape-walk, and towards the eastern side of the garden was its most interesting feature, the cedar-hedges, one plot nearly encircled by the cedars was used as a forcing garden for the early vegetables. The hotbeds and cold frames were on the extensive eastern slope and were well protected by the hedges. There were some unusual shrubs, a very handsome Irish yew being of special beauty. Multiflora roses, now rarely seen, formed what would now be styled a pergola, but was in those days called an arbor, down the greater portion of the central walk.

The forces of two invading armies visited Rock Castle. General Tarleton, during the Revolutionary War, at the head of a large cavalry force, swept off everything in his course, and he wreaked his special, petty spite upon the Flemings, his near of kin. He cut down, with his own sword, from the wall of the principal room, the coat-of-arms of Fleming and Tarleton and bore it away with him.

Later, in 1865, a marauding company of Federal cavalry, ordered to destroy the locks on the James River and Kanawha Canal, in the absence of the Rutherfoords, forcibly entered the house, broke into the wine-cellar and, despite the entreaties of the faithful house-servants, destroyed everything they could not carry off with them, leaving a desolate house and no provisions for Mrs. Rutherfoord and her little children, who returned by carriage from Richmond a few days later.

During 1864-1865 a box containing jewelry and silver was buried by Mr. Rutherfoord and his "head man" behind the hedge,

[126]

and careful measurements made so as to enable them to locate the spot. Months afterwards when the war was over, several men dug nearly all day without results and, just as the search was about to be abandoned, Mrs. Rutherfoord suggested making new measurements, allowing for growth of the cedars, and the box was discovered well under the edge of the hedge.

Near where the giant elm cast its shadows over turf like that of Old England, there was an arbor, and many a love scene was enacted there during the seventy years of the Rutherfoord occupation. Behind the hedge, under a great hackberry tree where the turf was like velvet, the girls would spend hours sewing and reading and the colored children be sent to remind them of meal times.

With the passing of slavery, the heavy pecuniary losses entailed by the War Between the States and the death of Mr. Rutherfoord and of Edward, the "perfect gardener," portions of the garden became gradually much overgrown, while the lawn became more beautiful as the trees attained full growth.

In 1908, Mrs. Rutherfoord, for more than fifty years the mistress of Rock Castle, passed away amid the scenes she had loved so well and under the old roof tree which her kindness and hospitality had made famous. In 1910, her daughter, Mrs. George Ben Johnston, took over the estate and she and her husband, a distinguished surgeon of Richmond, made many improvements on the farm and to the dwelling.

They employed a firm of Boston architects and landscape-gardeners, Andrews, Jaques and Rantoul, to lay out over again the garden, as much as possible on the same lines as formerly and, with a skilled Scotch gardener to carry on the work, Rock Castle garden took on new beauties and was a joy to its owners. Dynamite was used in many of the squares and the result, as shown in the extraordinary size and yield of the vegetables and fruits, was a proof of the efficacy of this treatment of our soil. Gourds grown on a vine were so large as to be regarded as curiosities and preserved as such. During this period our country was again plunged into war and, although no hostile forces visited Rock Castle, during the summer months the house was thronged with the young Virginians coming and going to the training camps, and again young couples sought the garden-walks and exchanged vows of love under the shade trees.

After the death of Dr. Johnston, Mrs. Johnston disposed of the place, and since 1918 it has changed hands several times. The last resident owner, Mr. Henry L. Pierson, was killed in a tractor accident last September, and dying intestate the estate reverted to his brother, Mr. Thomas H. Pierson, of New York, and to his sister, Mrs. Carlyon Bellairs, of Gore Court, Maidstone, England. Mrs. Bellairs, whose husband is a distinguished M. P., has relinquished her share to her brother. In the near future other strangers will take possession and feast their eyes upon this rarely beautiful landscape of which a convalescent Confederate soldier, during the War Between the States, said to Mrs. Rutherfoord on being summoned to dinner: "This is meat enough and drink enough for me."

ANNE SEDDON RUTHERFOORD JOHNSON.

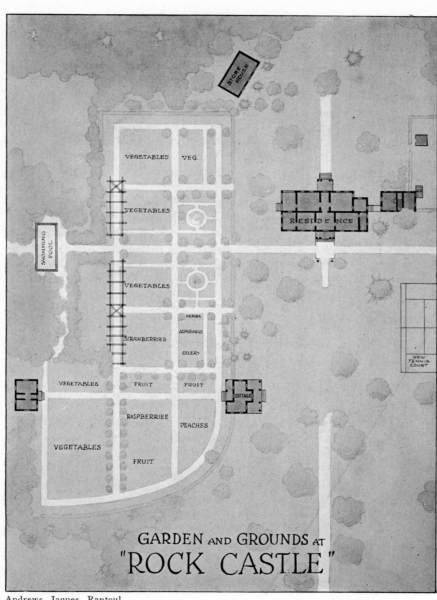

STORE HOUSE

VEGETABLES VEG.

VEGETABLES

SWIMMING POOL

VEGETABLES

STRAWBERRIES

HERBS

ASPARAGUS

CELERY

RESIDENCE

NEW TENNIS COURT

VEGETABLES FRUIT FRUIT

COTTAGE

RASPBERRIES

PEACHES

VEGETABLES

FRUIT

GARDEN AND GROUNDS AT
"ROCK CASTLE"

Andrews, Jaques, Rantoul

Box Trees at Elk Hill in Winter

ELK HILL

OVERLOOKING the romantic James, where the river bends on its course to Richmond, forty-five miles away, lies the twelve-hundred-acre estate of Elk Hill, so named, supposedly, from the number of elk that once grazed here.

Like many of the old homes in Virginia, this one seems to be resting under some strange, magic spell, which renders it impervious to time and well content to live on with the memories that lie back of it—memories which link it to other historic homesteads by ties of affection and consanguinity. In its early days, its isolated situation led Randolph Harrison to select it as a home, and, after nearly one hundred years, it is still fortunately sequestered.

The original estate, known as Elk Hill, contained a vast number of acres, and first appears in history in 1715, when it was granted by patent to John Woodson. In 1778 it was purchased by Thomas Jefferson. After various changes in ownership and many subdivisions, the estate became the property of the Harrison family, from whom part of it passed to Thomas D. Stokes, the present owner.

The house was erected by Randolph Harrison about 1845, and is structurally very substantial. The facade is dignified, and the effect of the building, with its white-stuccoed walls, set in the center of a lawn and garden numbering ten acres in extent and quite removed from the highroad, is noble and hospitable. A small and formal portico provides the entrance upon the north front, and here, against a western column, an aged vine at blooming time seems to be "a close-set robe of jasmine sown with stars."

Across the river front of the house a broad veranda extends. This is swathed with clematis and wistaria, with great knots of hydrangea otaksa huddling against the steps which lead to the serpentine brick walk.

Many and pleasing pictures have come down to us in the traditions of this old place. As court days, races, social or business appointments took the people along the saffron-colored road up and down the country, they found few inns. Instead of a tavern in this locality, hospitality was always sought, and found, beneath the spreading roof and ever-open doors at Elk Hill. The spirit of welcome has always stood at the gate here to lay hands upon the passing stranger and draw him into the green-shuttered house. This has been noteworthy even in a State renowned for good cheer and social graces. Neighbors, friends and strangers have always found a royal welcome in this fine old Virginia home.

The interior of the house, with its paneled door casements and wainscoat moulding carved in a design of classic detail; the pure Grecian carving in the drawing-room showing the egg and dart motif, and the remarkably high-pitched ceilings, place the building among the best of its type in the country. A large living-room occupies the width and depth of the house on the south end at the rear of the entrance hall. Here the most interesting object is the mantel of Pavanazzo marble. Most of the doors are opened by silver knobs; slat inner doors, that interesting detail of the best Southern houses of the early period, lend coolness in the summer and ventilation all the year. The first-floor halls and rooms are lighted by beautiful chandeliers of bronze which once hung in a famous old house in Richmond.

The lawn is studded with many elm trees. These, in May, look as if some fairy had touched their brown branches with a shimmer of green and gold. Other trees are here, too—birch, poplar and ash, chestnut, pecan and mahogany. Beneath the shade of one of the poplars—which boasts a circumference of twenty-one feet—General LaFayette is said to have made his camp.

Scattered in clumps about the broad lawn, between skyward-reaching magnolias and long-lived forest trees—some wrapped, trunk and bough, in ivy—are a wide variety of shrubs.

The garden is approached over the serpentine brick walk which leads across the lawn from the south porch. Sempervirens box-wood, eighteen inches in height, follows the walk along both sides. It is noteworthy that the six hundred and eighty-five specimens hedging the bricks were propagated at Elk Hill by Mrs. Stokes. Her hand also planted many of the shrubs and flowering trees that in the spring make of the place a double garden—half hanging, almost, in the air—the other half under foot. She was the presiding spirit who, short-handed at times during our day, yet continued to add so much to the old-fashioned beauty of the place by skill, personal care and indefatigable zeal. In a paper read some years ago before the James River Garden Club, Mrs. Stokes told the secret of her success with box.

"I am going to tell you very briefly just what I did in growing my boxwood," she said. "I took a square in my vegetable garden, had it deeply plowed and laid off in rows three feet apart. I opened the rows, mixed the soil with thoroughly well-rotted cow-pen manure, leaving the surface flat. I then broke off pieces from four to five inches from a hedge box in my flower garden, being sure each piece was pronged instead of being straight, as a root puts out much quicker from a pronged slip. I set the slips four inches apart in the rows, covering them so that only two inches showed above ground. These slips were put out in November, 1913— four thousand of them. The first winter I cut just the tips from each slip, laying pine brush between the rows to break the wind, as nothing is so disastrous to slips rooting as being blown to and fro by the wind. By the 1st of April, 1914, I could not tell from appearances whether rooting had taken place or the slips were dead, but, on pulling up several, I found the fine rootlets putting out. It was as though I had made a real discovery, for raising boxwood was with me a pure experiment. The weeds growing between the plants were pulled out by hand, and the soil between rows frequently worked with a hoe. I commenced by the first week in April to water the box plants each day, if it did not rain, so that the ground below the surface never lost its moisture. By the first part of May they were growing most encouragingly. I wish to emphasize that the most important thing in growing boxwood from slips, after they are rooted, is to water them incessantly. I don't believe you can use too much water. My boxwood is now eighteen months old, and from six to nine inches high. This November it will be transplanted to the walks throughout the lawn. Ever since a visit to beautiful old Brandon several years ago, I have dreamed of boxwood hedges, and I must have boxwood hedges. I found the one way I could get them was to grow them, and so I started in, and all of you practical gardeners know the joy of watching something grow hardy and beautiful, when in the beginning it was but an experiment."

South of the house and sheltered by it from the full sweep of the north winds, lies the garden which has long been noted in the annals of Virginia. In form it is semi-circular. A ten-foot turfed walk extends between clumps of althea, lilac and syringa, crepe myrtles, spiraea and mimosa trees, and beds rich in iris, paeonies and other perennials. Hackberry, ash and elm trees overshadow the rose-draped fence and trellises at the entrance. These are covered with a profusion of century-old damask roses of marvelous perfume, and scores of others, some of the names of which are all but forgotten amid the motley throng of modern blooms.

Beginning at the garden entrance and multiplying farther on stand sempervirens box trees, their tops modified in pointed arborescence. These splendid box trees, defiant of time and trimmed to perfect cones, throw their shafts fifteen feet into the sky. With scattering knots of dwarf box they add great dignity to this garden laid out many years ago. It is gratifying to tell that the

Sempervirens Boxwood at Elk Hill

Serpentine Brick Walk, Leading from House to Garden, at Elk Hill

Elk Hill—North Front

Elk Hill—South Front

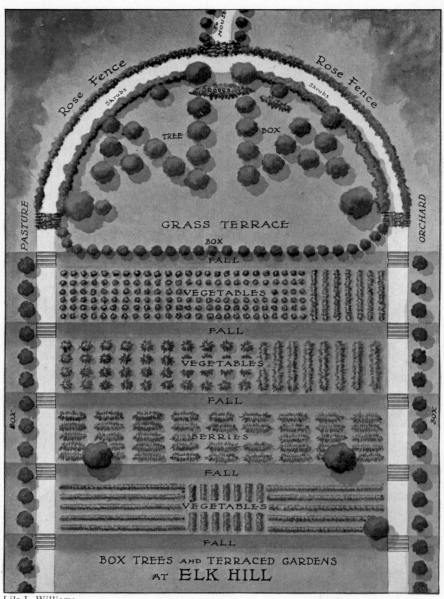

BOX TREES and TERRACED GARDENS
at ELK HILL

Lila L. Williams

boxwood at Elk Hill shows better and more consistent care than any in Virginia, excepting, perhaps, Mount Vernon.

Seven terraces fall vertically below these evergreen groupings, and upon the topmost stand twenty-seven conical box trees, ranging in height from ten to twenty feet, their soaring, dark green, glittering foliage standing out against the skyline. In lines of four, three, two and one, these trees grow ten feet apart, and below them, but still on the same terrace, a semi-circular grassy plateau hedged with dwarf box extends. From this, the six terraces of the kitchen garden, each grassed as it falls, drop to the lowest, which once was given over entirely to the cultivation of box.

To Randolph Harrison is given the credit for the beginning of the Elk Hill garden, which is supposed to have been laid off about 1845. There is a local legend that after the seven terraces were made, in order to enrich them, with the aid of teams of oxen, he had soil hauled from an island in James River, nearly a mile away. With this fertile soil he topped each terrace, with a result that has proven it well worth while.

The proportion of box to the other shrubbery at Elk Hill and the scheme of its distribution are as correct and effective for contrast and background to the transient foliage and flowers of June as amid the bare ramage of January. Both winter and summer, as the gravest item in the garden, the box retains its values and gives the year round a note both virile and conservative. There *is* a French saying, "Evergreens are the joy of winter and the mourning of summer months." Even if this be true, those who see it will agree that the effect of spring and summer color is doubled at Elk Hill by its splendid box, which, though dusky in winter, with spring, or "the sweet of the year," becomes bright with tender, green leaves. And all this box, even on dull days, makes the bright flowers look as if the sun were shining.

One reason latter-day Americans garden along lines of least resistance is that they are always in a hurry. The garden art is preeminently one of leisure. The designers of Elk Hill knew this,

[133]

and in planning their garden did much for future generations—much that has extended beyond the confines of their evergreen garden.

This garden is of the sort that can only be found about old houses where sweet and sacred memories linger like the scent of the box and the flowers which bloom within it. How cold and unfriendly modern gardens seem when compared to the old-fashioned ones! At Elk Hill, most of the flower inmates can trace their pedigrees back to the floral emigrants from England and Holland. The young plants that replace the dead ones are scions of the old stock. Strange blossoms, changing every springtime, would not be in good standing with the venerable day lilies and periwinkle, or the mock orange and althea, some of whom can remember the day when the elms and poplars that shade the lawn were only saplings.

In the following verses, "My Garden," written by Mrs. Stokes, we give a charming picture of Elk Hill at blooming time:

"Century-old boxwoods their vigils keep
Like sentinels on guard o'er the flowers sweet,
Lilacs, purple, peonies, pink,
Jonquils, hyacinths, tulips; think
Of the beauty, the fragrance, the charm—
Syringa, spiraea, lilies adorn
    My Garden.

"Ah! Roses twined with memories sweet!
With rapture many hearts in 'membrance beat;
Wars have raged under colors of the rose,
Lancaster and York cost England in throes.
A bier is covered! A bride's path strewn!
But return to the roses all—abloom
    In my Garden.

"As I sit in an arbor, all vine-clad
With yellow star-jasmine, I would I had
The power to picture on every side
Nature's canvas painted in springtide.

The bloom, the fragrance, the color apace,
Oh! The joy of life as I face
My Garden.

"Terrace on terrace rolls to the stream
That peacefully flows in a silvery gleam,
Bordered with honeysuckle, the red, coral kind,
O'er the fence the wistarias climb.
Purple and green, crimson and gold—
A pageantry of Nature brilliantly enfold
My Garden."

EDITH DABNEY TUNIS SALE.

BREMO

REMO, on the Upper James River, the beautiful century-old home, built by General John Hartwell Cocke, stands as a rare type of Greek-Colonial architecture, and commands a superb view of the fertile valley of the James and the Buckingham hills beyond.

This estate with its large stone barns and outbuildings, is one of the most notable places in its section.

Though he lived nearly one hundred and fifty years ago, General Cocke was as fanatical a prohibitionist as any of this later day. Believing that water—and water only—was the beverage for men to drink, he placed on the bank of the James River and Kanawha Canal, which ran through his property, an enormous iron pitcher or urn. Pipes from a nearby spring supplied the water which ran from the huge pitcher at all times except freezing weather. This curiosity, now known as the "Teapot of Bremo," stands on the lawn at the old place where it is a constant source of interest to visitors.

On the low-lying slope below the south lawn lies the old garden, famous in ante-bellum days for the beauty of its flowering shrubs, and its wealth of old-time flowers which pour out their fragrance to all who wander there.

Its broad, winding walks are shaded by semi-tropical trees, and the sunlight flickers through the rosy glow of the feathery mimosa or the dark green of the coffee tree. There one might linger under arbors and gather luscious grapes or stroll along the old serpentine brick wall and feast on figs worthy of the Orient. Or, they may emerge from the shaded walks to view the panorama of brilliant beds of roses encircled by the dark, rich green of the box-hedge which forms a gigantic star in the midst of the garden. Farther on, myriads of flowering bulbs once rejoiced on the sloping borders of a

[136]

River Front of Lower Bremo

The Hillside Garden at Lower Bremo

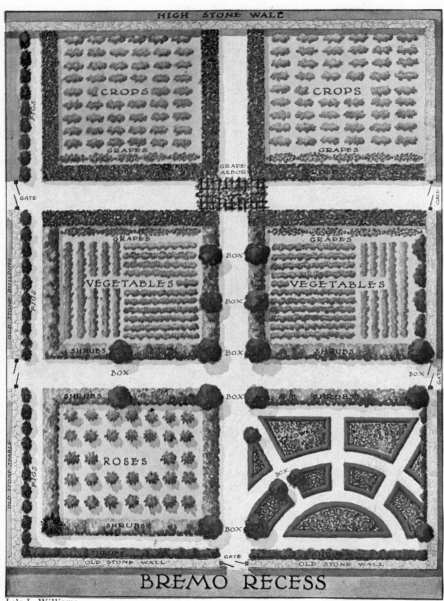

BREMO RECESS

Lila L. Williams

Stone Garden Wall at Recess

mirror-lake, whose calm waters reflected the beauty of the garden and rippled with the graceful motion of the swan upon its waters.

Where the lake narrowed to join the waters of the canal beyond, a graceful arched bridge led across to the orchard on the one side with fruits and nuts of various kinds. On the other, were the vegetable gardens with a luxuriance of all things for the bountiful table of the old house, within whose walls many noted guests were welcomed.

Near by there was a rabbit-warren, the soft, downy bunnies being the delight of all the children in early days who visited Bremo.

In one corner of the garden wall stood the brick cottage where Aunt Phyllis lived. She had special charge of the chickens that feasted in the adjacent barnyard.

Just after the War Between the States, General Lee was visiting Bremo, where his family had spent much time during the war. Aunt Phyllis had cared for Miss Mildred Lee's pets while she was at Bremo, and the General said he wished to thank her; so, accompanied by two college boys, he called at the cottage. Aunt Phyllis, who was the pure African type, stood curtseying in the doorway and hastened to tell General Lee of her war experience. She said that the Yankee soldiers in passing Bremo had induced her, under false pretences, to feed and house her large flock of chickens. They then entered the hen-house, caught all of the chickens, tied them to their saddles and were off, with the laugh on the old woman. Aunt Phyllis wound up her story by saying, "Mars Bob, dem Yankees is de mos' interruptious nation I ever did see." General Lee threw back his head with a hearty laugh and said, "Auntie, I have certainly found them so!"

With the passing of the old days and the old regime, many beauties of the garden also passed, and nature now runs riot with lavish luxuriance on the spot that the gardener's art once shaped into ideal beauty. The old home, mellowed by years, stands en-

[137]

dren and grown people with their delicious fruits—these ripen consecutively from June until November. When covered with their snowy veil of blossoms in the spring the trees looked like brides, so I heard one of their beloved mistresses say.

The next owners were a most devoted and flower-loving couple who added much to the beauty and fruitfulness of the garden in its variety of raspberries, peaches, pears, apples, and grapes. They also added to the large number of figs planted by General Cocke. How well I can remember those fig-bushes against the stone-wall! They have been a joy to friends and relations far and near; those visiting the family, or those dear ones near enough for the delicious fruit to be transported in large or small containers. Most of the late figs are gone now. All of the different kinds that are left are buried six inches below the surface of the ground and staked down about November 15th, to escape freezing weather. They are not taken up again until the middle of April, which treatment assures an abundance of fruit.

Not very long before the War Between the States, a friend sent General Cocke two scuppernong grapevines from North Carolina. He sent them to his daughter, Mrs. Arthur Lee Brent, to whom he had given Recess after the death of his son, John, who died unmarried. Mrs. Brent planted them in the lower part of the garden and they were busily running over the arbor in my early childhood. They would have run riot all over the whole garden by this time had they been permitted to do so. However, loving hands restricted them and now they are not only beautiful but have borne bushels of grapes, from which delightful wine and jelly have been made. It was some years before the scuppernong vines began to bear at all, and when they did, at first they produced but one grape at a time here and there; then two and three came, until now they yield good sized bunches, which hide themselves under the pretty leaves of the wonderful vine, giving forth a very sweet odor.

Another charming feature of the Recess garden of my child-

Point of Fork

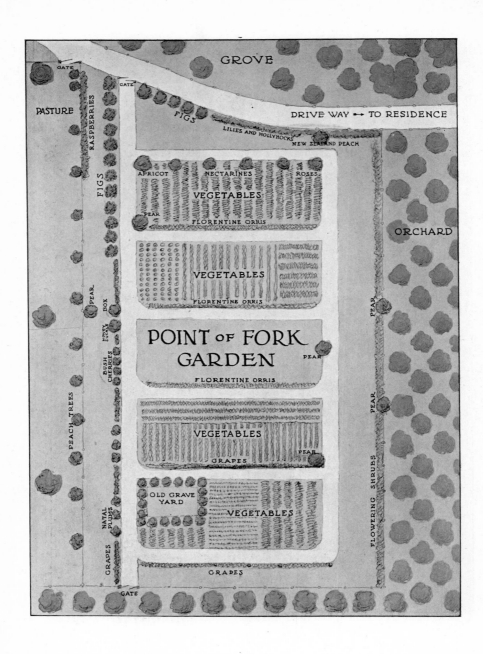

North Front of Upper Bremo

Recess

hood days comes to mind as I recall the arbors that stood there. Three of these, large and octagonal, were placed at the intersection of the walks and over them climbed roses and other vines. One, in particular, seemed very beautiful to me. It was covered with yellow roses called the Lady Banksia, which blooms in long wreaths and clusters.

Once, when a May party was the occasion of celebrating the birthday of a fair young girl who, after a great many years, became the mistress of Recess, ices and dainties of various kinds were dispensed to her companions from a new arbor covered with pink roses. Seats were built around this arbor and a pretty rustic table was placed in the center. It stood near the late figs, at the highest part of the stone wall which bounded the garden.

Shrubs of many kinds and great bushes of ivy formed quite a feature of the Recess garden. It is strikingly picturesque when the golden forsythia or tall, white lilies stand out against the dark, compact greenness of the boxwoods. The many beds of spice pinks of the same variety that used to be in the lovely garden at Mount Vernon, also give charm and sweetness to this old Virginia garden.

FANNIE G. CAMPBELL.

POINT OF FORK

OINT OF FORK derives its name from its situation at the forks of James River. One branch of this is here called the Rivanna (River Anna), and the other, which is the main branch, now the James, was formerly the Fluvous Anna (Fluvanna), both named for Anna, Queen of James I.

This was once a noted Indian stronghold, the capital of the Monacan nation, which was known by the tribe as Rausawek. The supremacy of these Indians at one time extended over the Alleghanies to the Falls of the James at Richmond and numbered many thousands. They carried their wars even into Canada. At Point of Fork, near the entrance into the garden, is the spot where one of their chieftains, famous for his warlike exploits and successful raids against the Iroquois, lies buried.

The spot was also on John Smith's map, and was reported by him as the principal settlement of the Monacans in his time. They had then been greatly reduced by disastrous wars in the North.

Point of Fork was regarded as a strategic point by the Colonial Virginians in Revolutionary days, and was an important barracks and arsenal where military stores were kept. Here, General (Baron) Von Steuben trained the Revolutionary troops, and the Battle of Point of Fork was fought with Simcoe and Tarleton, the latter having his headquarters here. During the War Between the States, Generals Sheridan and Custer made the present residence their headquarters.

The eminence, upon which the house is located, faces the convex of the bend in the river, and commands a beautiful view of the James for several miles. The dwelling was erected about one hundred years ago by William Galt, a rich Scotch merchant, who resided in Richmond. At that time, the estate contained five thousand, two hundred and ninety-three acres. On November 24, 1828, John Allen, executor and trustee of William Galt, deeded Point of Fork to James Galt, a nephew of the first owner of that name.

The red brick house, with white marble trim, is of Georgian design, and is still one of the handsomest in this part of Virginia. It is said that the massive timber of which it is constructed was selected with great care and allowed to season several years before it was used. The floors are hardwood, the doors and banisters of mahogany. In the wide hall, which runs the length of the house, there is a graceful elliptical stairway with mahogany rails. Broad entrance steps lead up to the porch, and this also extends the width of the house for about sixty-five feet. This porch is upheld by large white columns which extend up to the roof. The present owner has added many modern improvements and put in order the terraced gardens and shrubbery for which Point of Fork was once famous.

The gardens, which are large, were laid out with great care and expense. They lie some distance from the house, and on both sides, and many of their walks are bordered with Florentine orris. They consist of six terraces, each of which is sixty feet wide and one hundred and fifty feet long. There is a wide bed at the foot of the last and the corners of each are rounded by paths leading around them to the main walks. The latter, which range from one to one hundred and fifty feet in width, extend along each side of the terraces. On the other side are beds, thirty feet broad, running with the walks the entire length of the garden. Both walks and flower beds show the natural slope of the garden, which is very gentle, as the terraces range only from four to five feet in height. The exposure of all is southwest.

The soils on the various terraces are all different in character and composition, some having been hauled from a distance, some from the woodland, and still others from the rich lowgrounds, as was frequently done in the best old Virginia gardens. The front of the garden, which has the shape of a concave curve, opens upon

[143]

the carriage way leading to the residence. The bank here is a mass of lilies, spring flowers, and hollyhocks its entire length. Across the way a large grove of splendid old trees serve as protection from the north winds. This grove is bordered with shrubs and Scotch broom and in it, about seventy feet from the main entrance to the gardens, is the grave of the famous Indian chieftain.

Along the main walks of the garden many grapevines and foreign fruits are planted. There are at least twenty-five varieties of grapes and many kinds of fruits from Asia and Africa. There are still Chinese bush cherries and Chinese sweet cherries next, and plums from Natal and Russia; still other fruits came from the Himalayas.

Scattered throughout the garden are box and mimosa trees, honeysuckle, indicera gerardiana, and other flowering shrubs. At the main entrance, for thirty feet or more, are long rows of figs of two fine varieties. Every November these fig trees are bent to the ground, fastened down and covered with two feet or more of earth. In April they are taken up, and invariably yield two crops of delicious figs each year.

On one side, between the house and garden, lies the orchard of pears and plums. A driveway through this is bordered with many kinds of altheas, and at the foot of the garden, the apple orchard extends to the stream below and beyond to the hillside which it covers.

On both fronts of the house are extensive lawns, upon which grow many varieties of handsome old trees. Among the latter is a genuine cedar of Lebanon. The Department of Agriculture is authority for the statement that this is one of the few genuine specimens to be found in America.

J. ALSTON CABELL.

Westend, Louisa County

Lilies in the Garden at Westend

WESTEND

O neighborhood in Virginia exceeds that of the Green Springs in its rural charm. There are no magnificent views, no prodigies of nature, but the coloring and exquisite contour of the land, the woods that define and give value to every stretch of field and meadow, make this a country preeminently fitted for homes.

Years ago the little mineral spring, that gives this part of Louisa County its name, was a popular summer resort, but even the oldest inhabitant can just remember the decrepid bath-house that survived the hotel and cottages.

The rock formation about this spring is confined to a comparatively small area, several miles long, and two or three miles wide. The rock is soft and speckled throughout with green. It is said to be the bed of a prehistoric lake.

The soil in this section is particularly fertile, and that, no doubt, tempted the first Watson and the first Morris to come to Louisa County. They, with their descendants, owned the land for over a hundred years and built the homes that are standing today—Ionia, "The Old Place"; Sylvania, Bracketts, Hawkwood, Grassdale, and Westend. Most of these estates have passed in late years from the hands of their original owners and, as usual, when places pass from hand to hand, the gardens have suffered most. Now, there is barely a trace left of the early gardens with one exception, and that is the garden of Westend. This garden lives today untouched, a perfect example of the landscape art of its day.

The house at Westend was built in 1849 by Mrs. James Watson, who was Miss Susan Dabney Morris, of Sylvania. Mrs. Watson, so far as we know, designed the garden and planted the grounds at Westend herself, but just as we feel Le Notre, at

Brandon, and Sir Christopher Wren, at Westover, here Downing's influence seems to prevail. This is especially seen in the grounds, and nowhere could there be found a house more perfectly set. The broad, open lawn in front, the careful selection and grouping of trees, the avenue of elms, are all a monument to Mrs. Watson's taste, and an inspiration to the landscape architect of this day.

The site of Westend is on a part of Bracketts, the older estate of the Watson family. When Mrs. Watson began her garden here, the place was little more than a bare field. Under her efficient direction, however, it soon literally blossomed as the rose. Trees she ordered planted just where they would mean the most. Shrubs she placed where screens were needed to hide the more barren spots.

The grounds around the house, including the garden, consist of about twelve acres, all enclosed by a hedge of clipped osage orange. The garden itself is two acres in extent and is rectangular in shape. The lower part is for vegetables, and this is charming in its simplicity of straight rows and grass walks. This, too, has an osage orange hedge for border. The upper end of the rectangle is given over to the flower garden, which is divided from the lower by shrubbery, and enclosed by a boxwood hedge.

There is a raised circle in the center of the garden, about fifty feet in diameter. This is divided into small beds of roses that slope gradually upward to a center circle surrounding a pillar rose. The walks on the "mound," as it is called, are of grass, and the beds though originally bordered with box, are now edged with periwinkle. In addition to the roses, there are quantities of Madonna lilies; and these lilies, as well as almost all of the roses, were planted over seventy years ago. Unfortunately, no record of the names of the roses has been kept, but to a rosarian they are particularly interesting, as so many have joined the ranks of "old forgotten far-off things."

The beds that surround the mound are large and irregular in shape in order to conform to the circle in the center and to the rectangular boundary. The paths curve through them, half hidden by shrubbery, in a fascinating manner. Originally, the garden was pointed up with spruce-pine, now grown into large trees, some of which have died, detracting from the carefully planned "balance." At one time a summer-house stood just where the central path of the vegetable garden entered the flower garden; this, unfortunately, has not survived, but so many of the old shrubs and plants remain as they were originally planted, that our great-grandmother's garden of 1849 stands today a memorial to one who knew and loved "the art of gardening."

L. P. C. T.

The Tidewater Trail

The Garden at Lawson Hall

Lawson Hall, Princess Anne County

Sylvan Scene, Northampton County—Home of the Fitzhughs

LAWSON HALL

SEVEN miles from Norfolk on the road leading towards Cape Henry is Lawson Hall. The plantation originally contained over one thousand acres and was a Crown grant to Sir Thomas Lawson of England in 1607. It is said this same Sir Thomas Lawson was one of the company who sailed in the ship of Sir George Summers, which was caught in a gale off the Bermudas, and that it was from this stirring tale Shakespeare got the material for his "Tempest."

Formerly ships came from the sea through Little Creek and landed their stores near the site of the present house. Of these merchant ships the Lawsons are said to have had many, and brought in them, so the story goes, some of the bricks and much of the carved grey marble of which the original dwelling was constructed. In the latter, the walls were two feet thick and the drawing-room twenty-six feet square. Every room was finished in rich, hand-made wainscoting, but, unfortunately, this house was destroyed by fire several years ago. The residence we now see was built a few years ago by the present owner, Mr. C. F. Hodgman, who has built with appreciation and sympathy for the older home and has added greatly to the restoration of Lawson Hall.

However, it is the gardens which interest us most. It is not known just when these were laid off, but those who are familiar with the life of trees say it must have been over two hundred years ago. Here there are great beeches and laurel oaks with a spread of over ninety feet and many boxwood trees in formal rows; these are among the largest in America. The box-trees and the rows of cedars make it a scene as if summer were here the whole year round.

One feels in looking at the old place that one of these Lawsons brought with him the memory of some much loved garden in England and reproduced it here. For many years the estate suffered decay, and it was used as officers' headquarters during the War Between the States by both armies. Yet, during all these trying times, no one cut down the beautiful boxwood or harmed the larger trees.

A broad avenue one-half mile in length leads from the public road to the house. As one enters here, the road divides and circles to the marble walk which leads to the front door. On this front lawn are the very largest trees—beech, laurel, oak and maple. Across the front of the house and along the two sides are the box-trees which in front are kept low and clipped, but at the sides have been allowed to grow as trees will until now they reach above the middle of the second-story windows.

On the left of the house is a terrace with fine large box-trees on the edge. On this also is the formal rose garden, which has been planted by the present owner. Going down from the terrace by two stone steps and on for about thirty feet one comes upon a little stream with box-trees on either side, whose tops meet above it. This is a veritable bird sanctuary, for here the year around birds of some kind may be found. In summer the mocking bird, the cardinal and the wren make it their very own.

On the other side of the stream after another level of about thirty feet the ground is terraced again. Here, too, are box-trees in line with the trees of the other terrace. On this the red day lilies run wild and in June are a glowing mass. This is not seen until one comes on it suddenly upon descending the first terrace. There, too, the white narcissus is naturalized. Other native wild flowers have been moved here—the blood-root, trailing arbutus and others.

This year most of the box-trees have had their first clipping. To know that one thousand three hundred pounds of short clippings were cut and can hardly be missed, shows the number and size of the stately trees of England that have found a home here and seem to like it.

These Lawsons and their kinsmen, the Walkes, who occupied the place so many years, identified themselves with all that was fine in the history of the new country. One of them was always a vestryman in that ancient and most interesting church known as Old Donation, as well as the little church that preceded the present one. Another Lawson helped select the site of Norfolk. There were women, too, of charm and beauty. One, Mary Calvert Lawson, has had her name handed down from generation to generation always Mary Calvert, whether it be Lawson or Walke, Hill or Truxtun, as it is today.

When the moonlight streams over this garden, and lingers lovingly there, one feels that much of interest has happened in it. That these wonderful trees through their several generations have been revered is truly evident in that during these more than two centuries they have never been harmed, keeping their foliage green, and making of a lovely spot a perpetual summer, and well may the poet have applied to it:

> "A place of rest with swaying trees,
> A lovely garden by the sea."

CORNELIA HODGMAN.

POPLAR HALL

IT was about the year 1640 that the first member of the Hoggard family came to this country. Shortly after that, he obtained from the Crown a tract of land in Tidewater Virginia, and this grant, it is interesting to note, has never passed out of the possession of his descendants of the same name and blood. As the place has never been sold, it has never been identified with any other name than that of Hoggard.

Tradition says that the place name, Poplar Hall, originated from the numerous and very fine poplar trees planted about the house; there is also a story that these trees were brought from England. This, however, seems almost impossible. To begin with, the ships of the seventeenth century were too small, navigation was too difficult and absolute necessities were so essential, that the early colonists could not afford to consider anything else. But, even if the trees were imported and were put out, two centuries later not one of the original growth of poplars remains. Their place has been well taken by pecan trees, which shade the lawn; and add to this, their great commercial value.

The house, a plain brick structure, stands on a slight elevation directly on the shores of Broad Creek, a tributary of the Elizabeth River, which flows through Norfolk County. Though once far from civilization, the dwelling is now almost in the heart of the city of Norfolk. The exact date of its building is not known, but interior and exterior work and design, the type of brick used, and the general atmosphere of the smaller buildings, would seem to place it about 1645. The following poem, written in June, 1828, gives the best description of life at Poplar Hall to be had:

Poplar Hall. Norfolk County

The Park at White Marsh with Its Remarkable Variety of Trees

A Vine-Covered Outbuilding at Gordonsdale, Fauquier County

THE TRIP TO POPLAR HALL

(Seat of T. Hoggard, Esq.)

A TALE—JUNE, 1828

T. Hoggard was a widower,
  And a Farmer bold beside;
A pleasant country seat had he
  On Broad Creek's flowing tide.

Now Hoggard had a friend, who lived
  In Norfolk's famous town;
A Counsellor at Law was he
  Of credit and renown.

So to this friend he one day sent
  An invitation kind,
That he and his dear wife would come
  And leave their cares behind.

The Lawyer's spouse said to him, dear,
  We both lack change of air;
So let us to friend Thurmer's go
  All in a chaise and pair.

He soon replied, I do admire
  Of womankind but one;
And you are she, my dearest dear,
  Therefore, it shall be done.

Now Washington and Colonel Walke,
  Who were two gallants bold,
Were both together of one mind
  In what—you'll soon be told.

Quoth Colonel Walke—The girls are gone,
  As you and I both know;
So we must now our minds make up
  Right after them to go.

And as we 'proached fair Poplar Hall,
　　Beneath a poplar tree,
They were sitting all beneath its shade
　　And chatting merrilie.

Now welcomings on ev'ry side
　　Right cordially did greet,
And full glad in truth were we
　　Our fair young friends to meet.

We ate and drank and play'd and sung,
　　And walk'd about the grove,
Chatting of this thing then of that,
　　But wot not aught of love.

The morning come—and breakfast o'er,
　　And having bid good-bye,
They went with heavy hearts, I ween,
　　And many a heavy sigh.

Long live the girls of Cum'land Street,
　　And Hoggard, long live he,
And when he next invites them out
　　May I o' the party be.

The large garden, which was used both for flowers and vegetables, still has the original square central beds bound by long, narrow borders on each side. Its dominant feature is a very beautiful
and unusual Persian lilac, which stands ten feet high and throws out
its graceful branches with a span of twelve feet from the ground
upward.

And there are many roses of the old varieties at Poplar Hall.
But in the culture of roses, this garden has kept pace with the
times. Nearly all of the old-fashioned flowers bloom here at their
various seasons, but the lily of the valley, which has naturalized,
has spread about the garden in almost tropical luxuriance and is
easily the one flower thought of in connection with Poplar Hall.

It has been said that at least one acre could be planted out from the lily of the valley roots in this old garden.

Seven generations of one family have lived under this hospitable roof. More than one war has passed over it and left it still unscathed. The fires which wrought such havoc in the city of Norfolk seem to have respected both the age and dignity of "this pleasant country seat on Broad Creek's flowing tide."

FANNIE C. HOGGARD.

GREEN PLAINS

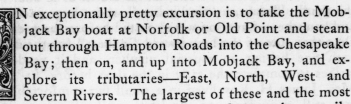A N exceptionally pretty excursion is to take the Mobjack Bay boat at Norfolk or Old Point and steam out through Hampton Roads into the Chesapeake Bay; then on, and up into Mobjack Bay, and explore its tributaries—East, North, West and Severn Rivers. The largest of these and the most beautiful is North River, twelve miles long, and more than a mile wide at its mouth. As the boat turns from Mobjack Bay, into this river, its course carries it very near the point of land on which is situated, in Mathews County, "Green Plains," the home of the Roys since the latter part of 1700.

"Isleham," the home of Sir John Peyton, a relative of Mr. James Henry Roy, and his marriage to Elizabeth Booth, of "Belleville," Gloucester County, just across the river, seem to have been the inducements to him to leave Essex, the home of his forefather, Dr. Mungo Roy of Revolutionary fame, and erect one of the most attractive and complete establishments in Tidewater Virginia, in a location incomparably beautiful. The river is like an inland lake, and on a bright day the handsome homes are reflected in the water all along the shores, as if in a mirror.

Green Plains mansion is of brick, composed of a large central building, of two stories and an immense attic and cellar, with wings on the east and west of one story. A broad hall runs through the house from north to south, with two rooms on either side on first and second floors. The stairway with two landings, the carved and paneled woodwork, the recessed windows with their broad seats and enchanting cupboards in the sides of the mantels, are interesting architectural features.

There were innumerable outbuildings, many of brick and most substantially built; the carpenter's shop, the weaving room, the tanning house, one of the conical-shaped icehouses peculiar to Tide-water Virginia, an unusual number of fine barns, and quarters for the house servants and field hands. The out-of-doors kitchen had an immense fireplace—crane, and a Dutch oven and, of course, in the good old days, a "tin kitchen," where huge saddles of mutton and haunches of venison were roasted before the great fire of logs. On either side of the house were "strikers" for the house-servants, each one having an especial number, and it needed twenty-one strikes to complete the tally in the days before '61-'65. Mr. and Mrs. James H. Roy lived in a small but comfortable brick building, still in evidence on the lawn, while they personally superintended the building of their home and the laying out of the grounds and garden.

The garden is surrounded by an unique scalloped brick wall. A broad, graveled walk extended from east to west as one entered, and another from north to south crossed it in the middle, where there was a latticed summer-house covered with jasmine and honeysuckle and fitted with seats inside. The walk from north to south was bordered by grapes carefully trained on lattices, while on either side of the entrance walk were raised borders, where many shrubs and flowers grew. On the north and south of this walk were flower-beds in circles and hectagonals where every sort of sweet old-time bloom was cultivated. Along the borders were arborvitae trees at intervals, and under them grew lilies of the valley in profusion, and such shrubs as calycanthus, smoke trees, tamarisk and English laburnum with, here and there, fine box-bushes.

In each scallop of the brick wall was a raised mound, covered with violets, out of which grew a rosebush. Against the southern walls pomegranates and figs ripened to perfection and French artichokes were successfully cultivated. The figs bear abundantly to this day, but the pomegranates have disappeared with the passing of the skilled gardeners.

A giant pecan tree on the lawn thrives as well as if in its native soil. Just back of the garden—down the shore—is the family burying ground surrounded with a high brick wall. Here lies the remains of William H. Roy, eldest son of James H. Roy and Elizabeth Booth, and beside him are the graves of his first wife, Anne Seddon, and of his second wife, Euphan McCrae. His only son who grew to man's estate, James H. Roy, died unmarried, and his sisters, the daughters of Anne Seddon, were Mrs. John C. Rutherfoord (Anne S.), of "Rock Castle," and Mrs. Thomas H. Carter of "Pampatike." Mrs. McCrae Washington, Mrs. Mc-Kendree Boyd, and Mrs. Richard H. Goldsborgh, were the children of Euphan McCrae, his second wife, and Mrs. Richard Goldsborgh (Ellen Douglas Roy), his youngest and only surviving child, now lives at "Green Plains." The dainty beauty of her face and figure stand out in the graceful old home like an exquisite miniature in an appropriate frame.

During the War Between the States, Green Plains was ravaged by the Federal troops. Gunboats came up the river and marauding parties scoured the neighborhood, plundering and destroying all they could not take with them. Mr. Roy died before this period and his widow and younger daughters lived in a constant state of anxiety. They had to endure stoically the sight of their most precious possessions being stolen before their eyes, or be insulted by officers, as well as men. Fortunately all wine and liquor had been secreted within the walls and, in spite of persistent search and tapping of the panelling, it was not discovered, or worse than insults might have resulted.

Green Plains is one of the few estates which still remains in the family of its original owners, and is kept up so as to be a pleasure to all who go there.

ANNE SEDDON RUTHERFOORD JOHNSON.

Green Plains, Mathews County

Poplar Grove, Home of Captain Sally Tompkins

POPLAR GROVE

IN the year 1725 Gloucester County embraced that little enclosure (for it is almost entirely surrounded by water) which is now Mathews County. It was here that Samuel Williams, of Northumberland County, received from George III a large grant of land which passed to his son, Thomas, who built the west wing of Poplar Grove in 1782. Ten years later it was sold to John Patterson, and he, it is said, having obtained the same architect who designed Mount Vernon, added greatly to the house.

About this time, the feeling between the two parties—Whig and Tory—was very keen and Mr. Patterson, in honor of his political affiliations, called his home Poplar Grove and planted on its lawn numbers of beautiful Lombardy poplars, the symbol of the Whigs.

With the lawn sloping down a few hundred feet to the water, a magnificent view is commanded of Mobjack Bay. To the south, just fourteen miles away, is Yorktown, and it was from there that schooners, laden with corn to grind for George Washington's army, sailed around York Spit and across the bay to the old mill at Poplar Grove. The old mill is still standing and is a continual inspiration to artists.

To the west of the house, and extending almost to the water's edge, was the old garden and, across the north end, ran a serpentine brick wall. Through the influence of Thomas Jefferson, this type of wall had become the vogue in Virginia about that date. Separating the garden from the lawn, ran a low brick wall capped with old English crescent-shaped brick. A part of the serpentine wall and all of the little wall still stand.

Like so many of the old gardens, the flowers and vegetables were in the same enclosure. Along the central walk were three large arbors covered with Cherokee roses. From the end of this walk, two rows of white and purple fig bushes extended. Some of these still remain, along with the old boxwood trees; with numbers of yellow tea and moss roses, whose bushes are known to be a hundred years old. The moisture of the atmosphere probably accounts for the longevity of these old roses.

Under the boxwood trees the periwinkle is still profuse. The yellow jessamine, the crepe myrtle, rose of Sharon, lily of the valley and jonquils still thrive as the daisies of the field. The smoke trees and flowering almond have gone, but the old Scuppernong grape arbor has been restored.

At the death of John Patterson, Poplar Grove passed to his daughter, who married Christopher Tompkins, the father of Miss Sally Tompkins, the beloved little "captain" of the Confederacy, who lived here until she was sixteen.

Captain Sally Tompkins, during the War Between the States, devoted herself and her fortune to the care of sick and wounded Confederate soldiers in Richmond. Appreciating the value and earnestness of her work, and realizing the necessity for as much freedom as it was possible to have, General Lee gave her a commission with the rank of Captain, C. S. A. It was through her influence that Christ Church, in Kingston Parish, was established. In its yard she now lies buried in the same grave with her sister, preferring this to the family burying ground at Poplar Grove. The latter is surrounded by a high brick wall, sheltered by four giant pines. These old trees tower so high above the rest of the landscape that sailors out in the bay use them as a landmark.

A winding lane of half a mile, with cedar and locust trees on either side, leads from the public road to the house. The poplar trees which were the glory of the lawn, and which gave the estate its name, have long since gone, but they have been succeeded by elms and maples, lindens and walnut trees.

The place passed from the Tompkins' to the family of John Tabb, who sold it to Christopher Brown. At the death of the latter, it went to his daughter, who married Judge Taylor Garnett, and whose family lived there until his death.

In 1910 Poplar Grove was bought by Arthur St. Clair Butler, who added the Colonial columns and modern conveniences. Thanks to him, the fields now produce the crops of the olden days, and the beauties of the old garden have been restored to a great extent.

MARY BUTLER POLLARD.

TODDSBURY

HERE is no more ideal place in America for country seats than along North River, an estuary of Mobjack Bay. The name of this sheet of water was given it by the sailors of long ago, who, when the echoes of their songs and voices were thrown back by the lush green shores, accused these silent banks of mocking "Jack" the sailor. Hence the name Mock Jack, now known no more, but substituted by the meaningless one of Mobjack.

Early in the seventeenth century Thomas Todd, emigrant, patented extensive lands in Maryland and Virginia; he was Burgess of Baltimore County in 1674-75, and in 1676 died at sea while on a voyage in the "good ship Virginia." With his will filed in the clerk's office at Towson, the county seat of Baltimore County, Maryland, and in which he left Toddsbury to his son, Thomas, there is a letter addressed "this to my son, Thomas Todd, at his home on North River, Gloucester County, Virginia, with all speed," and an old record says of the emigrant "he was very riche." There are many descendants of Thomas Todd of Maryland and Virginia scattered over the United States. Many of them have taken high positions, an ancestor of the Kentucky branch of this family having been a Justice of the Supreme Court of the United States.

In their veins runs the blood of the poet Lovelace and of our first Virginia poet, George Sandys. In Virginia, three of the descendants of Thomas Todd are on the bench—Judge Beverly Crump, Judge Crump Tucker and Judge John Rutherfoord. Another, Dr. Beverly Tucker, an eminent nerve specialist, is also a writer and poet of promise. In Maryland the families of Moale, Hoffman and Poultney are direct descendants, and in New York

Serpentine Brick Wall at Poplar Grove

Toddsbury—Gloucester County

the Townsend Burdens, the William R. Travers and Mrs. Ogden Doremus came from the same line.

Christopher Todd, great-grandson of the emigrant, dying without issue, left Toddsbury to his nephew, Philip Tabb, son of Lucy Todd and Edward Tabb of Amelia County, Virginia. Philip Tabb married his first cousin, Mary Mason Wythe-Booth, daughter of Elizabeth Todd by her first husband, Nathaniel Wythe of Williamsburg, and widow of George Booth of Belleville. In this manner, although Toddsbury passed from the name of Todd, it was owned by two direct heirs of the emigrant.

Mary Mason Wythe-Booth-Tabb was a personage in her day, as was her husband, Philip Tabb. Their home was the centre of the county's hospitality, and Mrs. Tabb was a model for wives, mothers and housekeepers. While Philip Tabb followed the hounds, bet on horse races and played cards, as did all of the gentlemen of his day, his wife became more and more devout; she joined the Methodists and the large church in that neighborhood was built by her. The story goes that after providing a bountiful supper for her husband and his guests, she would retire to the "chamber" and pray for their souls, while they cast the dice, swore brave oaths and drank merrily till late into the night.

The old house is of true Colonial architecture and has never been remodeled. The interior is like a jewel-box, so beautiful are the carvings and panelings. The dining-room, with recessed windows looking out to North River on two sides, is a spot to sit and dream in, and all sorts of visions come unbidden to the visitor. Near the entrance gate is one of the above-ground icehouses peculiar to the tidewater country; it is conical in shape and stands on a high mound overgrown with vines. At the back of the house is an old dairy with overhanging eaves, still in use. On the east of the lawn, which is nearly surrounded on three sides by water, is one of the most ancient family burying-grounds in Virginia. Here rest the ashes of seven generations of Todds and Tabbs, handsome stones and inscriptions preserving the records from the day of Thomas Todd, emigrant. Guarded by an ancient willow tree, this graveyard contains as many tombstones as any family seat in Virginia; among these there is one dated 1703.

In 1859, Thomas Tabb, son of Philip and Mary Mason Wythe-Booth-Tabb, moved to Texas and the property passed out of his family. In 1880 it was purchased by John Mott, of Long Island, the father of the present owner, Mr. William Mott. The children of the latter have been born and brought up at Toddsbury, and they all love and appreciate the history and beauties of the old Colonial dwelling; it is to the kindness of Mrs. Mott that I am indebted for the sketches of the house and lawn.

The garden was situated on the north side of the house and was much neglected before the days of the present owners, but there are descendants of the Tabbs who remember well its glories. It was surrounded by a brick wall not more than two and a half feet in height, and on top of this was a wooden railing, with a gate also of wood of pretty design. There is a similar wall and entrance in perfect preservation at Hickory Hill, Hanover County, the home of Mr. Henry Wickham.

The garden, which was a rectangle in form, was divided by a centre walk and cross walks, making squares for vegetables surrounded by dwarf box hedges, and with narrow borders for flowers along the edges. In these borders were grown all of the early and late flowers of that period, and at the junction of the walks were planted large and small shrubs, making a diversion to the monotony of the borders and hedges. Just inside of the gate, and across the south side of the garden, was a broad walk with flowerborders on either hand inside of the box hedges. On the lawn were set out trees of various kinds, a very fine pecan and a black ash remaining to show the taste of the early owners.

ANNE SEDDON RUTHERFOORD JOHNSON.

WHITE MARSH

FOLLOWING the Tidewater Trail from Gloucester Court House for six miles southward over a hard sand and shell road, one's attention is arrested by an imposing entrance which leads through a canopied avenue of such magnificent oaks, that the midday sun tapestries the driveway with shadows.

These monarchs of Nature's own planting guard the approach to White Marsh for half a mile. One is impressed with the majesty of the scene, and the silence unbroken except for the twitter of birds. Here was once the playground of the Red Man, who must have sighed at going, as did Boab-dil looking back once more upon his beloved Alhambra.

The main entrance, to the left of the lawn, discloses a circular driveway leading to the high-pillared house gleaming white against its background of crepe myrtle and magnolia.

From the portico, another vista is seen through the lawn of twenty acres, where leafy branches from the Orient lock arms with those of the Occident in a brotherhood of blended beauty. Forty-seven magnolia grandiflora, averaging twelve inches in diameter, lend grandeur, winter and summer, to lawn and gardens. Crepe myrtles, hoary with age, send their naked branches, capped with feathery blossoms of white, lavender and rose, high among the limbs of towering trees.

The bronze beech is here, the European horse chestnut, scarlet hawthorne, English yew and walnut. The varnish tree, white and black ash, sweet gum, elm, linden, tulip tree, locust, sycamore, and, practically every species of oak, maple, and pine interlace their branches over acres of greensward! It is marvelous how abundantly the grass grows beneath so dense a shade.

Trees—majestic trees, everywhere!

[167]

Wandering back to the house, one pauses enthralled by the size and perfect proportions of a Ginkgo biloba, or maidenhair tree, full eighty feet tall, with its trunk measuring twenty inches in diameter, standing sentinel at the right of the entrance. This tree is a fortune in itself—not commercially, perhaps, but because of its marvelous beauty.

To the right of this is a giant arbor vitae, cropped low to form a playhouse for children, its top a tangle of Cherokee roses. Nearby, a massive hemlock seems to frown upon such levity.

As one wonders at the planting, the romance comes to mind that a certain John Tabb, son of Phillip Tabb, of Toddsbury, wooed and won the fair Evelina Matilda Prosser, who inherited the White Marsh tract of three thousand acres from her mother. Their combined fortunes made John Tabb the wealthiest man in Gloucester County. Mrs. Tabb was loth to live so far from the social whirl, so her husband offered to make her the finest garden in Virginia, with every tree and shrub that could be grown in this climate, if she would but consent to make her home at White Marsh.

It was then, in 1848, that the present house was built and the lawn with its priceless trees planted. This was no mean undertaking in those days, when each foreign growth had to be specially imported. Thus, the collection stands a tribute to the planter's good taste botanical.

From the rear portico of the house are shown four terraces, a long grape arbor, and vegetable gardens with the meadows beyond.

Magnolia, elms and crepe myrtles fringe the terraces on both sides, affording many alluring spots for eager lovers, and the names inscribed upon window-panes prove they were not unfrequented!

In by-gone days "each terrace was laid out in a continuation of beds outlined by little boxwood bushes a foot high, and threaded by grass walks. The flowers in these beds consisted mostly of hyacinths, peonies, lilies, pinks, with the usual annuals and roses planted everywhere."

[168]

White Marsh, the Home of the Tabbs, Gloucester County

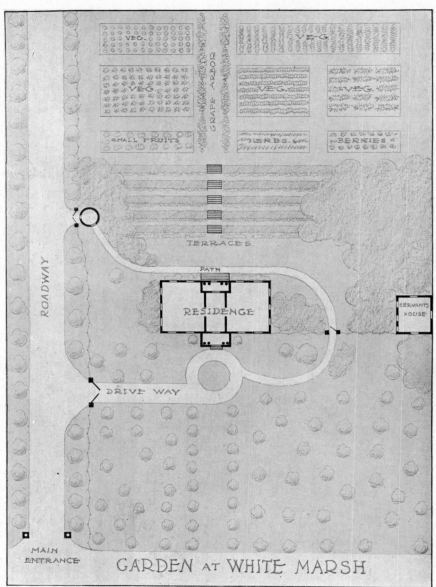

GARDEN AT WHITE MARSH

Lelia Scott Buchanan

Scalloped Brick Wall at Green Plains, Mathews County

Old Icehouse at Toddsbury, Gloucester County

Sherwood, Gloucester County

Snowballs, lilacs, flowering almonds, spireas and mock oranges held sway on the level stretch below the terraces, where the honeysuckle stealthily entwined itself about their branches.

To Mrs. John Perrin, of Baltimore, a granddaughter of John Tabb, the writer is indebted for the following description of the White Marsh garden as she knew it in her girlhood.

"Grandmother made a specialty of roses. I have heard she had five hundred varieties, which I rather doubt, though there were a great number. The arbors, of which there were four—two on the terraces, second and fourth—and two in the lower part, were all covered with white jessamine and running roses. So was the long porch at the back of the house overlooking the garden. The roses were not the ramblers we have today, but the sweetest little pink and white ones * * *. I can only remember a few of the names: 'Cloth of Gold,' 'Giant of Battles,' 'Safrano,' 'Le Marque,' and 'Lady Banksia.'

"The greenhouses were really wonderful! One in the garden on the left of the second terrace—all trace of which is gone now— one adjoining the parlour, and one in the front yard which is also gone. I have seen more than one hundred night-blooming cereus in bloom one night!"

With such a wealth of blossoms within and without, it is not surprising that General Robert E. Lee, who visited White Marsh for the first time in 1870, stood at the top of the garden and exclaimed, "This, indeed, is a beautiful spot!"

Beyond the shrubbery a grape avenue extends the full length of the main vegetable garden, a part of which in other days was subdivided into rectangular beds of small fruits, berries, and herbs. Ten miles of roadway encompass the present estate, now owned by Mr. H. M. Baruch, of New York.

Though the terraces no longer give forth fragrance and color as of yore, to the lover of magnificent trees, a pilgrimage to this old plantation holds a joy in store that will linger long in memory.

LELIA SCOTT BUCHANAN.

SHERWOOD

HEN Virginia was settled men were wont to follow where nature beckoned. Water still supplied society everywhere with its chief highways. Transportation by land was slow, tedious, difficult and expensive. Navigable streams were controlling factors in trade and commerce. A well-watered land was a populous and prosperous land. The many rivers that reach out of the inland sea, of which Virginia and Maryland are the mistresses, made for opulence, industry, and culture.

The wealth and prominence of Gloucester County followed as a natural consequence the fact that it is bounded on the south by one river, on the north by another, and has two others wholly within its own borders. Yet the county is a small one in actual area. It is questionable whether there is another county in Virginia, or any other State in America, that has proprietary rights in four such fine rivers as are the York, Severn, Ware and North. And in addition the whole eastern boundary of Gloucester is washed by Mobjack Bay. There is small wonder that the early settlers should have flocked to it in numbers; or that its scores of miles of bay and river front should be dotted with fine colonial residences.

Some of these houses date back to the seventeenth century. Some did not attain their prominence till a hundred years later. Homes of striking elaborateness and beauty were still being established when the nineteenth century opened. Among these none is more noteworthy than Sherwood, which for many years has been among the most admired residences in Gloucester.

A part of the present Sherwood house is of colonial construction, but it was not till the first three decades of the last century had elapsed that the old house attained its present spacious dimensions. At that time the property, which had known a variety of owners after the county was founded, came into the possession of Mr. Robert Colgate Selden, and for the last eighty-odd years it has been identified with the Selden name. Mr. Selden was a native of Norfolk; but his wife was Miss Courtenay Brook, whose mother, Elizabeth Lewis, had inherited Warner Hall, possibly the oldest and the most celebrated of all the Gloucester homesteads. Warner Hall, though the original house was burned in the nineteenth century, is still in the possession of a descendant of that original Warner, who came to America in 1628, and, some years later, established the estate that still bears his name. It was he who gave to the State of Virginia and the American nation such distinguished great-grandsons as George Washington and Robert E. Lee, not to mention a score of able men and charming women of less historic significance.

Mrs. Selden's association with Warner Hall, as well as her close relationship to most of the leading Gloucester families, probably was the controlling factor in inducing her husband to buy the Sherwood property, and to develop there the accessories of a famous Virginia home. Young Selden and his bride were both evidently endowed with a full measure of love for country life, which has from the beginning been a characteristic of the people of their native State. It is in the blood of every true Virginian. Their forebears brought it with them from England, Scotland and Wales.

Sherwood, in its eighty and more years of present existence, has known but three owners—the builder, his daughter, Mrs. Elizabeth Lewis Dimmock, and his granddaughter, Mrs. Henry A. Williams, the present owner who perpetuates in her Christian name Elizabeth Warner, wife of the first John Lewis and daughter of the second Augustine Warner, Speaker of the Virginia House of Burgesses in 1675-6-7 and 8.

Sherwood stands about a mile from the public highway that runs eastward through the little peninsular made in Gloucester by the Severn and Ware Rivers. Its back is to the Ware, an arm of which makes a most attractive western boundary for the park,

[171]

garden, and one of several orchards. The house and grounds of Sherwood, as the Seldens planned them, and as they are, for the most part, still maintained, occupy twenty acres. From the entrance gate, the lawn sweeps for half a mile down to the banks of the Ware River. To the east lie an orchard, numerous farm buildings, and a second orchard. To the west from the entrance, are part of the lawn, the beautiful old garden and a third orchard.

The house, flanked by the many quaint outbuildings of an ante-bellum Virginia homestead of its dignity, is of three stories. A wide veranda runs the full length of two sides of the building. The first and second floors have four rooms each, separated by wide halls that sweep through the building from south to north. On the third floor there are two rooms and another spacious hall. The windows here are deeply recessed and topped by gables.

In the furnishings of the house there are many rare and lovely old things in the matter of pictures, glass, silver, and mahogany. The wide, open fire-places are set off by mantelpieces that are simple in design but fine specimens of the classic period of the cabinetmaker's art.

But as charming as Sherwood itself is, the true glory of the place is to be found in its yard and garden. The former contains many superb trees, of which there are no less than a score of varieties. The latter is bounded on all four of its sides by giant trees of several kinds. Roughly speaking, the garden is two hundred by four hundred feet. The entire eastern side is occupied by a double row of crepe myrtles. Beneath them runs a broad walk, edged with slate, and flanked on either side by flower and shrubbery beds, ten feet wide. The crepe myrtles have attained a height of fifty feet. In some instances eight and ten stems spring from a single base more than a foot in diameter. When in full bloom, as they are during the greater part of July and August, they present a gorgeous spectacle of color—great pink pyramids forming an avenue four hundred feet in length. From the entrance gate a similar walk cuts through to the western arm of the river.

Giant Crepe Myrtle at Sherwood

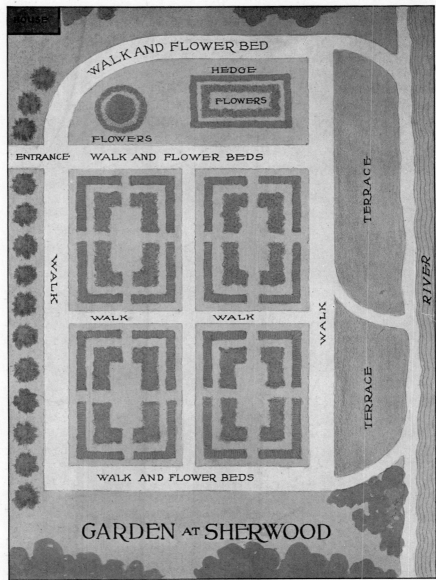

HOUSE

WALK AND FLOWER BED

HEDGE

FLOWERS

FLOWERS

ENTRANCE WALK AND FLOWER BEDS

WALK

WALK WALK

WALK

TERRACE

TERRACE

RIVER

WALK AND FLOWER BEDS

GARDEN AT SHERWOOD

This, too, is bordered and arched with towering trees and shrubbery. One looks down a fine vista of two hundred feet to catch a glimpse of water. The western slope of the garden breaks away suddenly in a broad terrace to the bank of the little estuary of the Ware. Along this bank, willows and cedars rise to a great height, the nearer distance being filled with crepe myrtle, Pride of China, lesser trees, and large clumps of shrubs. The terrace and its banks are given over to bulbs, ferns, and grasses.

The walk at the northern end of the garden is edged with numerous fruit trees. Originally the wide central space, allotted to vegetables, berry bushes, asparagus beds, etc., was divided into four squares, separated by lesser walks than those which sweep around the four sides. These have now been abandoned.

The space originally designed to contain flowers and flowering or ornamental plants comprises between forty and fifty thousand square feet. In it will be found today many of the original shrubs and bushes placed there by the Seldens. It is needless to say that, in eighty-odd years, they have achieved a growth which renders many of them conspicuously fine specimens of their several varieties. A hastily-made catalogue compiled recently showed the garden to contain more than forty kinds of shrubs and flowering trees. The display of lilies is especially intensive and fine. Iris of every hue; great beds of tiger lilies; lilies, white and yellow, and of other colors. These for the spring and summer. In the autumn thousands of chrysanthemums, dispersed in clumps that vary from one or two stems to a hundred or more, keep the eye well occupied.

The abiding interest and the chief distinction of the Sherwood garden are the "old" things it contains. There is a gnarled smoke tree the trunk of which is nearly two feet in diameter. Down another walk a yaupon tree, a veritable cluster of stems, has attained a height of thirty-odd feet. By its side there is a Camelia japonica that might grace the lawn as a shade tree. Before it came to Sherwood, it had formed a single item in a bridal bouquet,

[173]

four-score years ago. You will find here the yaupon trees in great profusion; huge clumps of bouquet and bridal wreath spirea, snowball, mock-orange, California gold-leaf privet, flowering horse-chestnut, deutzia, lilac, yucca, flowering pomegranate, althea, and butterfly plant or buddleia. About the bases of the great crepe myrtles is planted yellow jasmine which sets the garden aflame in the springtime, when the trees and shrubs are just beginning to bud. On the fences honeysuckle and trumpet vine have massed themselves into a veritable hedge. The roses comprise many of the old June and everblooming varieties. Some of them rise from base-stems a foot in thickness and reach to a height which enables them to hold their own with the larger and more formal shrubs. At the southern extremity of the eastern walk rises a well-trimmed tower of wistaria. At its foot is massed a great bed of lilies of the valley. A little to the north, the same walk is spanned by a great arbor of yellow jasmine at the foot of which are bedded iris of many hues.

Wherever one turns, the garden is reminiscent of another century, because of the prominence given to flowers that were popular with our great-grandparents. Possibly, you would scarcely recognize some of them by the names colloquially given them by those charming ladies. "Red-hot pokers," "butter and eggs," "fair maids of February," "butterfly plants," yellow and red cowslips, sage, lavender, balsam, blue bottles, mourning brides, and the old Roman hyacinths, which were so much more graceful than their more modern sisters. There is, indeed, an ineffable something imparted to a garden by age which time alone may supply. The best of taste may not provide its equivalent overnight. Money cannot buy it out of hand. It comes with the progress of many years and the vicissitudes of many seasons. Just when a garden becomes an "old" garden one may not readily say. But once a garden may be so designated, it has attained a beauty and a dignity all its own. It is the fact that the Sherwood garden enjoys this distinction in high degree that lends to it no small part of its attractiveness and charm.   JOHN MARSHALL.

[174]

BELLEVILLE

ORTH RIVER, an arm of Mobjack Bay, is a lake-like sheet of water around whose shores clustered the seats of "The Mighty" before the War Between the States. Here were the estates of the Taliaferros, the Tabbs, the Roys, the Dabneys, and others; but, of them all, none had Colonial significance except Belleville and Toddsbury—the homes of the Booths and the Taliaferros—of the Todds and the Tabbs.

Belleville was remodeled by its latest owners, Mr. and Mrs. Allmand Blow. A pillared portico now replaces the simple Colonial entrance of the English cottage, said to have been built in the seventeenth century by Thomas Booth, a member of a family of great antiquity and distinction in the counties of Chester and Lancaster, England. (See *College Peerage*.) In the old Booth burying-ground, near the end of Ware Neck, in Gloucester County, may be seen tombs with armorial bearings that date from an early period of the Virginia Colony. The Booths intermarried with the Throckmortons, the Cookes, the Carys, the Wythes, the Kendalls, the Lees, the Pages, and the Armisteads, so were connected by blood with nearly every family of note in what was called, then as now, Tidewater Virginia.

Originally there was only a large vegetable garden laid off in squares defined by box-hedges and flower-borders, like many of the gardens of Colonial days.

Frances, the daughter of George Wythe Booth, married Warner Taliaferro, thus bringing the Belleville property into the possession of the latter family. After her death, her husband married a second time and brought to the old home, as a bride of sixteen, Miss Leah Seddon. The second Mrs. Taliaferro, who became the chatelaine of Belleville in 1825, was the daughter of Susan Alexander and Thomas Seddon, of Fredericksburg, and a sister of James A. Seddon, Secretary of War of the Confederate States.

For seventy years she remained its mistress, and it was during that period that the garden and grounds of Belleville were laid off and developed.

There were two especial features to be considered:

First—The river which at Belleville sweeps around the grounds in such a manner as to make it nearly a peninsula. Mrs. Taliaferro, unusually gifted with taste and judgment, used this as a basis to work upon. On the broad lawn in front and on one side of the house she had planted singly and in groups trees which are still standing in their strength. Among them were the live oak trees, cottonwood, tulip-poplar and magnolia; there were also apple, and peach trees; plums, cherries and apricots, which gave bloom as well as fruit. Holly trees were planted in clumps, while a few handsome mimosas lent color and fragrance.

Along the bank of the river, cedars were planted at intervals. Near the flower-beds on the green in the rear of the house were many crepe myrtles; there, too, grew altheas, lilacs, bridal-wreath, snow-balls, smoke trees and yuccas. Fig bushes and pomegranates were also cultivated successfully in this old garden. Modern experts in landscape-gardening and planting might take lessons from this Virginia gentlewoman of the nineteenth century.

The second feature lay in the fact that in planting her flowers, Mrs. Taliaferro massed various colors in separate beds. There was infinite variety in the coloring of the borders, but each bed displayed a mass of bloom of the same color. She used, in great profusion, every sort of flower known in that day, and arranged them with such exquisite taste that the resulting harmony in color and form constituted the glory of the Belleville garden.

Among the flowers were the following: snowdrops, crocus, daffodils of many varieties. The small purple and tall white and purple iris, tulips, cowslips, narcissi, violets, lilies of the valley, and the single white hyacinth grew in great profusion in the borders.

From Collection of
Robert A. Lancaster, Jr.

Belleville

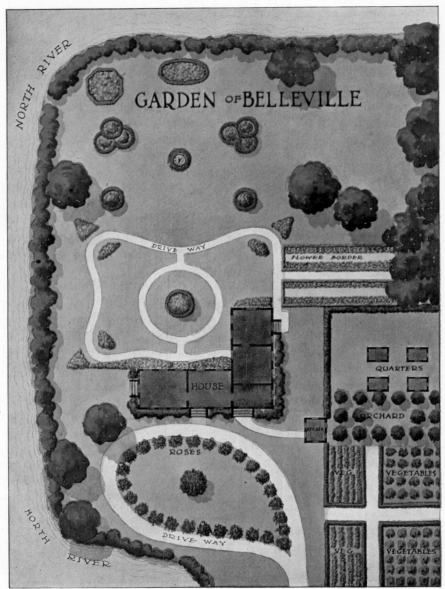

Lelia Scott Buchanan

Mignonette, heliotrope, four-o'clocks, lady-slippers, and blue Canterbury bells came year after year. The larger varieties of lilies were there with stocks and hollyhocks for background, while many roses flourished in the mild climate, especially the musk rose, the salmon-tea and the microphylla. Geraniums were used in the beds; in the large rustic baskets, too, and, in the autumn, chrysanthemums and other late flowers bloomed often as late as Christmas. Periwinkle covered what might have been bare spaces, and over the numerous arbors were trained white-star jasmine, yellow jasmine, honeysuckle—white and coral—in contrast to climbing roses. And over some, grapevines grew, affording a deep and grateful shade.

The outer boundary of lawn and garden, which were as one, was formed by the blue waters of North River. The completed work was marked by the simplicity and harmony that belong to nature itself, arranged with a taste so remarkable that many observers who visited Belleville have left their testimony that both lawn and garden were glorious in beauty and symmetry.

In a large octagonal summer-house, near the river bank, the ladies of the family were accustomed to sit on bright mornings with their sewing and embroidery, while some one read aloud a pleasing book.

To Mrs. Henry Alexander White, daughter of Susan Taliaferro and Judge Beverly Wellford and granddaughter of Mr. and Mrs. Warner Taliaferro, of Belleville, I am indebted for facts concerning this garden.

ANNE SEDDON RUTHERFOORD JOHNSON.

HAMPSTEAD

SOME twenty miles northeast of Richmond, in New Kent County, on the highlands overlooking the rich fields which border the Pamunkey River, stands in stately simplicity Hampstead. North of the house, the hill slopes suddenly to the valley of the Pamunkey, giving a magnificent view of the lowlands framed by the distant hills. This view is suggestive of the valley of the Medway, in the County of Kent, England. It was for this county that New Kent, Virginia, was named.

In the year 1827, Hampstead was built by Conrad Webb, the owner of vast acres in that section of Virginia. It was told by the oldest inhabitant, a descendant of one of his many slaves, that upon the occasion of the laying of the corner-stone, the proud owner, holding the hand of his young wife, walked three times around the foundation and had her lay the first brick, using a silver trowel provided for the ceremony.

There they built the stately dwelling with its four stories, its large, airy rooms, and wide, circular stairway. This stairway extends from the basement to the attic and is one of the most interesting features of the house.

The long and spacious hall, which runs through the house, is broken midway by Corinthian pillars, supporting an arch, and the woodwork throughout is carved to follow similar designs.

The floors are of unusual quality for the period in which they were laid, and it is said that in selecting the timbers for them Mr. Webb made what was then a long and arduous trip to Norfolk, to secure trees which had been cut and seasoned for masts.

One part of the English basement originally had built-in book shelves and was used as a library. In this basement are also the

A Corner of the Sabine Hall Garden

Formal Flower Beds at Sabine Hall

Hampstead

wine-cellar and the fat-cellar, the latter used for the storage of meats.

But it is in the wide lawn and old-fashioned garden that one realizes the real charm of the place. The brick walk is edged on either side by large boxwood, and a sun dial has been placed on the original column in the center of the box circle to mark the time as one did nearly a hundred years ago. Shading the sun dial is an unusually large mimosa tree, its glory of bloom in summer attracting many humming-birds which add glints of color to the already beautiful spot.

Conspicuous among the garden trees is an old magnolia with a circumference of more than twelve feet. This was somewhat the appearance of an English oak and is unusually handsome. There is a story that the boxwood, that once adorned the terraces, was taken to form a maze in a neighboring county.

The wide lawn has a remarkable variety of old-fashioned shrubs and trees. Magnolias, wonderfully suited to the climate, are there in their glory, also lindens, elms, tulip, poplars, white pine, and many other trees, including English walnuts and pecans. One of the latter stands with a spread of more than a hundred feet. This interesting collection testifies to the love and care bestowed by the founders of the home nearly a century ago.

As was the custom in those days, the family graveyard is near the house. It lies in a secluded corner of the lawn, surrounded by a low brick wall. There rests the only son and heir. His death at the age of twelve years was the tragedy of the hopeful parents and caused the home built with such care to descend to a collateral branch of the Webb family.

The present owners of the place have planted the old enclosure as a little rose garden with the time-worn tombstones resting among the flowers.

Not far from the terraced garden, and standing between it and the house, is the chimney of the original outside kitchen. This chimney, with its two Dutch ovens, is in size eight by fourteen feet and is now used as a picturesque water tower with the farm bell hanging midway. At its base is a great bed of red-stemmed mint— that pungent herb reminiscent of bygone joys when the making of a mint-julep was not a lost art.

With keen appreciation of the architectural beauty and value of the place, Hampstead was bought by William J. Wallace, in 1903, and restored without changing the original design. When purchased, practically all of the flowering shrubs had been removed from the lawn as, after falling into alien hands, the old place had been much abused. There were large gaps in the boxwood circle and hedges, made by the stock which was permitted to wander at will. Pigs had been running wild in the area, much to the detraction of both lawn and shrubbery. Even the great house had been commandeered to serve them, one enterprising tenant having built a trough to run out of the north drawing-room window as an easy means of disposing of garbage, or feeding the pigs from grain stored in some of the second-floor rooms.

It has been the policy of the present owners to work from the house outwards, replanting shrubs and flowers in the immediate surroundings—at the base of the house; by the steps; in front of the old-fashioned ice-house; around the little office on the lawn and in other places of that kind before completing the restoration of the wonderful old terraced garden. In this day of scarce and incompetent labor, this garden seems more a memory of what it was, though the original terraces themselves are still intact.

But to the lover of old-fashioned flowers, the peculiar charm of the terraced garden will be most striking. It lies to the west of the house beyond the shade of the lawn trees. The deeply-sodded terraces have endured the waste of years, and overhanging them are large crepe-myrtle trees in pale-pink, lavender, and cerise. Old-fashioned jonquils are there—iris, narcissi, peonies, and the Star of Bethlehem. Cherokee roses run riot and the little yellow Scotch or Harrison rose has found there a most congenial soil.

For those loving the memory of the years long gone, old songs

W. J. Wallace

Elevation of Hampstead

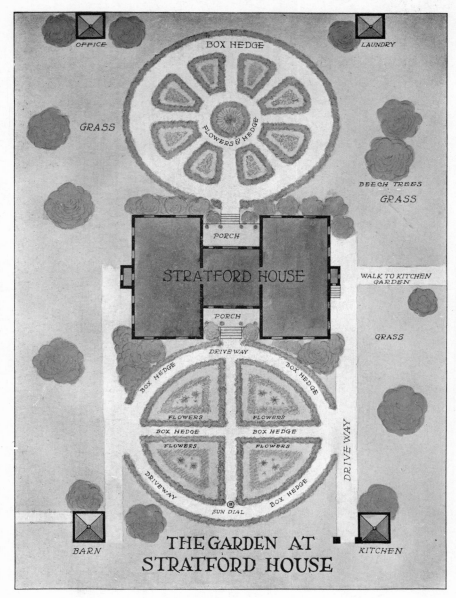

THE GARDEN AT
STRATFORD HOUSE

Redrawn from the Original Plan of R. C. Thurston by Lila L. Williams

and old flowers play a peculiar part in adding pleasure to retrospection, so the memory of Hampstead will ever live in the hearts of those so fortunate as to have known it.

KATE DUVAL HARRISON.

The Potomac and Rappahannock

STRATFORD

ICHARD LEE, of England, founder of a family
which made and brilliantly shone in American his-
tory through two centuries, and who brought here
a name destined to splendid immortality, patented
in 1640 the land on which Stratford House was
built. His home was established in a dense forest
of oak and sycamore, on a high bluff overlooking the Potomac where
it is broad, deep and beautiful. Nothing remains or is known of the
original building. Records prove that it was destroyed by fire.
The house now standing was built about 1725. Evidently the
Lees then were in high favor at the British court, and by some
special quality or service had won the good will of Queen Caroline,
because, we are told in Sale's "Manors of Virginia," that she sent
Mr. Lee "a bountiful present out of her own Privy Purse." From
this gift, the Stratford House, now standing, and in which General
Robert E. Lee was born, was built.

Such a mansion puts before us clearly, after the intervening
decades and vicissitudes, the customs, habits and mode of life of
the period in which it was created and first occupied. In itself it
is history: its rooms the chapters; its stories volumes; its furniture
illustrations; its inmates the characters; its garden the bindings.

Stratford House, with solid walls of glazed bricks and massive
rough-hewn timbers, represents and expresses well the strength and
solidity of the sturdy race of Lees which has stood always for what
was finest and best. They have given to their State one governor,
four members of the council of State, twelve members of the House
of Burgesses; to the State of Maryland one governor, two coun-
cillors, three members of the Assembly; to the American Revolution four members of the convention of 1776, two signers of the
Declaration of Independence and two brothers representing their
government at the courts of Europe. To the Confederate States

[185]

the Lees gave the great Commander-in-Chief of its armies and four other generals.

When Stratford House was built, the European colonists in America were few in number, and widely separated. They were hardly able to defend themselves against the Indians who peopled the interior and constituted an ever-threatening peril. The new-comers clung to the coast line and the banks of the larger rivers flowing to the sea, as if longing to maintain their water connection with the old country as closely as possible—like children loving the touch of the mother hand and fearing to lose it—and for the prac-tical reason that the easiest, safest, frequently the only, means of passage and transportation from point to point, family to family, was by water. Stratford House was built years before the moun-tains of Virginia had been explored; when the rich valley of the Shenandoah was an unknown land, shrouded by forest, mystery and fear, and an expedition to discover it was considered too dan-gerous to be undertaken.

Since the stately shape of the house, as it is, rose above the noble river this great nation has been born and come to its enormous strength. From the strip of territory and the few hundreds of in-habitants stretched along the Atlantic coast, it has extended from ocean to ocean and from the Great Lakes to the Gulf.

The Stratford House is built in the shape of the letter H, with a group of four chimneys in each of the wings. In one of these groups is a secret room, which evidently was occupied at times, as is proved by candle grease, smoke from lamps or candles, and traces of ink and grease on the floor. The centre room, or library, opens at each side on the garden by doors reached by stone steps. No lofty columned portico adorns the house. It was built before the architecture we call "Colonial" was generally adopted in this country. Plain and well-worn stone steps rise directly from the garden to the house. A somewhat unusual feature is a square brick house at each corner of the main building, a short distance away, used respectively as kitchen, laundry, office and cow barn.

The gardens were of the oval design customary for homes of important families before the Revolution. The shape probably was adopted not only because of its beauty and grace, but for the practical convenience of the driveway leading from the entrance of the ground to the house and making it easy to drive a vehicle in or out without need for turning. The oval at the entrance to Stratford was bordered with box, favorite evergreen and outdoor decoration of the colonists, doubtless brought from the old home gardens in the mother country. In this oval, convenient for observation, stood the usual sundial, infallible timekeeper so long as the weather allowed. The box-border enclosed the familiar flowers of the English garden—hollyhock, wallflower, cinnammon-pink, larkspur and the ever-cherished, beloved and admired roses.

Endeavoring to get clearly into our minds the picture of the old garden fronting the broad building with field and forest on one side and river on the other, we may assume that the oval was filled with beds, or "boutons," as they were called, of more or less intricate and fanciful designs, according to the fashion of the times. There was the box-walk, the box-maze and the rose-embowered summer-house. Fithian says a celebrated dancing master of the day held classes at Stratford on certain days, from ten in the morning until late afternoon, and it is pleasant to think of the pupils, in the intervals between lessons, wandering amid the box-borders, playing at hide-and-seek in the box-mazes, or resting in the shade of the towering oaks and beeches which had been left from the original growth.

The kitchen garden at the side of the house, surrounded by high brick walls, held squares of vegetables, outlined by the usual iris, grown for its roots, furnishing orris powder and perfume. The herb garden was a part of the equipment of every plantation house, the medicinal herbs furnishing much of the medicine used in days before convenient drug stores and doctors were in evidence.

The quiet, dignified gardens of old Virginia had a charm all their own, supervised as they were by flower-loving owners, with

[187]

plenty of docile and intelligent labor at command. Ovals, squares and circles were masses of color and fragrance, adding beauty and delight to the beloved homes.

In the bowered and perfumed privacy of these gardens, secluded from the world by miles of distance and density of woodland, lived those great makers of American history. Gone are some of their gardens, but who shall say what influence for serenity and right judgment and clear-cut honesty and dauntless courage were derived from the lovely gardens and quiet and inspiring surroundings of their youth and manhood!

At Stratford the mind is turned inevitably to the childhood there of Robert E. Lee, a handsome little boy, with his invalid mother, going from house to garden around the box-edged flower bed; and then on to the after years when that tall stately form, not wearing the robes of a conqueror, was homeless. From within a heart burdened with sorrows—not his own—rose a longing for the first home he had known, and he wrote, on Christmas Day of 1861, in a letter to his daughter, after Arlington had been taken from him, "In the absence of a home, I wish I could purchase Stratford." So passed that grand figure into history, leaving to us the rich legacy of his high ideals of right and duty, leaving to us, also, Stratford House, his birthplace, of which we can, with loving and justified pride, quote the Psalmist, "the Lord shall count when He writeth up the people that this man was born there."

LILA L. WILLIAMS.

Mount Vernon—The Home of President George Washington

Lila L. Williams

The Box Garden at Mount Vernon
The Garden of Mary and George Washington

MOUNT VERNON

THE estate of Hunting Creek, situated on the Potomac River between Doque Creek and Little Hunting Creek, was an original grant by Lord Culpeper in 1674, to John Washington, and in 1743 was left to Lawrence Washington by his father, Augustine Washington, son of John.

On the brow of the gentle slope, which ended at a thickly wooded precipitous river bank, Lawrence built his mansion. This is the nucleus of the present group of buildings. Before it swept the Potomac in a magnificent curve, its broad bosom thronged with graceful gull, wild duck, and other water fowl, while beyond the river lay the green fields and shadowy forests of Maryland. This house he called Mount Vernon, in honor of Admiral Vernon, under whom Lawrence Washington had served in the expedition against Cartagena, in South America.

Lawrence died in 1752, and left Mount Vernon to his little daughter, Sarah, with the proviso in case of her death that it should go to his half-brother, George, to whom he was tenderly attached. Sarah soon passed to that other land where so many little ones are gathered that it can but be a wonderful place of purity and beauty, and so George Washington came into possession of this beautiful tract of 2,500 acres. James McIntosh said of his visit to Mount Vernon:

> "The combination of what is grandest in nature with whatever is pure and sublime in human conduct affects me more powerfully than any scene I have ever seen."

To think of Mount Vernon and not of its owner, George Washington, would be impossible (so any article on his home must first give us the characteristics of its possessor). Pictures that we see

[189]

are so indelibly impressed upon our minds that their peculiarities of shape and form cling to our memories. In this way the American people must always picture George Washington as the dignified statesman, in full suit of richest black velvet, with diamond knee-buckles, and square silver buckles set upon shoes polished with the most scrupulous neatness, black silk stockings, ruffles at breast and wrists, his hair profusely powdered and projecting at the sides, tied at the back with a large bow of black ribbon.

But in writing a description of Mount Vernon, we must go back to him as he first became its owner; a young man, a young engineer, tall, rather large-boned, with deep-brown hair, his face rather long and slightly marred by illness, a sunburnt complexion. A young man, sensible, composed and thoughtful, gentle in manner, in temper reserved, a total stranger to religious prejudices, in morals irreproachable, a young man of determined bravery and independence of spirit. For such a man was Washington when he became the owner of Mount Vernon, at twenty years of age, in 1752.

Later his young wife of great charm came with her two little children, a boy of six and a girl of four. Then there were the four little children of John Park Custis and his wife, Eleanor Calvert. Two of these children, Eleanor and George Washington Custis, were brought up at Mount Vernon by General and Mrs. Washington, who took charge of them after the death of their father, the girl being at the tender age of two years and the boy only six months; in fact, there were ten children born or reared at Mount Vernon. Later came Washington's nephew, LaFayette Washington, who was entrusted to the General on the death of his father; also, young George Washington LaFayette stayed at Mount Vernon, and was lovingly protected during General LaFayette's imprisonment at Olmuts by the Prussians.

Let us, therefore, have before us in memory's picture a Virginian, young and vigorous, his gentle wife, and the little children always playing around them. Let us forget the lace and frills and seek a kinder view of the great man and great woman. Besides

Air View of Mount Vernon on the Potomac

Formal Garden at Mount Vernon

Mount Vernon Garden, Showing High Box Hedge

the twenty-five hundred acres he inherited from his brother, he already had inherited the paternal estate on the Rappahannock, and to those he added fifty-five hundred acres, making him one of the wealthiest planters and land-owners in Virginia, having many thousand acres of the finest land along the Rappahannock and Potomac. Mrs. Washington was, also, wealthy, having a large fortune in land and money, while her two children inherited comfortable fortunes from their father, Daniel Parke Custis. Washington's own description of his home is interesting:

> "A high healthy country, in a latitude between the extreme of heat and cold, on one of the finest rivers in the world, a river well stocked with various kinds of fish, at all seasons of the year, and in the spring the shad, herring, bass, carp, sturgeon, etc., in abundance. The borders of the estate are washed for more than ten miles by tidewater, several valuable fisheries appertaining to it, the whole shore, in fact, one entire fishery."

The plans and specifications for the house, the design for the grounds, the survey of the roads and gardens are all in existence, drawn by Washington's own hand. Every measurement was calculated and indicated with an engineer's exactness, and in every arrangement for his home, he appears to have made convenience and durability the prime objects of his planning.

As this article is on the garden of Mount Vernon, and not on the house, let us join the young engineer, and imagine him with his loved dogs—True Love, Sweet Lips, Mopsy, Music, and Rover—at his heels as he steps out in an early hour before breakfast to look over his estate.

On the river side is an undulating lawn, sloping gently with a slight rise at each end. On the points overlooking the river were summer-houses, resting places from which to admire the river or to watch the activities on the small wharf. Under the southeast summer-house, during Washington's time, there was a large, dry well, where he kept meat, butter, and vegetables cool in summer, for icehouses were unknown until later. Along the lower edges of the lawn were old English haha walls to prevent the cattle from approaching the house, but so arranged as not to break the view. These same cattle, however, of which there were many hundred, were driven over the lawns whenever cutting was necessary, as there were no lawn mowers in those days.

Below the lawn was a deer paddock, and the irregular shores of the river. On this southern lawn are beautiful old trees, almost all of which were selected in the woods and brought to their present situation by the young engineer himself. From the wharf a long steep ascending foot-path and a long easier driveway both led to the old burial-place of the family and to the newer tomb which now is the mecca of all tourists. Here numerous memorial trees have been planted by prominent visitors.

If George Washington had not been a great statesman and patriot, he would at least have been an eminent landscape artist, for nowhere in America have we such a splendid plan of landscape gardening carried out with such accuracy and beauty, and all this by a young engineer in his twenties. This makes one think more of rod and chain and tripod, than of lace and powder and velvets!

In the rear of the mansion, now the main entrance, was laid out a fine lawn upon a level surface comprising about two acres. Around it he made a serpentine driveway, and he planted a great variety of trees on each side. The list of trees mentioned in his diary which he selected in the woods and had planted on the grounds is long—including elm, beech, maple, ash—the different varieties of oak—gum, poplar, aspen, mulberry, dogwood, redbud, pine, cedar, magnolia, hemlock, many holly, and laurel. These trees terminated, by his own description, "By two mounds of earth, one on each side, on which were growing weeping-willow trees, leaving an open and full view of the distant hills. These trees were sixty yards apart."

Directly before the western front was a round grass-plot, de-

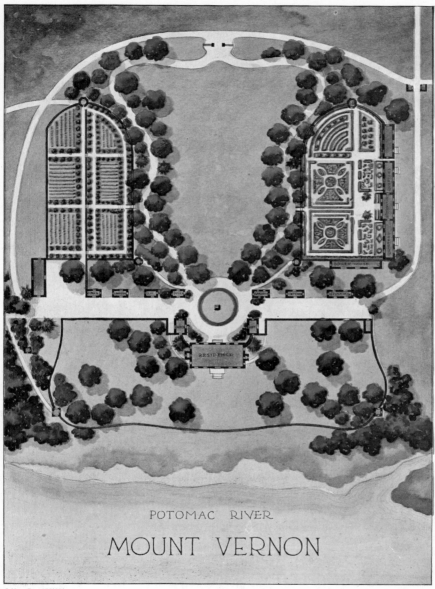

POTOMAC RIVER

MOUNT VERNON

Lila L. Williams

Gunston Hall, the Home of George Mason

signed with a sundial in the center and carriageway around it.
To the left, looking from the house, we find the kitchen, butler's
house, smoke-house, laundry and large coach-house. Also, an
enormous barn where many horses were kept, while to the right
we have the office, gardener's house, carpenter-shop, spinning-
house, and later, an ice-house.

The vegetable gardens are in terraces. During those early
years, doubtless, they held many fruit trees, but only a few pear
and apple remain. A grape arbor runs across the upper terrace,
and the whole garden is protected by the brick wall, topped by a
white picket fence. We still find some upshoots of the original
fig-trees. Amariah Frost, who wrote a description of the vegetable
garden during Washington's life, found this garden "very elegant."
"With abundance of fig-trees, currant-bushes, limes, oranges, large
English mulberries, artichokes, etc." At each side of the entrance
masses of bush box. In fact, there is so much boxwood at Mount
Vernon that we are led to believe that while it may be hard to
get established it is certainly very enduring and will outlast many
other evergreens.

At the far end of the vegetable garden is the seedhouse. In
his diary George Washington shows with what interest he studied
the English seed catalogues, and with what eagerness he exploited,
with more or less success, the latest improvement in horticulture.
The seedhouse and schoolhouse were of the same design, octagonal,
with brick foundations, and slabs of wood cut to represent marble.
The brick walls surrounding both gardens are in perfect preservation. These enclosed gardens are such restful places, shut in from
the turmoil and confusion of the outside world.

Let us cross the lawn to the flower garden as it is. Here, indeed, box reigns supreme. Masses and masses of it, in straight and
square beds, circles, hearts, moons, lozenges and double circles;
all healthy, strong and, best of all, planted by these dear young
owners of Mount Vernon. The box borders are so fine that one
wonders how they survived these long years. We of the garden

clubs owe a vote of deepest appreciation to the Mount Vernon Ladies' Association, which has preserved not only the home and its belongings, but these magnificent evergreens in their now perfect condition.

Numerous trees and shrubs were here planted by distinguished visitors. A charming custom which has always prevailed in foreign lands, and might be well emulated. The Mount Vernon trees are such beautiful, leafy monuments to Thomas Jefferson, General LaFayette, and others. Surely, these green mementoes of living men are more splendid than the carved stone and molded bronze marking their last resting place.

In an old book, it is claimed that the designs in house and garden at Mount Vernon were all Masonic, and while this is not in Washington's own diary, it does have some foundation in the designs themselves. As he was the leading Mason of the time, and a very enthusiastic member of that order, it seems only just that we should at least see what grounds there are for this belief. The circle before the front door represents a point within a circle, or, as the Masons say, "God is a sphere whose center is everywhere, and circumference nowhere." The twenty-four circle posts are the twenty-four hours of the day. These posts are bound together by a chain which stands for Time. The locust post in the center, with the dial atop, represents the sun, the source of time. The mounds at the entrance symbolize a newly-made grave—willows being substituted for the acacia, the Masonic emblem of sorrow. I will not touch on the Masonic emblems in the house, as they are too numerous. But in the garden we find the picket fence, with twenty-six in each section, which stands for the twenty-six weeks' progress of the sun to the north, and then twenty-six towards the south, or evolution and growth. The urns on top of the section stand for sacrifice and purification. The circular flower-beds are the fourth part of a circle, or ninety degrees. The square beds are the Knight Templar Cross, with camouflage. This cross stands for universal wisdom and consecration.

In the house border we find a tessellated border of box, each point a symbol of a human being, who is the termination of a line of ancestry, and the beginning of a line of posterity. In these box designs we also find open-grave designs, symbol of the Resurrection and humility—two bare feet designs, symbol of an oblique angle (heel of right to hollow of left)—open circle standing for infinite expansion—solid sphere or worlds prepared for human habitation—open squares representing Blue Lodge apron—solid squares meaning salt which cannot burn or freeze—a broken triangle and pendant, standing for faithfulness and regret. Whether these were deliberately planned by Washington, we do not know, but it seems likely that the young Mason worked out his emblems, just as in the Vatican at Rome, since time beyond record, the Pope's insignia is also worked out in box in his private gardens. Two lilacs stand sentinel at either side of the gate, to guard its privacy, and to extend a sweet, fragrant welcome to visitors.

In February, 1785, Washington writes in his diary:

> "Removed two pretty large and full grown lilacs to the north garden, one on each side, taking up as much dirt with the roots as could be obtained."

The conservatory faces the entrance, flanked on each side by the quarters of the household servants. This conservatory contained a collection of rare exotics, some of which were presented as tokens of esteem, and others purchased from the eminent botanist, John Bartram, of Philadelphia. Among these plants Washington had a small grove of lemon-trees, a sago-palm from East India, and a century-plant from Porto Rico. These plants were destroyed when the conservatory was burnt in 1835.

The rose garden is to the right. Here indeed is a lovely sight—borders of cowslip and ivy, and such lovely roses of all hues, with lilacs as a background. What a delightful combination—lilacs and roses and fresh perishable cowslips, with gray evergreen ivy. Long sidewalks bordered with ivy and masses of larkspur, lilies and Canterbury bells. To the left the same Maltese cross, with ivy and dainty cowslip borders, and masses of all our dearly loved Southern flowers. The many-shaped garden plots are filled with old-fashioned plants. The floral manuals of that period give lists of hollyhocks, peonies, iris, tulips, lilies, nasturtium, columbine, heliotrope, cowslips, pansies, pride of London, etc. Here, too, we find a calycanthus planted by Thomas Jefferson—a gentle shrub, bringing with its perfume a memory of those olden days of dignified friendships and courteous hospitality. A long, straight bed of roses, edged with ivy, helps out the design. Then we have long circular beds of roses, iris, and peonies with violet borders. In one of these beds is the Mary Washington rose, a small cluster rose nearly white, planted by young Washington, and named for his mother—(could any mother want a sweeter tribute from a son?) A row of fig-bushes stands behind the box-hedge, and doubtless the children after lessons would delight in their abundance. Turning at the little schoolhouse, we will come back to the conservatory. A long grass-plot, planted in shrubs, has next the wall a mass of lilies of the valley. In front of the quarters are long box borders, planted in squares and circles, open and solid, the outer box border tessellated, and an inner one of ivy. Outside of these are box designs in odd shapes, and other long borders planted in tulips. Two box-trees front the conservatory, near which we see also the shrub-magnolia planted by LaFayette—a glorious plant in spring—and in a bed, in all its glory the Nelly Custis rose—of creamy white—said to have been planted and named by George Washington.

And so we bid an unwilling farewell to these beautiful gardens of George Washington—so brilliant in the sunshine of our modern days, a design not yet equalled, of an historical interest impossible to approach. Here young Mr. and Mrs. Washington lived their lives of great contrasts—peace and war—isolated from the hurry-ing world, and yet crowded with earthly interests. Here they lived, and here they died. Lives full of sweetness of youth and the dignity of age. Here they rest amid the fine old trees and whispering evergreens on the banks of the Potomac. Mount Vernon is not merely the home of George Washington—it is also "the cradle of our national liberty," and the resting place of our national glory. No fitter ending for an article on the home of George Washington can be found than the sentiments of Rev. William Jay, of England, who wrote:

"There dwelt the *man,* the flower of human kind,
Whose visage, mild, bespoke his noble mind;
There dwelt the *soldier,* who his sword ne'er drew
But in a righteous cause of freedom true;
There dwelt the *hero,* who ne'er fought for fame,
Yet gained more glory than a Caesar's name;
There dwelt the *statesman,* who, devoid of art,
Gave soundest counsel from an upright heart.
But oh! Columbia, by thy sons caressed,
There dwelt the *Father* of the realms he blessed,
Who no wish felt to make his mighty praise,
Like other things, the means himself to raise,
But there—retiring—breathed in pure renown,
And felt a grandeur that disdained a crown."

LILA L. WILLIAMS.

GUNSTON HALL

UNSTON-HALL - ON - THE - POTOMAC, five miles below Mount Vernon and eighteen miles below Washington, the home of George Mason, of Revolutionary days, was built by him in the years 1755 to 1758.

The south front of the mansion faces the Potomac. From a little portico on this front one looks toward the river, between two rows of English box (Buxus Suffruticosa), twice the height of a tall man, and two hundred and twenty feet long. This avenue leads directly to a terrace overlooking wide stretches of meadows, interspersed and bordered with forest trees and commanding a view across the broad Potomac to the hills of Maryland beyond.

Doubtless it was Colonel Mason's intention, when he planted this box hedge (the slips of which were probably brought from England), to keep it trimmed in the low, formal style then customary, with a spacious walk between its rows. Through many years of neglect, the hedge was not trimmed, and, with soil apparently ideal for its growth, it has reached its present great height and beautiful form. A leading authority in this country estimates the box at Gunston Hall to be about forty years older than the box at Mount Vernon. Possibly, slips from the Gunston Hall box were sent to Mount Vernon to start the lovely planting of box there, for exchanges were frequently made, as we learn from Washington's diary, in which he acknowledges additions to his flowers and fruits from his friend, George Mason, at Gunston Hall. In 1763, Washington writes of "grafting cherries and plums from Colonel Mason's." Again in 1785, Mason, after spending the night at Mount Vernon, was sent by Washington back to Gunston Hall in his coach, "by return of which," adds Washington, "he sent me

A Garden View at Gunston Hall

Entrance Gates at Gunston Hall

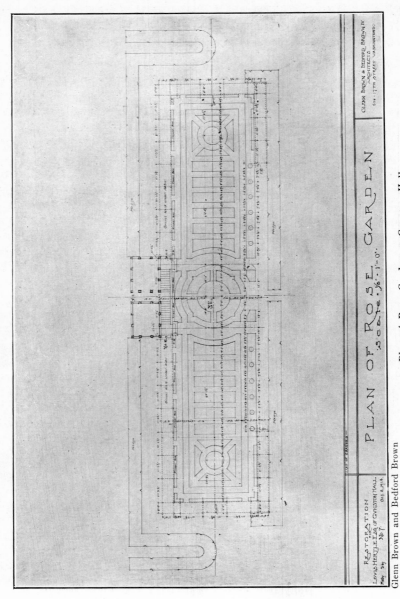

Glenn Brown and Bedford Brown

Plan of Rose Garden at Gunston Hall

slips of the Persian Jessamine and Guelder Rose." A month later, Colonel Mason wrote from Gunston Hall to General Washington, sending him a present of some cider. He had, he says, broached four or five hogsheads, and filled the bottles with the best, all being made of Maryland Redstreaks. "The cider this year is not so clear and fine," he tells his friend, and he wonders if grinding his apples late in the fall is the cause, and adds, "As the cider in bottles will not ripen for use until late in May, I have also filled a barrel out of the same, which I beg your acceptance of." He recommended that a little ginger should be put in, as it improves cider. At another time he sent Washington some watermelon seed, which he had promised him.

In the flower garden at Gunston are masses of heliotrope, phlox, delphinium, lemon verbena, rose geranium, ageratum, foxglove and many roses. In the fall the hardy chrysanthemums produce a riot of color.

In the center of the garden plays a bird fountain, made from the capitol and base of a discarded column from the United States Treasury building at Washington. This was found in a vacant plot in Washington, where it had lain for years. On its base it bears the date 1840. It is made of sandstone from the long since abandoned quarries of Aquia Creek, from which also were made the quoins of the Gunston house.

An arched brick step leads to the Falls' Walk, skirting the crest of the hill, from whence a sudden declivity leads to the lower field, which, in Mason's day, was a deer-park, studded with trees. The Falls Walk leads on to the dock, whence a recently constructed canal connects with the Potomac.

From the east end of the garden a lilac-bordered path leads toward the lawn, parallel to the spacious double walk, bordered by flowering cherry trees, under whose shade, in center beds, the spring bulbs bloom.

The bowling green, to the east of the box-walk, almost square in form, is enclosed by pleached fruit trees, and flowering shrubs;

while the vegetable garden, of similar form, lying to the west of the box-walk, is surrounded with a thick hedge of climbing roses. A break in the box-hedge bordering the center walk affords an interesting vista, extending from the cherry trees on the east to an ivy-covered sun-dial at the far side of the vegetable garden on the west.

From the crest of the high hill, bordered by a wide walk, an ivy and wistaria-covered tea-house and pergola overlook the broad water of the Potomac winding its way to the sea. One can easily imagine Washington's eight-oared barge sweeping up to the dock, landing the friend and neighbor coming in favorite fashion to pay a visit to Colonel Mason.

We learn from an unfinished manuscript that originally the entrance road, which curves through a native forest, then passes through open fields, "was girded by a double row of cherry trees, the common blackheart, raised from seed." (Page 98, *Rowland's Mason*), but they have long since disappeared. An avenue of magnolia grandiflora has now been planted, which will in time take the place of the stately, short-lived Lombardy poplars, placed there for immediate effect.

George Mason (1725-1792) was the author of the Virginia Bill of Rights and of the Constitution of Virginia. "The former, the most remarkable paper of its epoch, was the foundation of the great American assertion of right. Jefferson went to it for the phrases and expressions of the Declaration, and it remains the original chart by which free governments must steer their course.... The equality of men politically; the enjoyment of life, liberty and the pursuit of happiness; the responsibility of magistrates; the right of the people to abolish oppressive government; suffrage to all men having a permanent interest in the community; the freedom of the press; the subjection of the military to the civil government; the free exercise of religion; and an adherence to justice, moderation and virtue; these were to be the burning and shining lights to guide the new generation in their march to the Canaan of the future." (*Virginia,* by John Esten Cooke, p. 411.)

"From a porch which preserves the grace and beauty of Georgian architecture, one enters a wide hall extending through the house, as was usual in Virginia houses of its class. The first room on the right is finished with white woodwork delicately carved in Chinese-Chippendale fashion. The second and communicating room has still more elaborately carved woodwork, worked out with pilasters, and with broken pediments above the doors, the mantel place and the closet alcoves. Here, the mellow color of the pine walls, once covered with silken hangings, gives unusual beauty and dignity to the apartment.

"The first room to the left of the central hall was George Mason's study, where, often confined by his inveterate enemy, gout, he thought out and wrote out those documents which rank him among the founders of the government. Here Mr. Hertle has had a large photographic copy of the Bill of Rights placed as an over-mantel, thus linking up the place and the man. The dining-room looks out upon the gardens, the river and the distant hills. A stairway protected by a mahogany-trimmed baluster, delightful in design and delicately carved, leads to the chambers. The characteristic ornament of Gunston Hall, found on gateways without, over the stairway and on pediments within, is the pineapple, symbol of hospitality, a quality now as ever the outstanding feature of the place.

"If Gunston walls had tongues as well as ears, what conversations around open fires they might report; Washington and Mason discussing the Fairfax Resolves, that threw down the gauntlet of independence; Patrick Henry getting from the cool and philosophical Mason the fuel for the fires in his eloquence; Richard Henry and Arthur Lee talking of the French Alliance; Rochambeau and LaFayette journeying north after the victory at Yorktown; Jefferson and Madison, coming straight from Mount Vernon to get Mason's views as to the location of the nation's Capital. These early exchanges of opinion have been paralleled during the World War by the long discussions between Arthur J. Balfour and Secretary Lansing, which took place under Gunston trees." (Charles Moore, *Gunston Hall Sketch,* p. 3.)

From George Mason the Gunston estate passed to his eldest son, George, of Lexington; thence to the third George Mason. All three, with their families, lie in the quiet, tree-shaded grave-yard at Gunston. This sacred spot, until recently sadly neglected, is now enclosed within an appropriate brick wall. Here, beneath a chaste marble sarcophagus, imported by George Mason from England, lies his beautiful wife, Ann Eilbeck Mason. On this stone is inscribed the following verse:

"Once she was all that sweetens life,
The tender mother, daughter, friend and wife,
Once she was all that makes mankind adore,
Now view this marble and be vain no more."

The widow of George Mason III sold the estate in 1867, and thus the ownership passed from the Mason family. In 1912, Gunston Hall was purchased by Mr. Louis Hertle. The Hall was then seriously impared by neglect. Various additions had been made to the original building, sadly altering its character and appearance. The once well-tended gardens had almost disappeared, only their outlines remaining. The present owner, with the advice of a competent architect, has made a thorough and careful restoration of both house and grounds.

ELEANOR HERTLE.

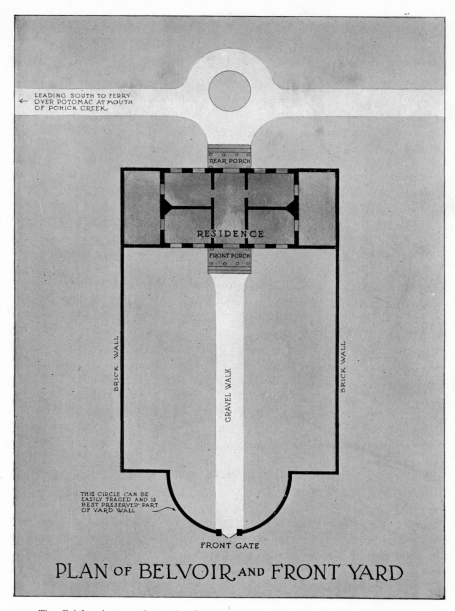

LEADING SOUTH TO FERRY
← OVER POTOMAC AT MOUTH
OF POHICK CREEK

REAR PORCH

RESIDENCE

FRONT PORCH

BRICK WALL

GRAVEL WALK

BRICK WALL

THIS CIRCLE CAN BE
EASILY TRACED AND IS
BEST PRESERVED PART
OF YARD WALL →

FRONT GATE

PLAN OF BELVOIR AND FRONT YARD

The Fairfax homestead on the Potomac, now the site of Camp Humphreys. The original house was partly burned in 1786. It was restored but shelled by the British in 1812. Many shrubs and spring bulbs still bloom here in memory of this charming garden of Colonial times.

Chatham, the Fitzhugh Homestead

CHATHAM

ON a terraced hill overlooking the Rappahannock River, with the spires and steeples of the historic town of Fredericksburg in the distance, Chatham lies, sleeping in the sun, dreaming of the romances of days gone by.

The charm of old books, the mellowness of old violins, the softness of old lace, the potency of old wine—all of these sensations are recalled when coming suddenly upon its green-shuttered windows and white walls, embowered in masses of box-wood and evergreen plants—all steeped in a strange allure.

From below, the old town has its memories, too; the boyhood pranks of no less a personage than George Washington; and long before that, the struggles and privations of the pioneer settlers. Then came the days of the coach-and-four, of clanking of swords, of powdered wigs and stiff brocades, of LaFayette's visits and of royal entertainments given in his honor. Then came the days that left their scars upon the gray old town during the War Between the States, when Lee's army defended it against overwhelming odds.

Through the quaint old streets, each house has its own story. There is the home of Mary Washington with its box-edged garden path which led to the home of Betty Washington, the wife of Colonel Fielding Lewis.

On a magnificent estate of more than fifty thousand acres, Chatham was built in the year 1728 by William Fitzhugh, that patriotic and able statesman, known as "Fitzhugh of Chatham." It was named, supposedly, after his friend, Sir William Pitt, Earl of Chatham, and there is a family tradition that the plans were brought from England by Pitt. The simplicity of the long low mansion with its ample wings has stood the test of time and today as it stands in the mellowness of its two hundred years, it breathes the spirit of hospitality and is in the broadest sense a home.

There was once a private race course, whose owner was the possessor of many famous trotters, a judge of fine horses, and a country gentleman of the old school noted for his lavish entertaining.

The site of the old garden, which was terraced to the river, is supposed to have been the spot where the courtship of General Lee culminated, for under the shade of an old elm tree overlooking the Rappahannock Mary Custis promised to be his wife. There is an old story that Lee refused to allow his troops to fire on Chatham while it was occupied by Union troops, so through his love for the place of so many happy memories, its life was saved.

Fredericksburg, lying on the road between Washington and Richmond, was a strategic point, and when the Federal troops occupied the Stafford hills, Chatham was used as General Burnside's headquarters. In those lovely gardens sloping down to the river, havoc was wrought by the blue-coated soldiers. From that vantage point could be seen the devastation of the picturesque old town. Clouds of smoke, the bursting of shells and the lurid glare of fire made a panorama of the horror and desolation of war.

Lincoln stayed at Chatham when he reviewed the troops, and many counsels of war were held in those panelled rooms. From early colonial days Chatham played an important part in both the social and political life of the country, and its spacious halls have been the scene of many important gatherings, both grave and gay. Many thrilling secrets those old walls could tell, if they only would! From the time of Madison's and Monroe's visits, nearly all of our Presidents have been entertained there, and have wandered through the gardens, with the river flowing beyond.

Originally these gardens were on the terraces, leading down to a river landing where boats brought each day the necessities as well as the luxuries of life. At one time a rose-garden, with more than two thousand bushes, bloomed here in such profusion that it was the pride of the entire countryside.

[204]

Now the formal entrance is on the river, and looking through the spacious hall, an open door gives a glimpse of such beauty that you must hasten through to see the fulfillment of the promise. A flagged terrace with two sentinel box clumps, just where the steps go down, is shaded by the spreading branches of an ancient tree. Sweet scents of flowers, the drowsy humming of bees, and the swift dart of a bluebird from the wistaria vine, truly, one could dream dreams and see visions in such a spot. No wonder that the famous ghost of Chatham walks here sometimes at night, when all the world is sleeping.

Beyond the terrace, the trim box-bordered walks reveal a startling mass of bloom, where delphinium, lemon day lilies, and hollyhocks vie with others in a riot of color, their brightness enhanced by the background of dark evergreen. Here and there a bit of white wall or a little white gate shows through, leading off to mysterious places—perhaps to the dairy, perhaps to the smokehouse, perhaps to the servants' quarters. Quaint rose trees line the paths; masses of white iris, daffodils, violets, and all of the early flowers bring each year their promise of eternal spring.

Though with the passing of the years, Chatham has stood a silent witness to the history of our country, it still stands so serenely that its life seems to have just begun. Through the loving care of its present owners, its youth is renewed, and today one sees the brightness of its tomorrow in the glory of its yesterdays.

ASHTON FITZHUGH WILSON.

MARY WASHINGTON'S GARDEN

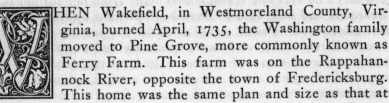WHEN Wakefield, in Westmoreland County, Virginia, burned April, 1735, the Washington family moved to Pine Grove, more commonly known as Ferry Farm. This farm was on the Rappahannock River, opposite the town of Fredericksburg. This home was the same plan and size as that at Wakefield. Eight happy years passed, then in April, 1743, Augustine Washington died after a brief illness. Mary Washington was a widow thirty-seven years old with five children under twelve years. Her stepson, Lawrence Washington, was living at Mount Vernon and was her sole advisor. Her son George was only eleven years old when he assumed the responsibilities of having grace and family prayers in his home. George said, "All that I am I owe my mother."

Washington, before setting out to take charge of the Colonial troops, after the battle of Bunker Hill, persuaded his mother to leave Ferry Farm and move to a small house he had bought a few years before in Fredericksburg. Betty Lewis, her only daughter, wanted her to live at Kenmore, but her mother had been accustomed to her own home, her own servants, and her own manner of life. The habit of command was strong within her. Her simple establishment had unfitted her to occupy a visitor's place in the fine home at Kenmore.

"My wants in this life are few," she replied to her daughter's invitation. "I feel perfectly competent to take care of myself."

Her home still stands in Fredericksburg. In 1775, it was a long, low cottage, with a hall and two rooms on the first floor and a half story above. The house was part brick and part frame. A detached building to one side of the cottage was the kitchen, with a room above for servants. The stables were on the corner; the garden and orchard in front and on the side.

The land was a part of the Kenmore estate. Mary Washington loved flowers and transplanted many from her former home. Calycanthus and box, said to have been planted by her, still grow in this garden. The same sun-dial marks the passing days. How we would listen could her flowers speak and tell us of those days! After the Revolution, when states had sprung from colonies, George Washington, on a visit to his mother, planted thirteen horse chestnut trees along a walk leading from this house to Kenmore. One of these trees still lives.

The change from Ferry Farm was great, for one who loved wide spaces and plantation life. Yet, Mary Washington made no complaint. "George thought it best," she said. Fredericksburg was in a direct line from eastern to southern colonies. Courier after courier would appear at this cottage door with dispatches that told of victory or defeat. Those trying years, when her son was leading the Continental forces, Mary was praying, and with calmness she remonstrated with her daughter for undue excitements. "The sister of the Commanding General should be an example of faith and fortitude," she said.

Knitted socks, garments and provisions, the fruit of her thrift and economy, were sent the General in camp for distribution among the soldiers.

November 11, 1791, Washington arrived in Fredericksburg with his staff of French and American officers, *en route* from Yorktown to Philadelphia. Leaving his retinue, he walked unattended to the unpretentious cottage, where his mother awaited him. She was alone. She bade him welcome, with a warm embrace and the endearing name "George." She spoke much of old times and old friends, but of his glory, not one word. Her only appearance in public as the hero's mother was at a ball given in Fredericksburg. In the autumn of 1784 LaFayette, for the sole purpose of paying his respect to Washington's mother, visited Fredericksburg, and staid at Kenmore. Madam Washington's one recreation was walking and working in her garden. Her love for her shrubs, flowers, and herbs was strong. LaFayette came by a side street unannounced and entered the side gate. "Ah, Marquis! You have come to see an old woman. But come in. I can make you welcome without changing my dress. I am glad to see you. I have often heard George speak of you." At the time she wore a short gown of linsey, a broad-brimmed hat over her plaited under-cap, and was raking leaves. She dropped the rake and took the hand of the nobleman in both of hers. He bared his head and bowed. Later, LaFayette said, "I have seen the only Roman mother living at this day."

April 14, 1789, she had a visit from her first-born. Washington had received notice of his election to the Presidency of the United States and it was necessary for him to leave for New York. He had galloped from Mount Vernon to spend an hour or more with his mother. Time pressed, but he lingered, realizing the fact that this might prove his last visit, as his mother was abed and stricken with a fatal disease. His premonition was fulfilled, for Mary Washington died August 25, 1789. New York was a week's distance by special post rider, and the President did not receive the news until September 1st. . . . .

Fancy and imagination can fill in these few facts and we can picture the grand old mother walking in this garden, both early morning and at twilight, thinking of her boy, her first-born, leading forces against the Mother country. How her heart ached for him, as he met trouble and dangers. How her heart throbbed as she thought of his glory. Prayer after prayer was offered for the Colony, his forces and her son. As we tread the same brick walk bordered by the same boxwood we feel a nearness to God, as this is hallowed ground—to God and our country.

ANNA MARSHALL BRAXTON.

Mary Washington Garden

The Mary Washington House, in Fredericksburg

Matthew Fontaine Maury's Garden

Blandfield, on the Rappahannock, Built by William Beverley About 1760

THE MAURY GARDEN IN
FREDERICKSBURG

ATTHEW FONTAINE MAURY! The name
scintillates in the realm of science in both hemis-
pheres. During several periods of his life this
great man was a citizen of Fredericksburg. Two
of the houses closely associated with him are still
here. Perhaps the old frame dwelling on Char-
lotte Street, so sadly in need of fresh paint—with the blacksmith
shop and the woodyard in juxtaposition—would never attract the
attention of the casual passer-by. But if he were keenly alive and
discerning, and appreciative of the historic lore of the old town,
a certain imperceptible and compelling influence would detain his
lingering footsteps. He would pause to read the inscription on a
bronze tablet which surmounts the granite block on the pavement
in front of this house:

Home of Matthew Fontaine Maury
1836-1842
Pathfinder of the Seas
Projector of the Atlantic Cable
Founder of the National Observatory
Father of Meteorological Science
Commander C. S. N.

He would note that the grounds on the east still bear traces
of former loveliness. Here is still the broad brick paving, and
the riotous tangle of the honeysuckle, with undisputed right of way,
usurps the choicest place, in what were once the formal flower
borders. Oblongs, ovals, and circles have lost their symmetry, and

only bricks at intervals are left to tell their tale. But birds still carol in the tall tree tops, and butterflies flit, and bees still buzz in the sweet-scented clovers and honeysuckle!

The interest of the stranger is awakened and unsatisfied. He inquires carefully and finds it was in the seclusion of that home with the high brick wall—a shallow wire fence has now replaced the wall—that Matthew Maury opened the eyes of the world of maritime science and took his first step on the rung of the ladder which carried him up to the heights of honor and fame.

It was here that he wrote that striking series of essays on naval reform, published incognito in the *Southern Literary Messenger*. It was also here that he made his *Survey of Southern Harbors.*

At the outbreak of hostilities in 1861, Lieutenant Maury was one of the first to sacrifice his own interests and ambitions to further the welfare of his own beloved State. He resigned his important position at the Naval Observatory in Washington to accept the position as chief of *The River, Harbor and Coast Defences of the South,* with headquarters in Richmond.

In April, 1861, he writes from Richmond to his affectionate kinsman, John Minor, of Fredericksburg: "Dear John. Bless your heart for offering us shelter in these times! . . . . "

The substantial brick structure which housed his family during the unhappy days of 1861-2, and also himself, whenever circumstances in those uncertain times made it possible, stands today, in all its well-preserved beauty and simplicity, on lower Main Street. It is now owned and occupied by Mrs. L. L. Coghill and family. Its every feature—the style of its construction, its hand-carved wood work, its interesting brass door locks and knobs—all are silent and accurate witnesses of earlier days.

An emerald lawn, which shows every evidence of loving care, ornaments the north side of the handsome old house. From its velvet surface a giant black walnut tree proudly spreads its protecting branches. What repose there was for Maury in its dappled shade! But fate denied him the bliss of that old armchair invitingly placed beneath its spreading boughs and the longed-for companionship of his own adored family, except on rare occasions.

When the Government appealed to patriotic Americans for certain woods to be used in the construction of ships during the World War, this walnut tree was generously offered by Mrs. Coghill, and her offer was accepted. Fortunately, however, when the inspector came to see if it was available, he was so struck with its magnificence that he recommended that it be held in reserve for a last call. The signing of the Armistice shortly after that saved the old tree from being commandeered.

Beyond the walnut tree is the old flower garden, radiant still with old-time favorites. In the fresh, sweet spring of the year, snowballs, lilacs, peonies, tulips, violets and jonquils vie with each other in perfection of bloom. And then when summer comes, geraniums, verbenas, phlox, mignonette. Everywhere, and during all the blossoming season, nearly all seasons, roses scent the air with their sweet fragrance.

The old plank fence in the rear, and the locust trees, half dead with age, support the strong and vigorous trumpet flower. The long serpentine brick-paved path, with its carpet of moss, which leads to the old kitchen of other days, adds a mellow note to the harmony of the garden, which, in the summer of today, is a joy to all who behold it.

In a lecture delivered at the laying of the cornerstone for the Maury monument in Richmond, Professor A. B. Chandler said: "He belonged to that very small circle of consummate masters in the field of research to whom every advanced nation is largely indebted for its present expanded commercial life. . . . . His work was not local but universal; not transient, but permanent; not benefiting a few, but all the earth. . . . He is, in truth, the father of the science of meteorology, and has been so recognized in all the world, save his native land. . . . Born within ten miles of

Fredericksburg, dead at Lexington, buried in Richmond, his life throughout was so steady, his heart was so pure, that the only 'crime'—God save the mark—he ever committed during his career was his allegiance with the incomparable Lee in the just cause that was lost."

DORA C. JETT.

FALL HILL

ALL HILL was built about 1738 by Colonel Francis Thornton, whose family was a very ancient one, tracing direct descent from William Thornton, Lord of East Newton, Yorkshire, 1313. It was built as a summer residence, and for this its situation upon the brow of a high hill, three miles outside of Fredericksburg, was eminently suitable. This property on the hill, and for many miles along the valley of the Rappahannock, was inherited by Colonel Thornton from his father, Francis Thornton I, who lived in the Falls house, half a mile from the river.

Colonel Francis Thornton II married Frances Gregory, in about 1736, she being the daughter of Mildred Washington, sister of Augustine Washington, the father of America's first president. When Colonel Thornton died, in 1749, he left a large property in different parts of Virginia to each of his two younger sons, and to his eldest son, Francis III, he bequeathed the Falls plantation and Fall Hill. He dowered his daughters handsomely, especially Mildred, upon her coming of age, when she married Charles Washington, youngest brother of the General.

In the old graveyard at The Falls eleven generations of the Thornton family are sleeping through eternity. Among the graves are those of Colonel Thornton and the infant daughter of Mildred and Charles Washington. After the death of Colonel Thornton, his family lived for some years in both houses, but when the Falls dwelling was destroyed by fire they moved to Fall Hill. Curiously enough, the latter house was not then finished, though the white panelling and fine mantel-pieces testify to the infinite care and taste with which it was being planned.

Francis Thornton III married Ann Thompson, the daughter of Lady Spotswood by her second marriage, to Parson Thompson.

At this time his mother moved into the Falls cottage, a commodious brick house, now in existence near the site of the original dwelling.

Of the six children of Francis III and Anne Thornton, Francis IV was the only son. His mother brought to Fall Hill with her Katina, an Indian woman, who had attended her from her infancy, who had been given originally to Governor Spotswood by an itinerant tribe of Indians when he was on one of his many exploring expeditions to the Blue Ridge Mountains. Francis IV personally told Colonel James Innes Thornton of Alabama, his son, that he could remember Katina's taking him and his five sisters into the woods and covering them with leaves while she called, with strange and beautiful cries, the birds of the forest, which would come and rest around them. Her grave is still well marked among six old oaks back of the Fall Hill house. After this, Francis Thornton was always a friend of the Indians, and the latter frequently called upon him at Fall Hill when they were passing near the place.

In 1837, when Francis Thornton IV died, his family scattered, and for some years the place was tenanted by the family nurse, Mammy Nancy. In 1843, his granddaughter, Bessie Forbes, inherited it in part. After her marriage to Dr. John R. Taylor, the latter, by purchase, added to his wife's portion many acres of the original plantation.

In 1868, General Robert E. Lee was a guest at Fall Hill, and Mrs. Taylor, who then owned the place, called his attention to the shattered trunk of a tree, the top of which had been shot away by a Federal cannon. Though rapidly being overgrown with ivy, Mrs. Taylor was preserving this tree trunk as an object of historic interest. Instead of showing the interest she expected, General Lee advised her not to preserve it at all, but to obliterate as far as possible every trace of the unfortunate war.

Mrs. Taylor died in 1876, and upon her husband's death in 1882 the property was divided by lot among his four sons and one daughter, Bessie Thompson Taylor. The house, with considerable land, went to the youngest son, Richard Taylor, who sold it, and for the first time the estate reverted to an outsider, Mr. Smith, who, in turn, sold Fall Hill to Colonel Hellier.

In 1909, upon the death of Colonel Hellier, Fall Hill came into the possession of the original family again, through Captain Murray Taylor, eldest son of Dr. Taylor. At the present time, his daughter, Mrs. Bessie Forbes Robinson, is chatelaine of the old place, which descends by entail to her daughter, Butler Brayne Thornton Robinson.

Though the garden, which suffered cruelly during the war, has been replaced to a great extent by modern shrubs and vines, the steep terraces and the thousands of naturalized jonquils, which make them glitter like gold in the spring, give a very good idea of what the spot once was. The driveway around the grass circle in front of the house is still lavishly bordered with jonquils, and ends at an old-fashioned stone carriage block quarried at Fall Hill.

Mrs. Charles Selden, daughter of Dr. and Mrs. J. R. Taylor, who once lived there, says of the old garden: "A broad gravel walk once led from the carriage block to the house, and from there followed the course of the lawn overlooking the Rappahannock River. The terraces which fall from the front of the house are bordered with jonquils of many varieties, and thousands of daffodils grow in large beds under many of the trees on the lawn.

"On the first terrace, which begins at the brow of the hill, some of the trees which once stood there are still left, though the trellises and arbors, covered with roses and Virginia creeper, that were at one time scattered over the lawn, have disappeared.

"Extending through the original flower garden at the rear of the house was a wide gravel path, bordered with masses of cowslips and hyacinths which bloomed beneath spiraea, pyrus japonica and magnolia conspicua. Microphyllae and damask roses were also in these borders, and beyond them were large beds of hundred-leaf roses."

[215]

Surrounding the house are many original oaks, said by experts to be among the finest in America. And in the woodland, as if in consolation for the garden that has gone, grow as many different varieties of wild flowers—especially hardy orchids—as may be found anywhere in the country.

ANNE THORNTON TAYLOR BAYLISS.

Gordonsdale, the Scott Homestead in Fauquier County, Noted for Extensive Boxwood Hedges

The Garden at Sabine Hall

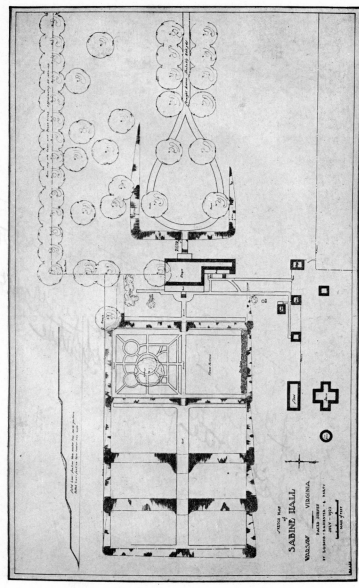

SKETCH PLAN
of
SABINE HALL
WARSAW   VIRGINIA

PACED SURVEY
BY LOOMIS · BANISTER · & PARTY
JULY — 1932

SCALE   FEET

Sabine Hall

SABINE HALL

HERE grow no strange flowers every year—
But when Spring winds blow o'er the pleasant places
The same dear things lift up the same fair faces."

Just such a garden is that at Sabine Hall, which is situated on a ridge one mile back from the broad waters of the Rappahannock River.

The house, Sabine Hall, was built in 1730 for Colonel Landon Carter by his father, Robert Carter, of Corotoman, who was called by his compatriots "King" Carter by reason of his very extensive possessions in the Colony of Virginia.

Colonel Carter, like many another squire of his time, found great delight in Horace, and legend has it that he named his estate for Horace's Sabine farm because of his interest in the Roman poet.

The house, with its high ceilings, spacious rooms and wide halls, remains today one of the finest among the Colonial dwellings of the Old Dominion. The walls of the drawing-rooms and great halls are hung with family portraits, among them being pictures of Landon Carter and "the three great ladies who successively bore his name." One of the family's most valued possessions is a fine portrait of King Carter. The estate, consisting of some four thousand acres, is on the Rappahannock, in Richmond County, not far from Menokin, the home of Francis Lightfoot Lee. It was at Sabine Hall that Colonel Carter, "retired from public praise," carried on his famous correspondence with General Washington and the Lees, much of which has been preserved. These historical documents show the great influence he exerted over Colonial and Revolutionary affairs.

On one front of the Colonial brick house are lawns many acres in extent shaded by stately old trees. On the other, commanding a beautiful view of the lowlands and river, is a very lovely terraced garden, an excellent example of Colonial gardens at their best. Fortunate in never having passed out of the family, this garden is beautifully cared for and still in perfect preservation. Practically unchanged since it was laid off about 1730 by English gardeners, presumably brought to this country for that purpose, it bears witness to the skill and good taste of former days.

The garden has a series of six terraces. Upon the upper a broad, level walk leads from the porch to its outer edge; on each side of this and running the length of the terrace, are grass plots, their green unbroken except in the center where clumps of crepe myrtle give a touch of color by their wealth of pink blossoms. At the edge of this terrace are wide borders beside which run gravel walks several feet in width. These borders are filled with a variety of rose bushes and yellow jasmine. At the far end clumps of hollyhock, weigela and stately white yuccas are massed. In addition to these, pink and blue columbine, Oriental poppies, peonies of different hues, golden coriopsis, delphiniums, sweet william, bleeding hearts, chrysanthemums and other flowers give a continuous succession of bloom and a riot of color.

To the right this terrace slopes to a portion of the lawn where the sides of a little ravine are covered with thousands of narcissi, and to the left it slopes to a lower level on which are the old-fashioned toolhouse, dairy, and smokehouse almost completely enveloped in ivy, wistaria and climbing roses.

One walks from the first terrace down a grassy ramp to the second. Here is the real flower garden, bounded on the left by an unbroken box-hedge, about eight feet tall, which extends the breadth of the terrace. In the far corners are clumps of lilac, althea, mock-orange, and smoke tree. Here, too, Japanese quince or cydonia japonica, calycanthus, Persian lilacs, snowballs, hardy white hydrangeas, hollyhocks, bridal wreath, and syringa growing on irregularly shaped turf beds form a background for the smaller flowers.

Still more to the right is a magnificent English broadnut

(hickory) tree under whose protecting branches merry children have for many generations played "flower ladies." A corresponding pecan tree which stood on the left was blown down a few years ago.

On this terrace narrower gravel walks branch off from the side. These lead one who traverses them through a maze of beautiful flowers which fill the quaintly shaped borders. Roses of many varieties and colors—lavender, whose blossoms are cut each year and placed among the linen—wall flower, foxglove, Canterbury bells, gaillardias, verbenas, orange and yellow calendulas, chrysanthemums, peonies, pink and white phlox, cowslips, snapdragons, petunias, flowering almond, Easter lilies, many kinds of iris, violets, lily of the valley in profusion, and others too numerous to mention fill the borders with sheets of brilliant bloom from earliest spring until latest autumn.

The next terrace is given up to grapes, figs, strawberries, raspberries, currants and other small fruits, while the fourth and fifth are planted with vegetables and the sixth with fruit trees.

It would be difficult to imagine a spot more suggestive of romance than this old garden. On a moonlight night, with the river a thread of silver in the distance, one can almost see the belles and beaux of bygone days emerging from the shadows.

It was in the garden of Sabine Hall that George Washington and Landon Carter walked together as Washington unfolded his plans for the campaign at Morristown. When the latter returned he took with him the young son of Sabine Hall to enlist in the Army of the Revolution. It well-nigh broke his mother's heart. Then followed a letter from General Washington to the boy's father full of tender sympathy for the mother, "understanding her fears and anxieties," saying he is going to "place the boy with so good a man as General Baylor," how he himself is sick of war and longs for the shades of private life.

Landon Carter's diary tells of the yearly Christmas house parties, when the Lees and Washingtons, the Spotswoods and other great men from all over the country were gathered there. He writes of the pipes of wine, barrels of oysters, saddles of mutton and other supplies laid in for their enjoyment. It is interesting to read of the colors the different brides chose for the walls of the house. One wants the walls green and the chariot painted yellow!

Landon Carter married Maria Byrd of Westover. Three months ago in looking over some of the old books, a leather volume of Thompson's poems was found. In it was the beautiful Byrd coat-of-arms and on the flyleaf was written, "Presented by Maria Byrd of Westover to Colonel Landon Carter of Sabine Hall." The book of poems she presented to her lover so long ago rests today on the library table at Sabine Hall, a bit of atmosphere linking the past and present together.

Sabine Hall has come down for eight generations, alternating with Robert Carter and Landon Carter until Robert W. Carter willed it to his grandson, Robert Carter Wellford, whose mother was Elizabeth Landon Carter.

Robert Carter Wellford, like the first Landon Carter, went to the banks of James River for his bride, and most of his wooing was done at Westover, then the home of Mrs. A. H. Drewry. Robert Carter Wellford and Lizzie Harrison, a sister of Mrs. Drewry, were married in the old drawing-room at Westover under an arch of roses, where had stood nearly two hundred years before Landon Carter of Sabine Hall and Maria Byrd of Westover.

Amid all the joys and sorrows that have come with the years the children and grandchildren of Robert Carter Wellford and Lizzie Harrison still gather in the old home. Their feet patter down the halls which echo with laughter and merriment, and in the old garden, under the old English broadnut tree, little ones still play flower ladies.

ELIZABETH LANDON WELLFORD JONES.

MOUNT AIRY

T

HE Northern Neck of Virginia is that long, narrow strip of land, lying between the Rappahannock and Potomac Rivers. Here were the homes of Washington, Madison, Monroe, and Lee—and many other noble and stalwart souls, whose lives helped to make the sum of human achievement greater for having lived.

This section is far from the centers of trade and commerce, and there are still no railroads or towns; so there one can find old-time traditions and conditions as perhaps in no other part of Virginia. Here one finds many fine old homes and churches left intact.

Amid the rural beauties, winding rivers, honeysuckled roads, great wheat and corn fields in Richmond County lies "Mount Airy," the ancestral home of the Tayloes. It is one of the greatest of Tidewater estates, and is like an old barony, with its vast lands and great mansion.

As you drive up the high, winding way to the top of the terrace, through grassy lawn and giant trees—alternate shade and sunlight—and come to the house, you feel that you *must* be in England, for it is very stately and beautiful, so softened and mellowed by time, that you are *sure* you cannot be in twentieth century America.

It was in the reign of Charles II that the first Tayloe came to the new land to live and brought with him the culture and traditions of an English gentleman, and transferred them to the virgin soil.

His grandson, Colonel John Tayloe, built Mount Airy in 1747, and the Tayloes still own the place, and live there, which makes it unusual among Virginia colonial homes.

The place consists of three houses, grouped about a central axis, and connected by curved covered ways, the whole enclosing a raised forecourt where the grass is very green and four symmetrical holly trees give color and dignity. There is ivy clustered against the wall and foliage massed behind the house.

Below the court is a circle of green, with an ancient sundial, and below and beyond, the many rolling acres in lawn and trees where, in olden times, many deer were kept. The worn stone-steps leading to the court have massive stone urns on pedestals at either side. The walk leads through the court to more stone-steps that lead to the loggia and hall. These steps are guarded by bronze dogs. The architecture of Mount Airy is not colonial at all, but rather English, and one unique feature is that it is built entirely of stone, native brown and grey sandstone. Time has weathered and softened it, and it is very lovely, surrounded by the beauties of Virginia landscape.

At the back are five grassy terraces, the central one being a perfect square of green. This was once used as a bowling green, and one easily imagines the gay gallants of long ago, bowling upon it, with might and main, and later going into the dining-room to drink a mint-julep, from the "Old Bowl of Mount Airy," which is famous in poem and story.

These terraces are most unusual and end in a vista of flowers and shrubbery, at the brink of the great hill, where one gets a view of surpassing grandeur. Before you lie extended many miles of farm and woodland—most of it still belonging to the estate. There the Rappahannock River, three miles away, winds like a blue ribbon, in the distance; and, on the farther side of the river, the houses of the little colonial town of Tappahannock, in Essex County, spread out upon its shores.

There was once a large, formal garden at Mount Airy. There were parterres and hedges and, several feet below the green, at the right, was the kitchen garden. But, in the sad days after the war, things had to be changed, and the kitchen garden was ploughed for wheat, the parterres lapsed into a lawn, in which paths and ornaments are still seen. It has never been restored to its original plan, but today is in smooth grass, trees, flowers, and shrubbery, and is much more charming and picturesque than in the days of its ancient, formal stiffness.

I will never forget a very large and symmetrical crepe myrtle tree, standing in the center of a square of this old garden and *every particle* covered with its pink, crepy bloom—the sunset red behind the trees and across the river, and the air musical with the songs of many birds, for there are thousands of birds at Mount Airy.

It is an unforgettable experience to have tea on the second terrace, the sun low behind the tulip poplar trees, and the birds coming quite close to pick up crumbs—mockings, red birds, thrashers, and robins, while two wood-thrushes sang their musical song from the woods. The old tulip poplar trees are magnificent and are believed to antedate the house. The view from the loggia of the five terraces, the flowers, and the vista, is very lovely. Off from the old garden are delightful walks to beguile one to rustic arbours, seats under trees, vine-covered "summer-houses," honeysuckle, shrubbery, and open woods.

In the wall at Mount Airy they show you the place where the old copper-still was placed in colonial times, where roses of the garden were distilled into rose-water for "my lady's" toilet and bath. And the garden, also, contributed a delicious drink, and many a distinguished visitor from afar has wondered if the far-famed cup which Circe gave to those she sought to beguile, could have been half so fragrant and delicious as the rose wine that was made at Mount Airy. It could be made only of damask roses, and must be made in a blue bowl!

Off to one side of the old garden site, there are picturesque brick arches draped with Virginia creeper and trumpet vine and backed by ancient box-trees, that lend a foreign touch; these are the ruins of the orangery or conservatory.

Here many a tropical and out-of-season fruit and berry was raised—pineapples, oranges, lemons, etc. One English visitor,

Mr. Baker, coming to this country in 1827 and visiting Mount Airy, speaks of "the large conservatory with orange and lemon trees put upon the grass." And in the biography of Thomas Dabney, of Gloucester, one reads of a famous dinner given to the Marquis de LaFayette. He says, "It was in the month of October, and there was a small dish of red Antwerp raspberries, sent by Mrs. Tayloe, of Mount Airy. They came from her hot-house, and were set before General LaFayette."

The present owners of Mount Airy use the three sides of the bowling green for flowers and, also, below the terraces on either side to the brink of the hill. The borders of the bowling green are a glowing mass of jonquils, narcissi, cowslips, iris in the spring. In summer these are followed by peonies, pansies, roses, poppies, hollyhocks, snapdragon, larkspur, phlox, sweet william, canterbury bells, ragged robin, and madonna lilies. Asters and chrysanthemums usher in the fall, making it possible to have flowers following each other in endless succession, the house always filled with them.

One could never forget the great central hall, so high pitched, so softly colored, and so restful, with over twenty vases of flowers, a strangely sweet and Oriental perfume coming from the sofa-pillows, filled with dried, wild sweet clover. In this hall are many fine pieces of old furniture. Everything at Mount Airy has grown old beautifully, through the care of and association with gentle, refined people, to whom living was an art.

Here is the large and gaily-decorated music box, where a hundred tunes can still be played. How often have the belles and beaux of long ago in knee-breeches and patches trod a stately measure to its music; for Mount Airy was as famous for its lavish hospitality as for its ardent patriotism.

The faces of these ancestral folk still look down upon one: Colonial Governors, Burgesses, Officers of His Majesty's Army, and beautiful ladies are there. One English visitor to this country said that the portrait gallery at Mount Airy was the finest private one he had seen in this country. One of the sweetest faces is that

Elizabeth Harrison Wellford

The Garden at Sabine Hall

Mount Airy, the Home of the Tayloes

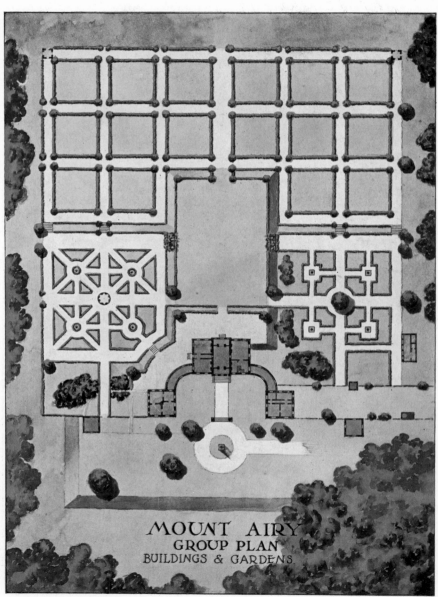

MOUNT AIRY
GROUP PLAN
BUILDINGS & GARDENS

Mount Airy

of Mistress Betty Tayloe who is the heroine of one of Churchill's books.

The library is filled with books and there are many prints of race-horses belonging to the three John Tayloes, for the first Colonel John Tayloe was a pioneer in the keeping of fine race-horses in Virginia. They had their own race-track at Mount Airy, and all the neighboring gentry came to the races—the Turbevilles of Hickory Hill, the Carters of Sabine Hall, the Corbins of Lane-ville, the Wormeleys of Rose Gill, the Beverleys of Blandfield, the Robbs of Gay Mont, and many others.

Among the fine pieces of silver are several trophies won by Mount Airy horses. They no longer keep race-horses, but the place, the people, the flowers, and the atmosphere are the same, and one hopes that time will deal as gently with them in the future as it has dealt in the past.

HATTIE BELLE GRESHAM.

AVENEL

IR WALTER SCOTT says, "Breathes there the man with soul so dead who ne'er to himself hath said, 'this is my own, my native land,'" and is there a Virginian whose pulses do not tingle when there lies before him a garden the beauty of which is almost eclipsed by the long series of historical memories that the name of the owners and the plan of the garden bring to his mind?—Avenel—home of the Beverleys—Avenel, with one-half of its garden copied from Tudor Place, the other, the copy of Blandfield.

With the very name comes the perfect picture of Virginia and Virginia's best life from the middle of the seventeenth century. For it was that William Beverley, the emigrant's own grandson, and his wife, Elizabeth Bland, who first laid out the garden at Blandfield. That same first master of Blandfield was the son of Robert Beverley and his wife, Ursula Byrd, daughter of William Byrd the first. This Robert Beverley, you remember, was the first native historian of Virginia. All honor to him!

The beautiful garden of Blandfield by long closure of the house has practically fallen into ruin; but we can picture to ourselves what a charm it had from frequent allusions to it in old letters; and one can well imagine that its master, William Beverley, would have brought to it the same intelligent interest that caused his grandfather, William Byrd the first, to write in 1690 to his correspondent in London, one Thomas Wetherold, that he had "saved many seeds, but all had been ruined except the ones he sent, namely: Poppeas Arbor, Rhus Sentisie, folias, Laurus Tulipfera." I believe that most of the seeds that were saved were seeds of trees, but what is a garden without trees!

In 1730, Catesby, the naturalist in London, wrote to his niece in

ENTRANCE

COPY
OF
BLANDFIELD
GARDEN

BOX HEDGE ALL AROUND

COPY
OF
TUDOR PLACE
GARDEN

DIAGRAM OF THE GARDENS AT
AVENEL

J. Bradshaw Beverley

Bridal Wreath at Prospect Hill

Prospect Hill, Caroline County

Virginia, Mrs. Thomas Jones, "Virginia cones, acorns and seeds would be most acceptable." Robert Beverley, the historian, writing about 1700, tells how easily and abundantly both fruits and flowers were grown in Virginia. He writes, *con amore,* of the tulip, "the perfection of flavor" and "all sorts of herbs," and "the charming colors of the humming birds revelling among the blossoms," etc. This Virginia historian of the long ago shows the same knowledge and love of flowers that his many-times grandson, Captain James Bradshaw Beverley, does in the following sketch of the old garden at Avenel—a garden designed more than a hundred years ago by James Bradshaw Beverley and his wife, Jane Peter of Georgetown, the grandparents of Captain Beverley.

The garden of Avenel was formed by two flower-knots, which are shown in the diagram. To quote from Captain Beverley, "the flower-knots which were at Avenel were copied by my grandparents, if I remember aright, the one on the right from 'Tudor Place' and that on the left from 'Blandfield.'" In drawing them, I have not attempted mathematical precision, as no instruments were available; to have done so would have been difficult. And no drawing could convey to you the beauty, the wooing welcome, the *dolce far niente* of it all.

Nothing but old-timey flowers! None of our grand new roses, not one. Nothing but old-timey flowers. And it has often struck me that our new productions, while each by itself, posing for its portrait, as it were, is indeed a prince of beauty, do not add much to the looks of a crowd. Have you ever seen, at a cemetery, a floral tribute composed only of wild flowers, which had been selected with taste and arranged with a sense of harmony? The florist's best effort meets its peer.

No drawing, I said—of course not—not even Paul deLongpre's brush could have done those flower-knots justice. And yet "the Sunburst" and "Mrs. Charles Russell" were not there. Only the old Damask, the Hundred-Leaf, the Hermosa and the Daily, the Harrisonian, the Champigny and Grevel. Then came the Giant o'Battle, and later, the Jacqueminot and the Bourbons of the Agrippina type. The first I recall of the wonderful Tea family was known only as the Tea Rose. I have often wondered if it had any other name.

Over the four arches (poorly suggested in the diagram) twined the Grevel or Seven Sisters. No regular order had been followed in planting; no bedding, no grouping. A great vine of yellow jasmine (Gelsemium sempervirens) monopolized the "diamond" on the left as you entered. Trained originally up a single post, it wound over and over the top until it took the shape of a huge shock of hay.

In the center of each circle stood a large iron vase, from which verbenas usually hung and vainly reached earthward. Spiraeas of several kinds, Rose of Sharon, deutzias, and a calycanthus were among the shrubs. Between and among the roses and shrubs bloomed, in the spring, bulbs of all sorts, and in summer, all of the old annuals. A dense honeysuckle hedge served as a background and obscured the vegetable gardens beyond. These terminated at the center walk in two large lilac clumps, and to the right in a great bush of mock-orange.

At the entrance, between two o'er-arching arbor vitae trees, were permanent seats. And many other seats, during the fair days of summer, were added, for here visitors were entertained, and here lovers knew they would not be intruded upon, if by good luck, they first occupied the position.

In each flower-knot, yet not in juxtaposition, stood a grand box-tree; the largest I have ever seen. Within one of these, when a lad, I constructed a seat, and hidden there, would study my lessons and then read Bulwer's novels and Scott's poems. The alleys were all evenly sunken about eight inches, and the beds and borders were held up in line by a narrow bluegrass edge. These grass edges were kept trimmed with a knife. No boy of the family has ever forgotten this part of it, nor, also, of helping old Moore, the negro gardener, work the beds. Speaking of Moore, how often have I laughed at his reply to my sister Rebekah. She had expressed her sympathy for us because of the scorching sun, yet added: "But, Moore, 'Man's work is from sun to sun, while woman's work is never done.'" "Yes, Miss Becky—that's sometimes because they never do it." (He had trotted her on his knee when an infant.)

And I must tell you of another apt rejoinder given here. A neighbor, who was a good farmer, but lacking in the esthetic, was deprecating the amount of time and labor "wasted on these flowers." Goaded by a positively dissenting view, he asserted, "I'll bet there never was a day when all of the flowers here would buy you a breakfast." "Perhaps not," was the rejoinder, "but in construction I do not happen to be all stomach."

I fear that I have allowed my memories to run on until I have wearied you. "However," say I, "alas that a time should be at hand when, with the country-folk, the struggle for a livelihood and the scarcity of labor should ever exclude the cultivation of the Beautiful!"

MARY MASON ANDERSON WILLIAMS.

PROSPECT HILL

HE Tidewater trail, from Fredericksburg to Norfolk, which passes the now sleepy, but ancient and historic, little village of Port Royal, is a popular and interesting highway, and many of the roads which lead therefrom extend to the tourist a call so inviting that the summons is irresistible.

About ten miles from Fredericksburg, an attractive roadway leads to the right in a southeasterly direction. Great branches of oak, sycamore, maple, and elm trees, garlanded with honeysuckle, interlock familiarly above, and form a graceful canopy over its hard, smooth, serpentine surface, carpeted here and there with pine-cones and needles.

This entrance-way to the interior of historic old Caroline County, with its sweeping hills, and restful valleys, is very charming.

Caroline County! which gave to our nation's history such distinguished men as Edmund Pendleton, William Woodford, Richard Brooke, and John Taylor! It also gave the Battailes, Fitzhughs, and Gordons. The latter of Flintshire, Belvedere, Santee and Prospect Hill. It was the home of the Hays, of Hayfield; the Corbins, of Moss Neck, and others are closely associated with the best in every phase of the social, political, and religious life in Caroline County.

Many of the homes of these old families, long past the century mark, exhibit a peculiarly picturesque age, with entire freedom from that detracting quality, often the result of years of indifference on the part of unappreciative inmates.

Santee, familiarly known as the old Gordon place, but which was originally one of the many Fitzhugh country seats, is among the most interesting estates in this section. Its vine-hung house was built by Battaile Fitzhugh in 1807, and here, as in days of yore,

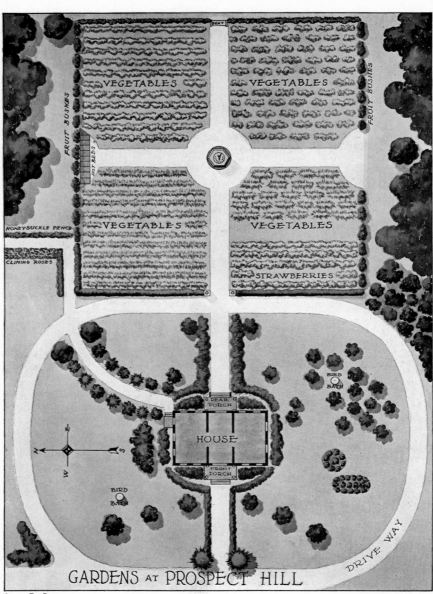

GARDENS AT PROSPECT HILL

Dora C. Jett

Gay Mont, Caroline County

are the same masses of boxwood and the same fine park with its kingly forest trees. There is still the old rose-garden to be seen, too, and the grapevine dell. It was in the latter place, possibly, that Patsy, the beautiful young daughter and only child of Battaile Fitzhugh, plighted her troth to Samuel Gordon, Jr., of historic Kenmore. "I love you," said Patsy, with a radiant blush, "but I cannot leave Santee."

Ever since that time the place has been owned and occupied by members of the Gordon family. Today, the infant grandson of the late Robert V. Gordon, holds sway at the loved old homestead.

From Santee, a half mile's stretch of woodland road leads to Prospect Hill. The vines clinging close to the substantial brick house; the great sprawling shade trees, with every evidence of hoary, but well preserved and worthy, old age; the fascinating brick walkways, overgrown with moss, all unite to give to Prospect Hill that charming touch of days gone by, which lends itself so irresistibly to many of the country seats in Old Virginia.

The present house on the old Battaile home site was erected by Basil Gordon, whose daughter, Mrs. Charles Herndon, one of the best loved, and one of the oldest residents of Fredericksburg, remembers distinctly when, as a little child, a workman held her up, so that she might have a wee hand in placing a brick in its corner-stone.

After several careful owners and tenants, Mr. and Mrs. C. L. Gage now have it in appreciative possession.

The house itself is most attractive, with its spacious rooms, breezy halls, and wonderful woodwork. The pillars of the porch, and the beams and boards (some of the latter being thirty-eight feet in length) were hewn from trees in the nearby woods. But it is the out-of-doors surrounding Prospect Hill that holds most charm. In the adjacent woodlands are some old gun-pits and breastworks, relics of the War Between the States. In the old family burying-ground, not far away, are interesting mementoes of days long gone.

[231]

In early days, one of the first requisites considered in building the beautiful homes of Virginia was a desirable location. This was not only from a practical, but from an aesthetic viewpoint. At Prospect Hill, the many miles of swelling hills, smiling valleys, whether dressed in spring verdure or autumn's glorious tints, make a landscape so pleasing that even the glint of silvery water is not needed.

But there is more to Prospect Hill than the mere beauty of its landscape. It has always held an unique agricultural value from the excellent quality of the grain grown there and the special flavor of its tobacco. Besides all these advantages, the place held a stronger magnet for young Henry Fitzhugh, of Bedford, across the Rappahannock. The rumble of his coach-and-four along the drive at Prospect Hill was no infrequent sound, and on a fair day in October, 1748, pretty Sarah Battaile became the bride of the wealthy heir of Bedford. A few years later, Henry Fitzhugh was appointed colonel of the Stafford County militia.

Go to Prospect Hill in the early spring season, when Nature's most pleasing plans have been perfected. Those splendid poplar, locust, linden, and walnut trees have lately donned their spring attire. Those symmetrical hollies guarding the entrance have freshened up their dress a bit. Those hedges, beyond the vine-clad house, are brilliant now with the blossoms of early spring roses. The robins, wrens, and bluebirds are caroling their song of satisfaction. Mating time is here, and homes, whether in the tall tree-tops, or in those picturesque bird-houses, scattered at intervals about the trees and shrubbery, are reasons enough for joyful warble. That lately trimmed hedge of privet, on the east side of the house, is groomed to perfection, and the breeze is heavy with aromatic odors from the dwarf-box, which borders the brick-paved path on the west.

And the bridal-wreath at Prospect Hill! Nowhere does this beautiful shrub attain the same grace and luxuriance. In wreaths and garlands and plumes it waves in the gentle wind on this Virginia hilltop. A forest of dainty white blossoms is massed on each side of the house on the west. Countless numbers of miniature roses they appear. On the east an avenue of the same shrub meets the privet hedge, still other avenues of snowy-white blossoms extend to the tangle of roses and honeysuckle, near the vegetable garden.

Then, when summer comes, shrubs and flowers sparkle in their gorgeous colors. There are masses of weigela, summer lilacs, phlox, clematis, and calycanthus. Roses, iris, and other gay perennials vie with each other in color and fragrance. They dot the emerald lawn, some in the blazing summer sunshine, others in the softened shade of the mimosa and the fir trees. Between the flowering quince and the euonymus bush is sunk the shallow, concrete bath for the birds. With hearts filled full of the joy of living, they chatter over their daily splash. Bees are lazily droning out their same old summer song. Butterflies are flirting with their favorite flowers. The timid squirrel peeps from the blossoming shrubbery; but, like a flash, he is safe in the tall treetop. All nature is in tune with the season.

If the Battailes and Gordons of the olden days at Prospect Hill were ambitious for the future of the loved old garden, their brightest hopes are realized. At every season it is one of the loveliest in all this section of beautiful garden spots.

DORA C. JETT.

GAY MONT

THE garden at Gay Mont lies on a high hill overlooking the Rappahannock River and Valley, twenty miles below the historic town of Fredericksburg. It is beautifully located and commands a wonderful view of the surrounding country.

This estate, which formerly comprised some two thousand acres, was part of the Miller grant. Unfortunately, the early records of Caroline County were destroyed or carried away by the Union troops during the War Between the States, making it difficult to obtain exact data. It is certain, however, that it was afterwards part of the Catlett estate, and was purchased from Mr. Catlett in 1790, by John Hipkins, of "Belle Grove," King George County, Virginia, who on his death left it to his grandson, John Hipkins Bernard.

The original house comprised only the central, or two-story portion of the present building and was erected about 1725. Two wings, one at either end, were added in 1798, and the octagon-shaped music room at the back in 1830. The latter opens on a small porch, from the steps of which one can look down the central garden walk to the sundial.

John Hipkins Bernard upon reaching his majority went abroad for several years and on his return brought with him many things for his home, including landscape wallpaper—then a novelty in France—for the Gay Mont hall, parlor and dining-room. The paper in the hall shows brightly colored Italian scenes, that in the parlor represents the Bay of Naples in soft grey tones, while that for the dining-room pictures mythological characters in sepia.

Mr. Bernard also brought over two English gardeners who remodeled the grounds and garden into their present form. That a rose garden antedated their arrival and was a feature of the

A Garden Walk at Gay Mont

The "Beauty Spot" at Gay Mont

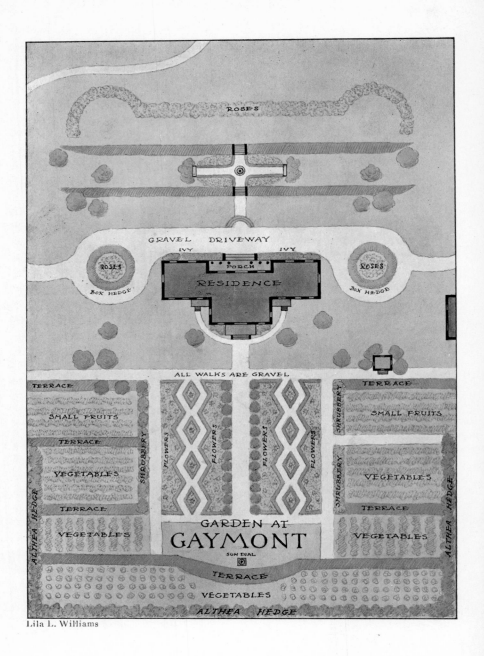

Lila L. Williams

place from its beginning, is apparent from the original name "Rose Hill" which Mr. Bernard changed to "Gay Mont" in honor of his bride, Miss Jane Gay Robertson, of Richmond, Virginia.

The portico at Gay Mont is supported by six large pillars with balustrades between, and is enclosed at each end by the wings. Between the windows opening on the portico and at either end are plaster busts of Washington, Franklin, Shakespeare, Milton, Scott, Byron, Napoleon and LaFayette.

In front of the portico is the driveway, and beyond are three terraces, each three hundred feet in length. The last terrace, twice the depth of the first two, broadens out at its base into a semi-circle at either end, and has a border of roses its entire length.

Between the second and third terrace there is a small formal garden, in the shape of a circle, consisting of four plots separated by gravel walks, with a fountain in the center surrounded by conch shells and ivy. This little garden was christened "The Beauty Spot," by which name it is still known. The water supplying the fountain was brought in lead pipes from a reservoir in the rear of the house, and after the War Between the States, when ammunition was scarce, the lead from the pipe was made into "slugs," and used instead of shot by the huntsmen of the family.

In connection with the fountain there is an amusing story told of a small dog which had been trained to turn the wheel which supplied the water. He would sit on the lower terrace overlooking the avenue, intently watching for visitors, and on seeing them approach would dash to the wheel and work violently in order to have the fountain spraying freely by the time the host greeted his guests at the front door.

At either end of the house there is a circular rose garden surrounded by box-bushes. Formerly this box was kept neatly trimmed, but it has long been allowed to grow at random and has now assumed the form of great, round masses, higher than a man's head.

At the back of the house, separated from the lawn by trees and shrubs, is the garden proper, consisting of a gravel walk, three hundred feet long, parallel to the lawn, and three lateral walks, ending in a wide terrace. Mr. Bernard is said to have brought shiploads of gravel from Bermuda for these walks, as well as conch shells for the fountains. The walks were bordered with shrubs— pyrus japonica, forsythia, spiraea in all varieties, lilac, snowball, weigela, althea, syringa, mock orange and others. These were trimmed to form arches over the paths. Between the walks were formal gardens laid out in the shape of diamonds and filled with many old-fashioned flowers. Peonies seem to have been the favorite centerpiece. On either side of this flower garden, separated by walks, were two large squares devoted to small fruits and vege-tables. A hedge, formerly of roses but now of althea, encloses the whole garden.

In addition to the lawns and garden, a large part of the estate of Gay Mont was given over to what might be called pleasure grounds. On the north side of the hill was a deer park of eight acres, with clumps of beautiful holly and enormous tulip poplars. Mr. Bernard had a great love for trees and imported many kinds, not only for the immediate grounds but also for the hillsides. Some years ago fifty varieties were counted within a comparatively short distance of the house, among them a variety of French chestnut, still vigorous and bearing nuts.

To the south of the hill ran "Golden Vale Creek," the name given it on an old atlas printed before Washington was founded. Its waters were dammed to form a pond, and stocked with fish. Here Mr. Bernard loved to entertain his friends, and it was no doubt, the scene of many gay parties. A large, round stone table, and a spring enclosed by stone slabs are all that now remain to mark the spot.

As horseback riding was the favorite pastime of Mr. Bernard's daughters, he built for them a private road through the woods and "the long meadow." This road crossed a small creek seven or eight times by rustic bridges; the upkeep of both road and bridges was given over to "Uncle Roly," a faithful slave. "Uncle Roly" loved to tell stories of the past and always began his tales by saying, "He had more recollections than he could remember." He loved to boast that "Ole Missis' flowers was so sweet you could smell 'em a mile away—jest as soon as you turn'd into de abenue."

During the War Between the States, Gay Mont, from its commanding position, narrowly escaped having a battery placed on the hill. This would have made it a target for the gunboats which shelled Port Royal and vicinity. The officers sent to place the battery desisted at the earnest entreaties of the women of the family. Two of Mr. Bernard's daughters remained at Gay Mont with their faithful servants during the entire war, thus no doubt saving the place from destruction. General Abercrombie, the Union commander stationed in Port Royal, showed them great courtesy and kindness. Many nights these young ladies sat in a low window holding by the bridle their favorite horses, "Ariel" and "Empress," to prevent them from being stolen. These horses were finally taken, however, but were instantly released when the owners appeared next day at headquarters and begged their return. General Abercrombie then sent a special guard to protect Gay Mont from further interference while the Northern troops remained in the neighborhood.

The Confederate officers encamped around Fredericksburg— General J. E. B. Stuart and his staff among them—were frequent visitors at Gay Mont. General Stuart was very fond of a music box in the library and would often enter the house unobserved and announce his arrival by playing some familiar air. A chair much scratched by his buttons was long kept as a souvenir of his visits.

Major Duncan McKim, "the gallant Pelham," and other officers were dining at Gay Mont the evening before the Battle of Fredericksburg, when a courier arrived summoning them to headquarters. So furious was the cannonading in that battle that the big bell over the kitchen and the smaller servants' bells which hung outside the several windows, all rang while the battle was in progress. Several of the guests of the preceding day were killed in this battle.

The servant bells attached to the windows at Gay Mont deserve mention only as relics of by-gone days. Each room had its bell, rung by means of a cord within, to summon a servant whenever wanted. One wonders how many servants were required and where stationed to catch and locate the sound of these bells, hung into space from any window of the rambling old house.

Like many Virginia homes, Gay Mont suffered severely during the War Between the States and the years following, when the labor necessary for its upkeep could not be obtained. But so well had the original plans been carried out and moulded into terraces and other enduring landmarks that today Gay Mont reflects honor on those who planned and those who carried the plans to completion.

In the division of the estate, Gay Mont was bought in by Helen Struan Bernard, youngest daughter of John Bernard, who in 1865 was married to Philip Lightfoot Robb, whose children still make it their home.

JOHN BERNARD ROBB.

The Famous "Ring of Oaks" at Newmarket, the Caroline County Home of Colonel George Baylor, Aide to General Washington

Oak Hill, the Home of President Monroe

The Piedmont Section

OAK HILL

"By a garden is meant a place of spiritual repose—stillness—peace—refreshment—delight."—Cardinal Newman.

AK HILL, the stately home of James Monroe, in Loudoun County, Virginia, was built by him while President of the United States.

The place took its name from an avenue of giant oaks towering above all other trees on the spacious lawn. At Oak Hill today there may be seen a letter from President Monroe written from the White House to William Benton, the manager of the estate. In this letter the President gives instructions regarding the avenue leading from the house to the public road and states that it is to be lined with Lombardy poplars planted as he directs.

This President chose wisely in selecting Loudoun County as his home. In the distance the Blue Ridge Mountains, ever veiled in a blue and violet haze, and around him an undulating, varied landscape whose climate, except for one district in the hill country of Bavaria, has been shown by health statistics to be the most healthful region in the world.

The plan of the house is said to follow that of the White House, and is a striking example of the taste in the early years of the Republic for the severely classical in domestic architecture. It is built of brick, and its great portico is graced by seven massive Doric columns, nine feet in circumference and thirty feet high.

The flower garden lying at the rear of the house is overlooked by the porch which, in most Georgian manor houses, characterized the rear, or more private entrance. The ground slopes slightly from the house, and while the garden is not a large one, it is laid out in fine proportions, and with taste. There are three terraces, and with such a setting one can imagine the beauty of masses of lilac bushes on either side of the terraces; the most beloved flower of spring. In many colonial dooryards, it was the only shrub, known both to lettered and unlettered folk as Laylock and spelt Laylock.

In the original Oak Hill gardens were, no doubt, scores of old-time favorites—flower-de-luce, peonies, daffodils, merry phlox, and as a background, the green of massive oaks, which revealed President Monroe's love of trees.

Although the Oak Hill garden does not now bear comparison for elaborateness with other gardens in historic Loudoun and Fauquier, it has been the care of various flower-loving women from time to time. With its changes in ownership the garden has never lost its distinction.

During many years of her occupancy of Oak Hill, it was the pleasure of Mrs. Henry Fairfax to see that the garden preserved its beauty, and she welcomed into it with gracious hospitality many discriminating guests.

Describing the garden Mrs. Fairfax says, "The Oak Hill garden is very simple but sweet and satisfactory with a profusion of bloom from early flowering bulbs and shrubs to the cosmos and chrysanthemum of late autumn. It slopes to the south and the west and comprises about one acre enclosed on three sides by a privet hedge. The fourth or north side is bound by a wire fence almost covered and concealed by rose vines. This gives the appearance of a continuation of the garden as a part of the lawn.

"The entrance gate is in the center of the garden and has a rose-covered arch above it with box bushes on each side. At this gate one looks through three rose-covered arches—one on each terrace—down a turfed path to a white marble sundial beyond which range the lovely Bull Run hills or mountains. Within the gate, one finds on either side a border of roses along the fence. A three-foot path runs with the first terrace east and west for one hundred feet. Below this are two more terraces about thirty feet wide which extends east and west. That on the east is flanked by a long terrace running north and south for perhaps two hundred feet and gradually dwindling away into the natural slope at the south end. This natural slope gives the appearance of a sunken garden. The east and west terraces are divided into beds and borders by grass walks and are planted with shrubs, roses, perennials, and many varieties of the best flowers for cutting. At one time the rest of the garden was given over to small fruits, grapes and vegetables."

Monroe retired from the Presidency in 1825, and the remaining years of his life were divided between Oak Hill and the residence of his daughter, Mrs. Gouverneur, of New York.

After his strenuous life as an officer in the Revolutionary Army, member of Congress, member of United States Senate, twice President of the United States, and three times ambassador to foreign courts, one loves to think of Monroe's joy in his home, surrounded by friends and loved ones. Among the latter was the Marquis de LaFayette, who came to this country as his guest, and with whom the closest bonds of friendship existed. They had shared the dangers and privations of the Revolutionary Army. It is said that Monroe, while Minister to France, effected the release of Madame de LaFayette, when the latter was confined in the prison of LaForce, hourly expecting to be executed.

In the house are exquisite marble mantels, presented by LaFayette, and many pieces of handsome furniture.

The beloved wife of James Monroe died at Oak Hill in 1830 and was buried on the lawn, under the majestic oaks, as was also his daughter, Mrs. Gouverneur. After his death, the bodies of the wife and daughter were removed to Richmond, Virginia, by the Legislature, and rest in Hollywood Cemetery on each side of the illustrious husband and father.

Samuel L. Gouverneur, Jr., grandson of the latter, was greatly distressed when Oak Hill was about to pass from his family in 1852. He had spent many happy hours there and a few days before the place was sold wrote a Farewell to the place.

"The autumn rains are falling fast,
Earth, the heavens are overcast;
The rushing winds mournful sigh,
Whispering, alas! good-bye;
To each fond remembrance farewell and forever,
Oak Hill I depart to return to thee never!

"The mighty oaks beneath whose shade
In boyhood's happier hours I've played,
Bend to the mountain blast's—wild sweep,
Scattering spray they seem—to weep;
To each moss-grown tree farewell and forever,
Oak Hill I depart to return to thee never!

"Oh, home of my boyhood, why must I depart?
Tears I am shedding and wild throbs my heart;
Home of my manhood, oh! would I had died
And lain me to rest by my dead mother's side,
Ere my tongue could have uttered farewell and forever,
Oak Hill I depart to return to thee never!"

In after years Mr. Gouverneur could never be induced to visit the place.

One could dream dreams of lovely women and brave men who walked under the lilac bushes. Fascinating Dolly Madison, with the stately LaFayette, Thomas Jefferson and lovely Mrs. Monroe, Martha Jefferson and the distinguished owner. The ladies' hair piled high in puffs, ornamented with tall tortoise-shell combs, the sleeves bouffant with cushion of feathers, pointed waists, and flowered skirts.

One can imagine them pause by the sundial inscribed:

"Time is too Slow for those who Wait,
Too Swift for those who Fear,
Too Long for those who Grieve,
Too Short for those who Rejoice,
But for those who Love
Time is Eternity."

MARIA POWELL THOMAS.

Driveway Planned by President Monroe at Oak Hill

The Portico at Oak Hill

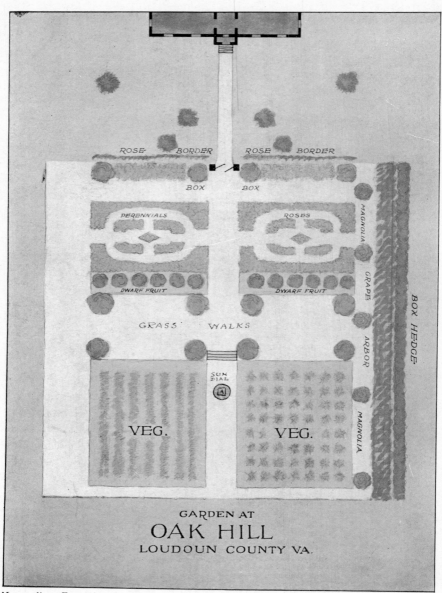

GARDEN AT
OAK HILL
LOUDOUN COUNTY VA.

OATLANDS*

IT is about forty miles from Washington and a little off the beaten track, perhaps, but it is well worth a visit because the house and garden are not only old, as age goes in America, but beautiful besides. That part of the country where it is situated is sometimes called Piedmont Virginia—"the foot of the mountain"—with the Blue Ridge some twenty miles away, and the upper Potomac River not far off to the east. The place itself is known as "Oatlands House."

The house and garden at Oatlands were built almost one hundred and twenty years ago by George Carter, fourth son of Robert Carter, of Nomini Hall. Robert Carter, known to the Virginia of Revolutionary and post-Revolutionary days as Councillor Carter, was a man of great distinction, whose family life is described in terms of no unusual interest by his children's tutor, the author of Fithians Diary.

But the earliest Carter to stamp his mark on Colonial Virginia was Councillor Carter's grandfather, another Robert, whose vast acres, derived from crown grants, gained him the patronymic of "King Carter"—in all the colony, one of the foremost land-owners and influences of those days.

King Carter lived at Corotoman, and his eldest son succeeded him there, but his grandson built Nomini Hall, and his great-grandson left Tidewater Virginia, to settle in what was, then, the backwoods, the frontier almost, of the Old Dominion. One of thirteen children, he was given three thousand acres by his father, north and south of Goose Creek, and some six miles south of the little town of Leesburg, in Loudoun County. There, still imbued with the Eng-

---

*In 1902 Oatlands became the property of Mr. and Mrs. William Corcoran Eustis, under whose appreciative guidance it has been restored and beautified.

lish traditions which governed in the more civilized portions of the State, he built a Georgian house and a walled-in terraced garden. The garden recalls the English formal garden, which derived some of its inspiration from Italian models—yet its atmosphere is typically Virginian.

George Carter started the building of the house in 1800, from bricks made on the place by his slaves, and was, in large measure, his own architect. He ordered the Corinthian columns from New York, however, giving minute directions as to their size and carving; and, old books on architecture, in the possession of his family, and his letters, besides, show that he devoted much time to the planning of the house and the right proportion of doors, windows, cornices, etc. It would be interesting, if one could but look backward with clear enough vision, to see the house rising from its foundations, black labour under white overseers, piling brick upon brick, to the accompaniment, doubtless, of old plantation songs. Then the arrival, after long, devious journeys, on boat and over single track, corduroy, or deep mud roads, through the forest wilderness, of those white columns from the North.

How self-sufficing they were, the country land-owners and planters of those days, turning to account all the resources at hand, living on what the land could furnish, and converting it into bread, meat, clothing, building and hard cash! The Virginians, however, did more than this, they derived an aesthetic enjoyment from the development of things beautiful about them, and so George Carter, when he had finished his house, turned to the building of his enchanting garden.

No papers remain to show where he got his ideas, nor how he put them into execution. Suffice it to say, that this garden was his hobby, that he cut oak trees, on the hillside to the east of the house, to build it; brought the soil from the meadow-lands near the creek, to make easy the growing of the things he wished to plant, and walled it in with home-made brick. No other gardens were being built in Loudoun County at that time, perhaps very little interest was taken in gardening, but, the proverbial Virginian hospitality must have brought many visitors to admire beauty which the owner of Oatlands was creating, not by the aid of landscape gardeners, but from his own good taste modified by the study of English patterns. He planted box—the American tree-box—seeing, with the eye of a prophet, the time when those dark branches should meet over a descending path, forming an archway of rare beauty. He planted it, also, by the side of a steep staircase opposite brick buildings used as tool and lumber-rooms, now long since crumbled into soil and, surrounding the vault where he was to be laid. But he did not neglect the English hedge-box, either; and his grandchildren tell of places where the box edging set off, to their best advantage, roses and other vari-colored flowers. These low hedges have gone—remaining only as memories—with most of the shrubs and the old-time blossoms. But enough stays, as a background and a setting to all the beauty which modern taste and knowledge have brought to it.

The Oatlands garden, especially in May or June, when the spiraea and flags are in full bloom, when colour runs riot everywhere, has that indefinable flavour of the past wrapt around it which marks it as a thing separate from the garden of today or even of yesterday. For people walked in its alleys and paths, by the shade of its walls, made love under the shadow of its trees, when America was very young, when President Monroe was building his country home, some three miles away, beyond the creek; before the years of strife and war, and when tragic memories still hung low over the Virginia hills. Federal troops passed through the grounds, cavalry trampled over lawns and flower beds, and in the house, the daughter-in-law of the builder of Oatlands guarded a secret hiding place for Confederate scouts when hard pressed by Northern raiders.

So that those walls and terraces have known of gay days and sad; of romance and grief; and if spirits revisit their old haunts on earth, many may flit about on moonlight nights, along the bowling green, or by the vault, or in the wistaria arbour, near the south gate. It is this atmosphere that gives the garden its charm, and makes it speak a different language from that of the most beautiful gardens of this age.

When the present owners bought it—not from the Carters— but from one who had not sensed its beauties, the Oatlands garden was falling into ruins; bricks were crumbling, weeds crowding the flowers and yet the very moss-grown paths seemed to say, "We are still what we were." It was a thankful task to restore the old beauty, although the thoughts and conceptions were new, but they fitted it, and every stone vase or bench, every box-hedge planted, seemed to fall into its rightful place and become a part of the whole. Certain improvements were made—improvements the old designer and builder would have approved; fruit trees, hiding huge box and yew, were cut down, and a rosary laid out as a counterpart to the box-grove. It was not always easy to get the right effect.

More than one-half of the garden can be seen from several vantage points: from the upper balustrade, looking down; from the oak grove, looking up, and from each separate terrace. The things to be striven for—mystery, variety, the unexpected—were difficult of attainment; but in certain places they have been attained. The tall north wall, with brick coping and its small beds above descending stone walls—just the same as in Carter days; a shady, almost neglected spot, where the grass grows too tall sometimes, is a thing apart from the rest. Then the rose garden with its background of tall box and pine, in an enclosure of dark-green fencing, cedar posts and chains, overhung with Dorothy Perkins roses, cannot be seen until you turn a corner and are on it unawares. And the bowling green, a long stretch of greensward, bordered by euonymus, flowering shrubs and Oriental Biota, is nearly always shaded, giving that sense of stillness and remoteness which a hidden mass of green so often suggests. At one end of it, the tall north wall shields it from blustering winds; at the other a sunny, white-pillared tea-house overlooks a grove of great oaks which, more

Oatlands

The Garden Stairway at Oatlands

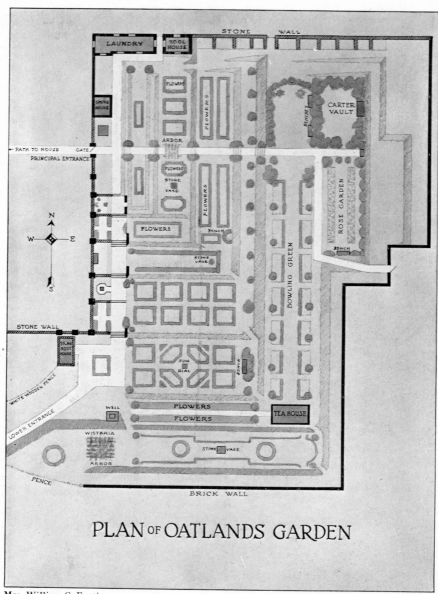

PLAN OF OATLANDS GARDEN

Mrs. William C. Eustis

Montpelier, the Home of President Madison

than house or garden, is the living glory of Oatlands. The rest of the garden—the staircase, box-hedges and brick pilasters to one side, with a great ivy-clad wall to the other, a larch tree crowning the whole; and, looking down and southward, an old pink Venetian well head, protecting a deep, cool well. Then the terraces, bearing some vases, a sundial, many low box-hedges, and innumerable flowers—they finish the tale. But the brick walls and, in one place, a slender white fence, shut it all in and give it that sense of separateness, of a certain aloofness almost, befitting the guardian of treasures, the storehouse of old secrets.

The Oatlands garden should be visited in the springtime first, I believe, so as to see the peonies and iris, after the tulips have faded. Later, the hot summer sun robs it of some of its charm; but the late afternoon hours, before or after twilight, call you imperatively to wander over the grass walks when the heliotrope and mignonette smell strongest, and the mocking-birds and catbirds speak to each other incessantly. Or, again, there are the lovely autumn days, days of cosmos and chrysanthemum, and in November or December, when the barberry berries give the only bit of colour to the beds, although the red-birds flash their scarlet notes through the upper foliage, it is always quiet and sheltered under the lea of the walls, even when the most biting northwest wind is blowing. But, take it all in all, the best of the year is generally June, because the roses are in bloom then on every wall, and the colours of the other flowers—larkspurs, pinks, lilies, with humming-birds among them—vie with each other against backgrounds of stone or brick, ivy or box.

There are winter scenes, too, worth remembering; mornings after a sleet storm, with the sun reflected on every leaf and twig, every blade of grass, and the stillness so intense that it seems to speak, and to bid one pause. One feels, then, as if the world must be pausing, too, for a moment in its mad rush. At all events, some fragments of an indefinable peace seem to have been caught within its walls, by this old garden. EDITH EUSTIS.

MONTPELIER

ONTPELIER, in Orange County, Virginia—such a lovely spot! and one filled with memories of those picturesque early days when James Madison, our fourth President, sought rest and relaxation from his strenuous public life. There, with his charming and gifted wife, he dispensed such hospitality as nowadays seems scarce believable.

Montpellier (for then it was always spelled with two l's) is charmingly situated, overlooking a broad sweep of lawn—with fertile fields stretching away to the Blue Ridge Mountains in the distance. Although most of the famous country seats in Virginia were in Tidewater, some of the Colonists felt the call of the hills— or was it the greater fertility of the soil that lured them on? Be that as it may, John Madison, the first of the name in Virginia, obtained land in 1653 in Gloucester County, near York River; but his grandson, Ambrose Madison, in 1723, along with Thomas Chew, patented four thousand six hundred and seventy-five acres of land in what was then Spotsylvania, but, in 1732, became Orange County.

A large part of the Chew-Madison patent was inherited by the son of Ambrose, James, who, by purchase at different times, acquired the whole tract which has come down in history as Montpelier. Here, in 1756, on a commanding site, James Madison built for his home a plain rectangular brick edifice of four rooms. This was enlarged at different times and the most important improvements were made by his son, President James Madison, in 1809. In this he was aided by his friend, Doctor Thornton, the architect for the Capitol in Washington. Latrobe also lent assistance in adding the wings.

But when Montpelier, the home of the Madisons, is mentioned

it is not so much of the distinguished stateman that we think, as of his lovable lady—Dolly Madison. Time has not dimmed her charm. Washington Irving speaks of her "plump beauty" in contrast to her husband's delicate and feeble figure and wizened face. Even in his prime, Madison was as Henry Adams says, "a small man, quiet, somewhat precise in manner, pleasant, fond of conversation, with a certain mixture of ease and dignity in his address." But Dolly was sprightly and lovable, with gifts of mind and character and a vivid personality that has made her name beloved through all these many years. Strange, is it not, that such a beautiful butterfly should have burst forth *en seconde noce* from the drab chrysalis of Quakerism? That Dorothea Payne Todd, of Philadelphia, should have become the first lady of the land and the most brilliant mistress that has ever held sway in the White House? True, she was originally from Virginia, and that accounts for many wonders.

Indeed, Montpelier was a suitable setting for the far-famed Virginia hospitality that was so freely dispensed by its genial master and his gracious lady.

In a letter of Mrs. Madison, in 1820, she says, "Yesterday we had ninety persons to dine with us at one table fixed on the lawn under a large arbor. The dinner was profuse and handsome and the company very orderly. Many of your acquaintances were here, among others, the two Barbours. We had no ladies except Mother Madison, Mrs. Mason, and Nellie Willis. The day was cool and pleasant. Half a dozen only stayed all night and are now about to depart. President Monroe's letter this morning announces the French Minister. We expect him this evening or perhaps sooner, though he may not come until tomorrow; but I am less worried here with a hundred visitors than with twenty-five in Washington." Great indeed was the social talent of this charming chatelaine. In the words of one of her contemporaries, "She never forgot a name she had once heard, or a face she had once seen, nor the personal circumstances connected with every individual of her acquaintance.

[251]

Her quick recognition of persons, her recurrence to their peculiar interests produced the gratifying impression in each and all of those who conversed with her that they were especial objects of regard." What charm! What tact!

President Madison must have equaled, if not excelled, his good wife in tact, for did he not have two separate establishments under the same roof; with everything that might rupture the harmony of the household—separate and apart? One side of the house was occupied by Mrs. James Madison, Senior; and there, attended by her old family servants, constantly visited by her children and grandchildren, the venerable dame preserved the customs and habits of an earlier generation. In the basement were two kitchens, one for "Mother Madison," the other for Madame Dolly. There were separate living apartments, and separate stairs led to the bed chambers. Indeed, our President Madison solved the problem that has caused so much havoc in otherwise happy homes.

The central part of the old house and the arrangement of the two stairways are just as they were in the "good old days." Nor has the library been changed, where the ex-president received when so feeble that he had to recline on a couch, which caused him to remark merrily, "Strange as it may appear, I always talk better when I lie." But the wings of the house have been rebuilt and broadened, so that the house now is many times larger than it was originally. The Tuscan portico, flanked by huge box-trees, the old cream stucco and the general spacious atmosphere of hospitality is there just as it has been for these hundred and more years.

We must go through the house, across the beautiful turf with peacocks strutting under century-old trees; under a cedar of Lebanon (which President Madison planted himself) to the brick-walled garden with lovely wrought iron gates, which give an added feeling of seclusion to the peaceful spot. Here one enters under a tunnel of box-trees; at the end of this the garden itself is spread out in all its glory. Certainly one feels the French influence, and rightly, I believe, for in 1824 when the Marquis of LaFayette

Hildreth Dunn Scott

The Garden at Montpelier

Woodberry Forest, Built by General William Madison

visited ex-President Madison, one of his suite laid out the garden to please the charming Madame Dolly. Tradition has it that this gentleman was Major L'Enfant, but this is extremely doubtful. The young Frenchman took as his plan the hall of the House of Representatives in Washington, and this amphitheater design affords wonderful opportunities for terraces and steps. When emerging from the shadow of the overhanging box-trees, the vivid panorama of the garden is one never to be forgotten.

For many years a French gardener (at the then fabulous price of $400 a year) tended the elaborate parterres and clipped the hedges and made wonderful topiary designs in the box-bushes. But, alas, the lavish hospitality, the dissipations of the graceless stepson, and the too great generosity of Mr. and Mrs. Madison caused considerable financial stress, and the French gardener had to be dismissed and his place filled by one of his black assistants. This was but the beginning of pecuniary embarrassments which harassed the last years of Madison's life.

When, in 1900, Mr. William duPont took over this historical estate, the garden was surrounded by a rail snake fence. The terraces had been ploughed down and were planted in vegetables, and only the wonderful box, extending down the center of the garden, remained; the latter so straggly and overgrown that one could hardly walk down the path. Mrs. duPont had the terraces graded and turfed, the flower beds laid out and planted. She had the paths made of gravel with tiled edging. Under her direction steps were built and garden ornaments added, but it has taken years of patience and toil to bring the garden back to its present state of perfection.

I like to pass swiftly over the years of neglect and think of the garden in all its old-time glory—as it is now in June with roses everywhere. Ramblers drooping over the walls, tree-roses standing about in prim precision in gay beds of larkspur and lady slippers and brilliant phlox and the white marguerite, without which no French garden is complete.

Then there are rose-beds—nothing but roses—on either side of the box tunnel at the upper end of the garden. In the center of each group of beds is a carved Italian column, and, too, there are eight large marble vases sentineling the upper tier of terraces and adding dignity to the whole. One goes down into the garden between walls of box and with parterres of flowers circling around on either side; past a sun-dial, on one of the landings; until, at the very end, the speaker's desk is represented by a lovely marble stand filled with gay, growing flowers.

The unusual layout of the Montpelier garden, the evergreens, the garden ornaments, and the beauty of the surrounding hills make it a place to rejoice in at all seasons and at all hours. With the snow everywhere, it is indeed as lovely as when the blossoms are most luxuriant.

HILDRETH DUNN SCOTT.

WOODBERRY FOREST

HE estate of Woodberry Forest, the home of General William Madison, brother of the President, is situated along the Rapidan River, at the lower end of Madison County. The exact date of the erection of the dwelling is uncertain, but it is known to have been in existence in 1785, prior to the separation of what is now Madison from Culpeper County, in 1792. The house is one of the many homes the planning of which is authentically attributed to Jefferson. The plan of the building, drawn by Jefferson, is still in existence. But the accepted family tradition was to the effect that while Jefferson made the sketch for the plans, three Presidents had a hand in the designing—Jefferson, Madison, and Monroe. It was built for General Madison on the occasion of his marriage, and remained in the possession of his family till the close of the War Between the States. For several generations Woodberry Forest was the center of the social life of the community, drawing to its hospitable doors many whose names were familiar in the early traditions of Virginia.

During the War Between the States it was occupied at times by the Confederate, and again by the Union Armies, and was the scene of lively skirmishing, as the various fords on the Rapidan River, lying just below the house, were strongly defended by the Southern forces. This was especially true during the winter of 1863-1864, when Lee's Army was encamped between Orange and the Wilderness, and the Northern troops were making every effort to reach Richmond.

The house and place suffered, as needs must, from their continued occupation by military forces; outbuildings were destroyed, shots penetrated even into the house; the furniture was broken and much carried away, while the garden was completely torn up and laid waste. Evidences of war's devastation are still visible—bullet holes in a mantelpiece and in some of the heavy timbered doors— the remains of the old brick walks leading to the outside kitchen, which was totally destroyed, and pieces of mutilated furniture. A fine old Sheraton sideboard was found, after the estate was sold, lying out under some trees, with its drawers, which had been used as horse troughs, lost or broken.

Woodberry Forest lay idle for some years after this, and it was not till 1870 that it was given to Captain Robert Stringfellow Walker by his father, who had bought it when it was offered for sale at the close of the war.

The house is beautifully situated on a hill, to the right of which the valley stretches out into the foothills of the Blue Ridge Mountains, with the mountains themselves only about fifteen miles distant. On its left, the steep slope is terraced to the Rapidan River, which at this point half encircles the place. The opposite hill, with its wooded sides and, now and then, cleared fields, forms a lovely setting to the southern frontage of the garden.

The site of the old garden was the same occupied by the present one, though the latter has far outgrown the original. The hill, stretching from the residence to the Rapidan River, is completely taken up with the ten-acre vegetable garden, and the slice at the top devoted to flowers. The old flower garden was a simple one, typical of so many Virginia country homes—several long borders, as they were called, stretching the whole width of the garden enclosure, and lying at the top of the slope which extends to the river. It is entered by a wicket gate, and half way between that and the vegetables was the sun-dial, the beloved object of the children, whose never-failing source of delight was that Grandfather's Clock and the sun-dial both told the same kind of time! A group of old purple lilacs, cut down during the war, bordered the walk, and the beds of roses were noted through the community—Harrison's Yellow, Cabbage, Lorraine, Damask, Musk,

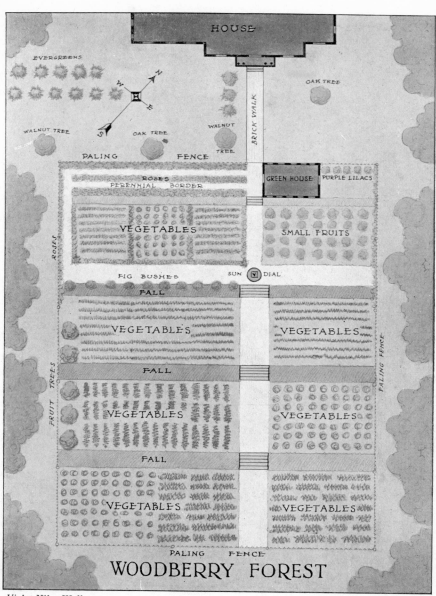

WOODBERRY FOREST

Violet Niles Walker

The Garden at Woodberry Forest

and Chinquapin roses gave an individual charm remembered even today by those whose childhood was passed in the old house.

The devastation of the war period, with the succeeding years of neglect, had done much to destroy the substance of the garden, but when the present owners took possession in 1870, there were still traces of the old planting, and a few surviving perennials gave the main details of the former garden. The vegetable squares lay in terraces below the flower borders; fruit trees, fig bushes, and some flowers, were planted about their edges. Shrubs, lilacs, trumpet creepers, grapevines, honeysuckles, yuccas, and narcissi, whose age is unknown to persons living, still live and flourish, though they have been divided and moved to make place for the changing of the flower borders and the development of the present terraced vegetable garden.

The chief beauty and pride of the whole place are the dozen or more trees surrounding the house—oaks, gums, and hickories—all relics of the primeval forest. The oaks are estimated at between four and five hundred years in age, and some have a spread of one hundred and fifty-nine feet; their limbs hang high about the long, low one-storied house, with its quaint roof, nestled below the great branches. So tall are the trees, that the fine lawn of old bluegrass flourishes like a green carpet, and the whole setting presents a picture, glowing in color, and restful in its quiet, simple charm. It has been said that the designers of the house were better Presidents than architects—it may be so—but surely their sense of fitness and beauty was keenly developed when they chose the site for William Madison's home, and placed the type of house it demanded within such fitting environment.

VIOLET NILES WALKER.

BARBOURSVILLE

ARBOURSVILLE, in Orange County, once held the honor of being the loveliest home in the foot-hills of Virginia. It was built by Governor James Barbour, about 1815, and was much like Frascati, the home of his brother, Philip Pendleton Barbour. Both of these houses were designed by Thomas Jefferson, who was generous with his talents in building houses while building a great republic, and left a conspicuous monument to himself in the home of his friend, James Barbour. There were the characteristic red-brick and white Doric columns, but never have they been assembled with more beauty nor in more dignified proportion.

To the mistress of Barboursville we give all the credit for the garden, although its surrounding serpentine wall, like that at the University of Virginia, suggests again the helping hand of Mr. Jefferson. There must have been hundreds—perhaps thousands—of box plants set out at that time, for today you may see a veritable forest of box trees both inside and outside the garden. Double avenues of box lead off to where the stables used to be, and the front lawn is entirely surrounded, except for an open vista just in front of the house through which the eye is lured to the long, green field and the meadow beyond. Here was the location of the "Riding Greens"; and one can, in imagination, complete the picture with red-coated riders on prancing horses following the hounds into the distance.

The original garden covered nearly three acres, and was entirely surrounded by the serpentine wall of red brick. Old records show that these bricks were brought in ox-carts from Fredericksburg. Truly we have not inherited the patience of our ancestors, for we try to build a garden in a day.

Barboursville—From an Old Painting

Frascati, Home of Judge Philip Pendleton Barbour, in Orange County

The design of this old garden is in formal squares, which are separated from each other by wide grass-covered walks. Each square is deeply bordered with flowers and the inside filled with small vegetables. A bold stream, along whose banks were naturalized daffodils, narcissi, and forget-me-nots, runs through the garden; and, at intervals, this was spanned by three rustic bridges.

In the borders were all kinds of old-fashioned flowers of that day, and its many varieties of peonies were known far and wide. The serpentine wall was covered with English ivy, and in its curves were violets and lilies of the valley. There was a huge cherry tree in the center of the garden from which radiated the rose arbors. There were avenues of lilac and other shrubs, with blossom or decorative berry for each month of the year, as well as sunny corners of sweet herbs, as essential to the excellence of old gardens as old cooks.

With Thomas Jefferson, James Madison, and other distinguished neighbors, the garden at Barboursville was not infrequently the scene of merriment; nor did they need the local moonshine to give snap and sparkle to these occasions, for the cellars near by were amply stocked with imported liquors, and mint flourished in every nook and cranny, so no guest ever left Barboursville without at least one sip of the favorite beverage of old Virginians.

One of the distinctive features of the house is the wide grass ramp leading up to the high front porch. The house was burned on Christmas Day, 1884. The interior is gone, but the vine-clad walls and tall white columns, draped in volunteer grape and ampelopsis, are still standing in their picturesque ruins.

A large walnut tree has grown up through the house and has sympathetically spread its branches in place of a roof. A long, low wing at the right of the house is all that is left of the grand old mansion; but this serves as a charming retreat for a descendant, Governor Barbour's granddaughter, who lives there in the shadow of past glory and who cordially extends the old-time welcome.

CAROLINE COLEMAN DUKE.

HORSESHOE

THE county of Culpeper, which was carved out of Orange in 1748, found its way first into the pages of history through its gallant Revolutionary soldiers of whom John Randolph said, "They were raised in a minute, armed in a minute, marched in a minute, fought in a minute and vanquished in a minute." Upon their picturesque green hunting shirts the motto, "Liberty or Death" was so conspicuous that a would-be recruit begged that it be modified to "Liberty or be Crippled."

Since the time of these brave Minute Men, Culpeper has held its place in the annals of the country through the bravery of its people and the beauty and charm of its homes, some of which antedate the Republic. Among the latter, the lands granted by the English Crown to Governor Alexander Spotswood naturally come first.

In William Byrd's "Progress to the Mines," after a description of the Spotswood family and Germanna, he wrote under date of September, 1732, "In the afternoon we walkt in a Meadow by the River side, which winds in the form of a Horseshoe about Germanna, making it a peninsula, containing about 400 acres." As the present estate of Horseshoe contains approximately that number of acres it would seem that this very property was part of the estate of the colonial governor.

History tells us that John, the son of Alexander Spotswood, lost by debt, his inheritance of four hundred and sixty acres, "known as the Horseshoe tract," and that on April 15, 1767, the place was purchased by James Pollard. Still later it became the property of the Reverend John Thompson, who married the widow of Governor Spotswood.

John Thompson was a conspicuous figure in Virginia church

Horseshoe, Culpeper County

REARRANGEMENT OF
PERENNIAL GARDEN
HORSE SHOE FARM
ESTATE OF
R.M.BRADY ESQ.
RAPIDAN, VA.

Charles F. Gillett

history and though in wooing the Lady Spotswood he met vigorous opposition from her children, the following bit of a letter proves that his cause was plead well:

"Madam: By diligently perusing your letter, I see that there is a material argument, which I ought to have answered, upon which your strongest objections to completing my happiness seems to depend, viz.: That you would incur ye censures of ye world for marrying a person of my station; by which I understand that you think it a diminution of your honour and ye dignity of your family to marry a person in the state of a clergyman. Now, if I can make it appear that the ministerial office is an employment in its nature ye most honourable, and in its effects ye most beneficial to mankind, I hope your objections will immediately vanish, you will keep me no longer in suspense and misery, but consummate my happiness."

That the gentleman of the cloth won his suit, history well knows and though he was the master of Horseshoe but a short while, his name and that of his Lady will always add lustre to the old place. From the Thompsons the estate went to William Morton from whom it passed to Charles P. Moncure, who, in 1859, built the splendid house that is much admired today.

Overlooking a bend of the Rapidan River, the form of which gave the estate its name, the white columned house stands upon a slight rise of ground. An avenue of over-arching trees leads up to it from the high road, and immediately around it, on all sides of the lawn, venerable shade trees spread their branches.

A wide porch upheld by lofty columns, proves the southern front of the house, the walls of which are of brick washed with buff cement. The interior presents an effect of spaciousness. A wide entrance hall opens into a stair hall which runs at right angles across it and separates the two rear from the two front rooms. Where these halls join are pilasters which seem to permit the use of a paneled wainscot around the walls. To the right of the entrance door is the office; to the left, the morning room. Passing through the stair hall one finds a graceful spiral stairway which ascends upon the right to the upper floor.

The house possesses at least one unique—and strictly Southern—feature. Upon the second floor, each room has large slat doors used both for ventilation and as screens. It is significant of both the material and design of this dwelling that it has never been remodeled. Modern luxuries have been permitted to keep pace with the times, and certain innovations have been allowed. Up to the present, however, none of its owners has been willing to sacrifice one line of the original structure for a more modern idea.

In olden days, the inconspicuous service door at one end of the hall gave access to the out-door kitchen. It must not be forgotten that in colonial as well as ante-bellum times, the great families lived in the manner of their English ancestors. Their houses were not planned to permit the quick passage of food from kitchen to dining-room. Today, a modern kitchen stands as an addition at Horseshoe, though the old one still remains as an interesting and historic landmark.

A quaint little side entrance opens out of the stair hall on one side of the house, and it is through this that the visitor is led to make a tour of the garden which lies in the rear. Here, after leaving many roses, one sees long, prim borders stretching, perhaps a hundred feet, to reach a stone bench nestling among white and purple lilacs. Again, we are reminded of William Byrd, for we wonder if the present bench stands in the self-same spot as that where, this Genial Seigneur tells us, "Miss Thecky," Lady Spotswood's sister, "sat and bewail'd her virginity."

This garden, a survival, is said to have had its beginning in 1815, and is intersected by wide turfed walks between borders of flowers and shrubbery. Any search for box gardens would not be complete without a visit to Horseshoe, where the garden plan follows the line of the estate and both explain the place name. A grassy pleasaunce, studded at intervals by six-foot trees of sempervirens boxwood, forms its controlling note. While not so tall as much that may be found, this box, thanks to good care and constant clipping, is particularly broad of girth, the polished leaves being as thick upon the inner as on the outer side. And though the garden has been rearranged by the present owners, under the guidance of Charles F. Gillett, its old lines have in no way been destroyed, the new ones only serving to enhance the charm of many years ago.

The latter-day flowers blooming here lend the accent of comparison to their old-fashioned sisters which grow in greater profusion. And the garden calendars the seasons as they come and go. Tall hollyhocks and riotous sweet peas glorify the garden in June, while masses of lily of the valley and violets bloom in a sheltered corner before the May flowers come. All the flowers, every shrub, each tree is planted in accord with the dominate feature of the garden—the stately boxwood lifting its head along the center length.

Screened by a fragile wall of clematis and morning glories, the orchard adjoins the flowers. Near here grow many varieties of small fruits and old-fashioned herbs. Down toward the branch of the river which waters the estate lies a fairy forest where trumpet vine runs riot among the trees; where hawthorn has its day in June and Jack-in-the-pulpit nods his sprightly head among a phalanx of splendid ferns. A tiny hill which slopes into the stream has in its season a carpet of frail wood lilies, while among the birch and maple trees the pink moccasin flower blooms in bold rivalry to its sister orchid.

When the Federal troops marched through Orange and Culpeper when the Civil strife was aflame, Pope's army brought desolation to fair old Horseshoe. Soldiers rifled the barns and stables; they destroyed waving grain fields and burned outbuildings. But it was when they entered the house by battering down doors that they wrought their greatest injury. Maples and the long avenue of other trees beneath which we stroll today were leafless when news was hurriedly brought to Horseshoe that a body of Pope's soldiers was marching towards the place. Silver was

[263]

buried in the earth, papers and other portable valuables were huddled into portmanteaux and the horses and roomy chariot were ordered out for instant flight.

But happily, Horseshoe has known few vicissitudes with the exception of the war-time raid and those occasioned by the ruthless hand of time. It is now in splendid condition, having been restored and beautified by its present owner, Richard Meldrum Brady, Jr., who, in 1912, purchased the place from Colonel Joseph Wilmer.

The old estate seems a link between the present and those far-off days of 1716 when Governor Spotswood led his Horseshoe Knights to drink the King's health upon the mountain top. The neighborhood has greatly changed since it was a Royal Governor's grant. The junketings and progresses between Germanna and Williamsburg belong to an irrevocable past. But the daily routine at Horseshoe still has in it today much that reminds one of the country life once led here by the gentry of colonial days.

EDITH DABNEY TUNIS SALE.

Tree Box Which Dominates the Garden at Horseshoe

Castle Hill, the Home of William Cabell Rives

Tree Box at Castle Hill

Redlands, the Albemarle County Seat of the Carters

CASTLE HILL

IN beautiful Albemarle County, at the foot of Peter's Mountain, the Monarch of the Southwest Range and called by President Madison "The Chimborazo of our Andes," lies one of the famous old estates of Colonial days.

Castle Hill, standing among the lovely Virginia fields which slope gently away in all directions, is one of the best known homes of this historial part of Virginia.

It was here in June, 1781, that Jack Jouett was given food, drink, and a fresh horse when he made his famous ride from Cuckoo tavern in Louisa County to warn the then governor of Virginia, Thomas Jefferson, and the members of the Assembly in session at Charlottesville of their danger from the proximity of the British forces under Lieutenant-Colonel Tarleton. A few days afterward this energetic leader at the head of his notorious raiders, was welcomed by the lady of Castle Hill, who proved such a charming hostess that his stop on the march was prolonged into a social visit.

Amid such diverting environment, the soldier made the never-to-be-forgotten acquaintance of the genuine Virginia mint julep served in a silver tankard whose polished surface was filmed with frost. Green sprays of fragrant mint were fastened in by sparkling particles of crushed ice and luscious ripe red strawberries combined with the flavor of the *eau de vie* to produce that subtle and alluring taste, delighted vision, and entrancing odor which made it easy for the rigorous Briton to temporarily forget the stern demands of war.

He saw—tasted—and was conquered. One julep followed another until, when, some hours later, he finally reached Charlottesville, his quarry had flown. The wood near the dwelling at Castle

[265]

Hill is still called "Tarleton's Wood," for it was here that his men encamped while waiting for their leader.

How long the old garden at Castle Hill has been in existence it would be difficult to say, but probably somewhere between the granting of the land in 1727 and the completion of the present house in 1765. It has no intricate plan, no winding walks. It is simply a great square, bounded on the north side by a high brick wall against which stand fig bushes, and enclosed on the other three sides by a Colonial arrowhead picket-fence. The garden lies in four deep terraces.

At the top stands one of the great box-hedges, for which Castle Hill is famous. The highest terrace, where one enters the garden through an arch in the hedge, and down a flight of old brick steps sunk deep in the bank, is devoted entirely to flowers. There are the old garden shrubs and flowers, some so old that their names are now almost forgotten. The borders are a tangle of lovely color, and the air is filled with a penetrating sweetness that goes to one's head like wine.

Leaving the upper terrace by more old steps, deep set in the terrace side, a broad turf walk leads down to the second and down more steps to the third level, and so to the lowest terrace of all. The great square beds on each side of the walk are bordered by fruit trees, and grass paths lead everywhere around the terraces. Beginning on the second level, a grape arbor stretches over the broad turf walk, and as one passes down from terrace to terrace, one sees the orderly rows of vegetables stretching away on either side, for the Castle Hill garden is not only beautiful and full of old world charm, but it is noted throughout the countryside as the best vegetable garden.

No changes have been made since it was first laid out by Dr. Thomas Walker, of Indian fame. In Colonial days, he was Major and Quartermaster-General of the Colonial forces in Virginia, Member of the House of Burgesses, and the Committee of Safety. In this garden have walked many famous men—Washington, Jefferson, Madison, Monroe, and even LaFayette, who was a visitor at Castle Hill when he was last in America.

From her grandfather, Dr. Thomas Walker, Judith Walker inherited Castle Hill. She later became the wife of William Cabell Rives, United States Senator, and twice Minister to France. Additions were made to the old house during her life, and the present lawn was laid out under her direction. It is interesting to note that the father of Judith Walker, the eldest son of Dr. Thomas Walker, was not only a Colonel and Aide-de-Camp on the Staff of General Washington, but he was a United States Senator as well; so not only was she the daughter of a Senator of the United States, but her husband held also the same high office.

Dr. Thomas Walker, who married Mildred Thornton, a cousin of General Washington, completed at Castle Hill, in 1765, the house which stands today in excellent preservation. It is one of the few homes still standing on the soil of Virginia that is older than the beginning of the War of Independence. This house is still the home of the descendants of its first owner, who do honor to their lineage. For five generations, it has been a seat of hospitality and culture. In the great square hall, the youthful, music-loving Jefferson once played the violin, while the still younger Madison danced. Here the doors have opened to welcome five men who were Presidents of the United States.

The wonderful box-hedges, the tallest of them all now almost fifty feet in height with its broad arches, through which one catches glimpses of the garden and the mountains standing guard beyond, tell the story of the eventful years that have passed since the building of Castle Hill and the planting of its garden.

GERTRUDE RIVES POTTS.

REDLANDS

EDLANDS, belonging to the Misses Polly Coles and Sally Randolph Carter, is situated in Albemarle County on a high hill at the southern end of a range of mountains known as Carter's Mountains; on the northern end of this little range of hills lies Monticello, the home of Thomas Jefferson. It is rather interesting that there are marked similarities between the interior plans of these two houses, a fact to be accounted for by the intimate friendship which connected the original owners and their families.

Redlands, on its high hill, overlooks a fair and smiling country which stretches on one side to the ever beautiful and poetic curves of the Blue Ridge, and spreads on the front to the far extended, rolling, wooded plateau, which for thirty miles or more stretches its length through Albemarle and Fluvanna counties. It overlooks the "Big Woods," home of the partridges and wild turkeys, and, with its far extended sweep and beauty, seems to challenge the imagination of all who see it through the blue, sunlit, misty veil peculiar to these foothills.

The house was built in 1789 by Robert Carter, son of Edward Carter, of Blenheim, the younger brother of Charles Carter, of Shirley, and grandson of Robert Carter, of Corotoman, who was known as "King Carter." Robert Carter inherited the southern portion of his father's large landed estate in Albemarle County, and on his marriage to Miss Mary Eliza Coles (known to her family and friends as Polly), of Enniscorthy, he began the erection of the dwelling. Together they laid out the lawn and garden and the latter still retains the original plan on which it was designed in 1798.

Like many Virginia and English gardens, that at Redlands was a combination of vegetable and flower garden; it was and is laid

The Garden at Redlands

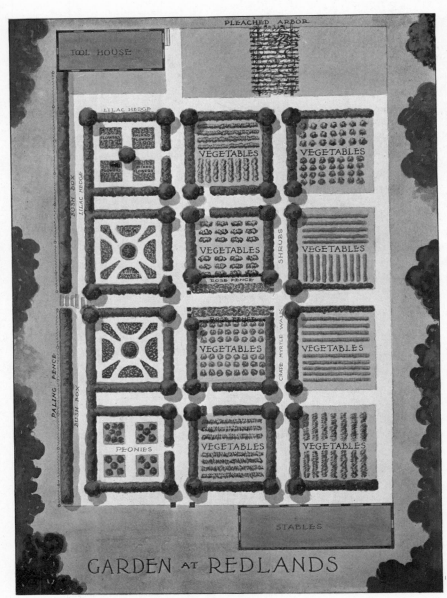

GARDEN AT REDLANDS

Lila L. Williams

off in squares, separated by broad, intersecting grass walks. The upper squares are devoted to flowers and the lower to the vegetables. As was the case in so many of the older Virginia gardens, the flower beds, within the upper squares, were laid off in a pattern that formed an insignia of the Order of Masons—here they outlined a Maltese cross. This arrangement, according to Masonic insignia, indicated that the owner of the estate belonged to that order. An illustration of this may be seen in the garden at Mount Vernon.

The corners of the squares in the Redlands garden were marked by shrubs, many of which are still there, notably the fine old boxwood bushes which guard the entrance and those that separate the vegetable squares from the flowers. These bushes are very unusual examples of the enormous size boxwood of this type can attain, though, of course, they are by no means so tall as the tree-box.

The Redlands garden is screened from view from the lawn by the original lilac hedge, which makes indeed a fragrant wall of blossom in the spring. In olden times this garden must have been an enchanting spot with its upper squares laid out in beds of blooming flowers; its long borders, down either side of the main or central walk, of cowslips, hyacinths, jonquils, white narcissi, butter and eggs, violets, peonies, bleeding hearts, Madonna lilies, chrysanthemums, four o'clocks, Jacob's ladder (I never see Jacob's ladder now), larkspur, Star of Bethlehem, and lilies of the valley, with here and there a lovely daily fragrant damask rose, or red June roses growing low and blooming lavishly, and yellow Harrisonias. There were coral honeysuckle and white jessamine or white roses with hearts of gold, but quaintest of all, the oldest of American garden roses—the queer, little, almost ugly, cinnamon rose.

Under the box-bushes were shy white violets, not to forget blue-eyed periwinkle and the flowering shrubs—mock orange, snowball, syringa, smoke tree, flowering almond and just a little Southern yellow jessamine and the smell and bloom of lilacs everywhere.

[269]

At the bottom and down the sides were broad, grassy walks and spaces where plum and small flowering fruit trees blossomed; here apple trees stretched their long limbs out lazily in the spring air waiting until the great cherry trees, which towered above them, should have shed their snowy bloom. There were birds—birds everywhere.

Underneath these fruit trees, blooming untended among the grass, are yuccas and iris; only they were called in those days bear grass and flags, and the leaves of the yucca, when shredded and knotted together, served as twine for the garden and plantation.

Perhaps the enchantment of the spot lay largely in the eyes of the beholder, because those who knew it and lived with it loved it. In all the hundred and twenty-five years of its life it has always been very dearly loved by some woman, its mistress, who found in it happiness and tranquility of mind, even serenity of speech in watching and tending it as best she might. So, though lacking many things that make other gardens beautiful and desirable, yet Redlands has one requisite, that is a prerequisite of every garden, and is best set forth in the old well-known lines—

> "A garden is a lovesome spot,
> God wot."

SALLY RANDOLPH CARTER.

Morven, Albemarle County

The Garden at Morven

MORVEN

MONG the records of Albemarle County, in the courthouse at Charlottesville, is that of a deed drawn up and signed by Thomas Jefferson in his own handwriting. This paper states that on December 8, 1796, William Champ Carter and his wife, Martha, sold to William Short, of Philadelphia, a certain parcel of land known as Indian Camp, lying on the southeast side of the Southwest Mountains. This land was sold for one thousand five hundred and sixty-seven pounds and nine shillings.

In the deed witnessed by Mr. Jefferson it is interesting to note that there is mention made of the rentals of the tenants going to the buyer of the property.

Again, in February, 1813, William Short, who was an aide on the staff of General Washington, sold the property to David Higginbotham. The name of Morven was probably given to the place when the present brick house was built by Mr. Higginbotham, about 1820. Plans for the latter are said to have been drawn by Thomas Jefferson, who also ordered for it from Paris the mantel of Carrara marble which adorns the drawing-room. Near this house there still may be seen at Morven an old and very attractive cottage, which was probably the only dwelling on the place in 1796.

After the death of David Higginbotham, his widow, as executrix, in 1853, sold the place to Daniel Smith. At this time, all the property pertaining to the estate was disposed of as the heirs were scattered. The servants were sold from the old cottage steps, bringing something over eighty thousand dollars. An old darkey, Uncle Lee Jones by name, who still survives, tells with pride that he brought one thousand eight hundred dollars. He stayed with the Smith family during the devastating years that followed the

[271]

War Between the States, and was always a faithful friend and overseer.

In 1906, Mr. Samuel Marshall bought Morven from the Smith heirs, and since that time the old garden has been renewed. Uncle Lee Jones, to whom reference has been made above, came one morning to see his old home under its new master. He walked into the garden and said, "Praise God, I lives to see Morven bloom again."

The big box-tree, the white violets, and the striped grass by the garden gates, the tall bamboos and the lovely hollyhocks that take possession every year, are the plantings of other hands than the present owners. The old terraces have not all been restored, but there has never been found any drawn plan of the original garden. Some say that the view from the garden is lovelier than anything in it. Ash Lawn, the old Monroe home, lies to the north, on the east are flat woods that give the effect of a sea view, and the "mountain on the place," as a previous owner described it, commands the view on the west.

Monticello, being only three and one-half miles away, tradition says that Thomas Jefferson rode on horseback to trade at the country store which stood at the foot of this mountain and within the confines of the Morven estate.

The present garden has on one side a hedge of box grown from cuttings taken from the big box-tree. Around the driveway, which leads to the entrance to the house, there is a new box hedge which the owner calls her "war hedge." This was bought in February, 1917, from a Belgian salesman who told her that these plants were the last shipment that could be made out of Belgium, as the German submarine ultimatum had gone into effect. Happily, the plants have all survived and flourished, taking courage, no doubt, from the soil which started them.

JOSEPHINE P. MARSHALL.

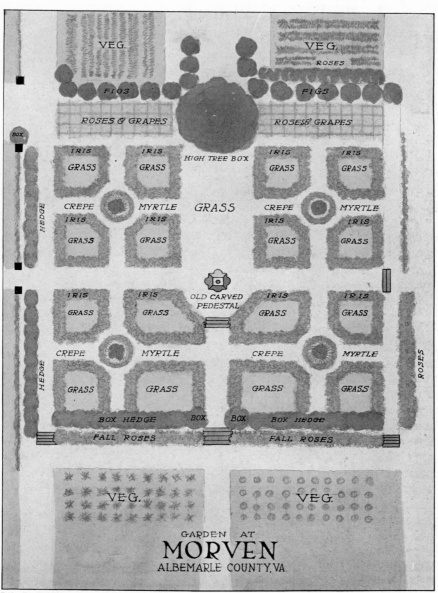

GARDEN AT
MORVEN
ALBEMARLE COUNTY, VA.

Lila L. Williams

Farmington, Albemarle County

FARMINGTON

ARMINGTON, the home of Mrs. Warner Wood, situated three miles west of the University of Virginia, has long been noted as one of the most beautiful places in Virginia. The charm of its hospitality, the beautiful paintings, and other objects of art in the house, and its unsurpassed landscape view are known throughout the United States.

The history of Farmington is quite interesting and reads like a romance. The tract of land on which the house is situated originally consisted of about four thousand four hundred acres, and was first patented and owned by Michael Holland, in 1744. In 1745, Holland sold his patent to Charles Lewis, of Goochland County, and he, in turn, sold the place to Francis Jourdone, in 1758.

In 1760, Jourdone (now spelled Jerdone) began the erection of the present stately dwelling, which commands such a beautiful view of the Blue Ridge Mountains. The massive brick walls range in thickness from two feet on the sides to three feet on the gable end, and show the quality of the material used. Even now, after more than one hundred years, they look as if the builder intended them to stand, as the pyramids, for all time. In 1785, Jerdone sold the estate to George Divers, who is said to have been a great friend of Thomas Jefferson.

Being a man of considerable wealth, and holding Mr. Jefferson in high esteem, Mr. Divers asked the Sage of Monticello to design for him a fine home. Jefferson's design is seen in the octagonal front of the present residence, which was begun in 1803, and which is said to have been inspired by the country house seen by him while abroad. The tradition is that one day Jefferson drove out to Farmington and, finding that his plans were not being carried out as he designed them, he dismissed all the workmen, thus ending for a time the remodeling of the Farmington house. Mr. Divers was away from home at the time. He died soon after his return and the house fell to his heirs in an unfinished state and remained so until 1852.

Upon the death of George Divers, the large estate was divided among his many relatives, and Farmington fell to Isaac White, who held it until 1842. The next owner was John C. Carter, who lived there until 1852, when it became the property of General Bernard Peyton.

Neither White nor Carter ever finished the house, which had been begun by Mr. Divers nearly fifty years before, but General Peyton, who is said to have spent thirty thousand dollars upon it, did much towards its completion. The last addition, however, was made in 1897, after Farmington came into the possession of Warner Wood.

The house had remained unfinished so long that it became a common superstition among the negroes that whoever finished it would die when the task was done. Strange to say, this superstition was fulfilled. The very day the finishing touches were put on, General Peyton, who had done so much to beautify and preserve the estate, though apparently well a few hours before, died that night.

In 1860-61, Joseph Miller, a wealthy and distinguished British marine engineer, came to this country for his health, and bought Farmington from the widow of General Peyton, in February, 1861. Being a man of great cultivation and a lover of art, Mr. Miller brought all of his furniture, silver, china, and many of the paintings from Europe with him; these still adorn the old house and charm the visitor who is fortunate enough to enter its portals. Merely to enumerate them would fill a space larger than is allotted to this little sketch. The house and a large part of the estate was next inherited by Joseph Miller's sister, Mrs. Mary Anne Harper, then a widow with two small children, Warner and Lucilla Woods, by a former marriage.

CONSERVATORY

BOX GARDEN
AT
FARMINGTON

STEPS

SHRUBBERY

GATE

CORRIDOR

ROSES
AND
PERENNIALS

FENCE

Robert Woods

Small Box Garden at Farmington, Showing Corner of the Conservatory

Boxwood in Sweet Briar Garden, Amherst County

The lovely box garden was designed and made by Mrs. Harper. This is located at the southeast side of the house, and one approaches it from the portico or conservatory, or through a little gate opening on the large lawn. This garden is very small and just as unique. In it there are thirteen beds, the majority diamond shaped; each bed is edged with dwarf-box. In all of them roses are planted, but now and then may be seen such old-fashioned perennials as lilies, larkspur, and mignonette. On the lawn are many handsome native trees and beautiful shrubs; some of these are quite familiar to our gardens, but others, from England, are not so common. The double pink hawthorne is a particularly decorative shrub, and this was sent over from England. There is also a walled garden at the southwestern end of the house, which covers one-half acre. Within its boundaries many kinds of fruits adapted to the temperate zone were planted, and against the walls were trained different varieties of delicious figs. Many of the fig bushes still remain and each season bear large crops.

ROBERT WOODS.

BLOOMFIELD

O go to the garden at Bloomfield, you leave the main road five miles west of the University of Virginia, cross the crest of a hill and descend into the chill, damp atmosphere of a little hollow, which always seems to have a cool climate of its own, no matter how hot the day elsewhere. Then the lane, whose red clay banks are hung with honeysuckle vines, leads up a steep incline, and you find yourself at the gates of Bloomfield. The lawn, shaded by elm and gingko trees, slopes from the big brick house on the summit down to the gates, where the road separates, forming a huge circle up to the door.

The garden cannot be seen from the front, although you may go into it through a small gate in the hedge; but the proper entrance, and the one most used, is from the door at the east end of the house. Descending the steps, one first emerges from a mass of box-bushes and spiraea grown to the height of trees. These are probably the oldest plants in the garden, unless the veteran oak, which towers above the tiny masonry of the bird's bath, is more ancient, and next, I am sure, is the gnarled old seckel pear tree in a far corner, still bountifully bearing its reddish-gold fruit in the fall. However, there are a number of shrubs, quantities of figs, and some roses still living which were also residents of the original garden, planned and planted nearly a century ago by Paul Goodloe, a native of Louisiana, who built the house.

When the box-trees are passed, there spreads before one a level plateau, enclosed on three sides by a high hedge, at the foot of which is a wide, well-kept border of flowers. In the center of the plateau stands a summer-house, built of stone by the present owner, with tiled floor, vine-covered, and cool even in the noonday sun.

[276]

Isabel S. Marshall   *The Bloomfield Garden With Blue Ridge Mountains—Mountains in the Distance*

A Garden Walk at Bloomfield

From an Old Print

Bloomfield, Albemarle County

The wide stretches of velvety grass are shaded with fruit and mimosa trees, and interspersed with flower-beds, so long and wide that you wonder how enough flowers to fill them are ever planted. Fortunately, however, very little planting is now necessary, for, in between the crepe myrtles and lilacs, flowering shrubs and roses, the transient flowers sow their own seeds with the assistance of the wind, and come up every spring with no less grace because planted "by an Unseen Hand." They represent, surely, those "flowery beds of ease" spoken of in the old hymn.

If the garden-viewer has spent her youth in the mountains, as I have, and then had to live away from them, she will only vaguely realize the garden at first, because she will have to sit down in the summer-house and not merely look at the mountains, but let the sight of them sink into her soul until she is satisfied. For the view is the great feature which individualizes this garden, and makes it the most beautiful of all others, and the most beloved by me.

In the tropical garden, described in "The Garden of Allah," the beholders looked out over the wall at a marvelous view of the desert, and neither the flowers nor Larbi's flute could lure them away from it. There is no wall to the Bloomfield garden, and the hedge is low on this side; the adjoining country spreads out kindly below in rolling hills and homesteads, the latter only recognizable by position, for that miniature cluster of trees, with the big gable peeping out, is the stately Spring Hill—where my grandmother's grandfather lived when Bloomfield was built.

Above, the Blue Ridge range, extending from one side of the horizon to the other, with its huge ragged outline against the sky, is a sight to leave one breathless. The dim-blue mountains lie in the distance, the slate-colored and soft-greys nearer, while the few in the foreground are a shaggy dark-green; white clouds floating over them make shadows in strange shapes. A winding trail of smoke—but, no! it is all too dreamily delicious to describe! Words only *un*-naturalize a beautiful impression.

Unlike most old places, whose gardens were in their prime

before the War Between the States, the glory of this one lies even more in the present than in the past. Its future was assured when J. Tatnall Lea, a Northern soldier, captured and carried through this Piedmont country as a prisoner, was so impressed by its beauty, that he eventually returned to make his summer home among its hills. Here, some years later, he brought the mistress of Bloomfield, who quickly overcame any sectional hostility by outdoing the Virginians at their own game of impetuous and lavish hospitality, thus proving herself utterly lacking in the ability "to calculate," considered at that time to be the characteristic of all "Northerners."

Here, also, came the youngest daughter, the real garden-builder or restorer, to plant her first flower beds as a little child. Later, as a young girl, she left Philadelphia every spring, coming down for a week in April, armed with varieties of plants and seeds. She then proceeded to plant (with the aid of the gardener and, often, the coachman, the carpenter and any others she could commandeer in the absence of a pretendedly irate, but over-indulgent, father) the flowers which were to make the garden so wonderful later in the season and indeed for all time. So it seems natural that, after it had been the stage-setting for many romances, this beautiful girl later on elected to be married in the garden instead of a church. Remembering that the "God of the Open Air" sets his altars everywhere, surely no more fitting place could have been found for the ceremony, which transplanted the garden-builder permanently to Virginia soil. She is now the owner of Bloomfield, Mrs. Nancy Lea Marshall.

Although, to many people, the Bloomfield garden may look its loveliest in the spring, when the fruit trees and lilacs are in bloom, the first week in September is the favored time for me, and no happiness compares to spending a morning there then. I go out early, when the dew is sparkling over everything and the spiders' webs are made of diamond necklaces, and take a seat in a chair facing the mountains, underneath the oldest mimosa tree.

The flower-beds are brilliant, though their abundance does not give the impression of individual flowers so much as a profusion of color—color that fills the artist in you with delight! Beds of indigo and topaz; masses of orange, shading to cream; beds filled with branching candelabra of red gold. Carpets of pansies, purple and mauve; white clematis above, waving its star-sprinkled sprays with the wind, and thorny vines with vermilion buds tangling behind white lilies; immense hydrangeas, tinted like diatoms; long avenues of pink gladioli stretching away to the west.

On days like these, the hazy mountains look perfectly enormous and give you a strange uplifting-of-the-spirit sensation. An hour later I drag my eyes away from them, for the advance of the morning brings many important occupations. There are my old friends, the fruit trees, that must be visited; to dispute the bees' title to the softest seckel pears, to find the first ripe figs, to waylay "Kritty," the pretty octoroon, as she passes through with a tray of purple grapes—and to eat of these fruits under the mimosa tree. There are three of these mimosas, a large young one, which is the daughter of this older, and a tiny one, surely its grandchild. Every year I plan to adopt the grandchild mimosa and carry it home to Richmond to raise—but it is there still.

Finally, the garden-builder herself comes out to join me, accompanied now like the delightful Elizabeth in her German garden, by three babies, their laughter tinkling through the box-bushes even before they appear. A moment later, perhaps, with dimpled arms outstretched and squeals of excitement, they chase, toddle and tumble after, but never overtake, the bright-hued butterflies, flying in and out among the flowers, while the mother sits down to her knitting by me.

Nothing can surpass the Bloomfield garden now! A few locusts may be singing, "Good-bye, Summer"; a dead leaf falling may remind the rest they will not be here always—but "let their loveliness fade as it will," for this immediate moment it is flawless, no flower fears the frost and every vine "entwines itself verdantly still."

NAN MAURY LIGHTFOOT.

[279]

MONTICELLO

THE home of Thomas Jefferson is situated on a high hill four miles southeast of Charlottesville. It is called Monticello (Little Mountain) and is approached by a winding macadam road which clings to the side of Carter's Mountain, the adjoining peak to Monticello and one of the Southwest range.

The steep drive offers many sources of interest to the lover of nature. The trickling of the mountain streams was music to the traveller in the old days, for soon one came upon a moss-covered rocky basin, or spring, embowered in ferns, which was welcomed as refreshment for man and beast. Native shrubs and trees frame with artistic beauty the vistas of the valley below, where lies the town of Charlottesville; the view extending a mile to the west embraces the classic buildings of the University of Virginia, behind which stretch in undulating lines the Blue Ridge Mountains, one spur of which, the Ragged Mountains, was made famous in the writings of Edgar Allan Poe, one time student of this great seat of learning.

At the crest of the mountain and at the point at which the county road begins to fall to the other side into the eastern valley, there is a gate at one's left which is the outer entrance to Jefferson's estate. A lodge has recently been built there by the present owner.

The drive to the house through the woods is enchanting in early spring, and the luxuriant growth of Scotch broom, with its pendant yellow blossoms, carpets the ground beneath, forming a veritable cloth of gold.

On the right, one passes a sacred spot, the family graveyard. Here lies interred the mortal remains of Thomas Jefferson, his beloved wife, his children and grandchildren.

A monument is inscribed with the epitaph written by Jefferson

Monticello—East Front

Monticello—West Front

Ridgeway, One of the Notable Gardens of Albemarle County

Edge Hill, the Home of Martha Jefferson Randolph

Serpentine Wall at the University of Virginia

himself, "Here lies Thomas Jefferson, author of the Declaration of Independence, of the Statute of Virginia for Religious Freedom and Father of the University of Virginia."

The second gate opens out on the lawn, and here the house comes into full view; on the left of the driveway are the servants' quarters and on the right the garden.

This garden is arranged in a chain of rectangular plots, with grass walks between. Originally, vegetables were planted here in long rows to be easily worked by horse and plow. There was a background of native shrubs and trees through which one caught glimpses of the valley below and the distant strip of the pine belt. Old-fashioned shrubs were scattered throughout the garden near the paths and in the angles. Further on, just before one approaches the overseer's house, there is seen a small graveyard owned by the Levy family, the present owners of the property.

On the left of this driveway was once a greensward running along the side of the quarters, or southern pavilion, and in the spring it was a mass of bulbous flowers familiar to old homes, such as jonquils, single blue Roman hyacinths and Stars of Bethlehem. The blue feathered hyacinth (Muscari comosum monstrosum) found congenial environment here. This was a rare flower in those days, and today is not generally seen here.

With such evidence of remains of a garden, one readily conjectures that on this gentle slope, protected from the north by the servants' quarters and work shops and exposed to the warm rays of the sun from the south, Jefferson must have laid out here an ornamental and terraced garden.

In an old book we read that "The nail factory, the machine shops and weaving room were on the southeast of the house, beyond which was the terraced garden in which he delighted to exhibit his horticultural products."

His granddaughter, Sarah Randolph, in her "Life of Thomas Jefferson," constantly refers to his love of trees and shrubs and of their intimate walks in the garden. One pictures them strolling

[281]

down the path from the house, emerging through an avenue of old-fashioned shrubs into the full sunshine of the formal flower garden.

Just at the point where the visitor alights from carriage or motor may still be seen the old-time shrubs on either side of the path leading to the house. A large clump of lilacs and syringa with modern privet hides the exit of the underground passage to the house. From this it is said that Jefferson escaped on the occasion of Tarleton's raid. Two wonderful copper beeches flank the north and south sides of the house on the western lawn and other handsome trees testify to Jefferson's love of the beautiful in nature. In 1793, in some of his writings, he mentions that "The trees planted nearest the house at Monticello are not yet full grown."

The Arnold Arboretum calls attention to the fact that in the year 1784 Thomas Jefferson, in his "Notes on the State of Virginia," published the first comprehensive list of the plants of Virginia, among which are some of the most beautiful trees and shrubs of the world.

The Marquis de Chastellux, who visited Monticello in his "Travels in North America," speaks of the scores of deer in the park.

Many trees from foreign countries are planted on the eastern and western lawns, and his granddaughter says "much time and expense were devoted by him to improving his house and grounds. While in France and England, Jefferson visited gardens with a view of reproducing them in Virginia, and of importing trees and shrubs from other countries. In a notebook of his is found a description of Blenheim, the home of the Duke of Marlborough. His granddaughter speaks also of a garden book, and says, "This book, in which he began to make entries as early as the year 1776 and which he continued to keep all through life, except when from home, has everything jotted down in it from the date of the earliest peach blossom to the day when his wheat was ready for the sickle."

Thomas Jefferson was known as an intelligent and progressive farmer and was most careful to keep account of the operations of his farm and household. The achievement dearest to his heart was the founding of the University of Virginia. Through a telescope he watched the building operations from a room in the domed roof of Monticello. Scarcely a day passed that he did not visit the site itself, overseeing the building of his own design, which is a monument to his ability, foresight and wisdom.

Much credit is due the present owner, Mr. Jefferson Levy, from the fact that when he inherited this estate from Commodore Levy, who purchased it from Jefferson's heirs, he made no change in house and gardens, but restored Monticello to its original beauty.

JUANITA MASSIE PATTERSON.

MIRADOR

MIRADOR, originally the home of Colonel James M. Bowen, in Albemarle County, is perhaps one of the finest examples of early American architecture to be found in Piedmont Virginia.

The ancestors of Colonel Bowen, who landed on the cold, unfriendly shores of Massachusetts in 1644, seem to have steadily moved southward with each succeeding generation, until in the beginning of the eighteenth century we find them settled in Virginia, where, in 1758, Richard Bowen "Soldier" was granted land for services in "Captain Rutherford's Rangers" in the French and Indian Colonial Wars.

The grandson of this Richard Bowen was the owner and builder of Mirador between the years 1825-30. Here in the beautiful Greenwood Valley near the Great Blue Ridge he placed the homestead in the center of an extensive plantation, from which can be seen the high peaks which tower above the dividing lines of Albemarle, Augusta and Nelson Counties. Mount Humpback, which overlooks five counties, and on which one of the first Weather Bureaus in Virginia was stationed, can be seen in the distance.

Because of the magnificent view and for love of the soft Spanish names, Colonel Bowen called his home "El Mirador," a Spanish derivation from the verb Mira—Look! Behold! El Mirador meaning a place commanding an extensive, a great view; the El has long since been dropped and only Mirador used.

This house, like those of the preceding century, was a square building of brick with two stories and an attic; it had a wide hall and four large rooms on each floor. The four chimneys and the outbuildings used as office, schoolhouse and kitchen, were also of brick. The spacious stairway with its mahogany rail, the fan-shaped lights above the doors, and the fan-shaped wood trim throughout the building added much to the beauty of this stately old

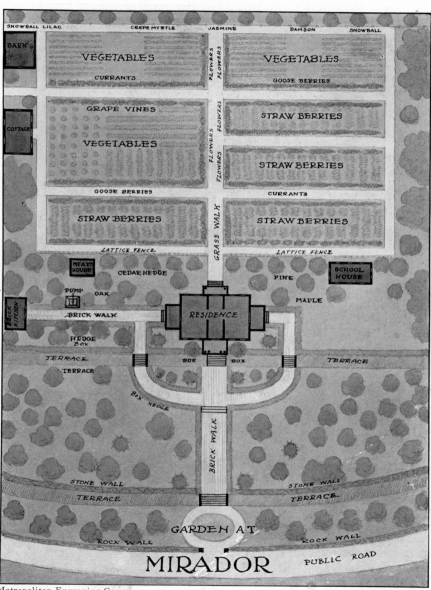

GARDEN AT

MIRADOR

From Collection of
Robert A. Lancaster, Jr.

*The Beautiful Garden at Greenfield, Home of the Reads,
in Charlotte County*

home. The wings were added after 1890 by Mr. C. D. Langhorne, as was also the beautiful rock enclosure and handsome gateway.

Hospitality at Mirador was part of its atmosphere. The Virginia woman from her earliest training knew that she was expected to be a good neighbor and a gracious hostess, however hard and inconvenient it might often be, and from old letters and diaries it would appear that Mirador was continually having what today we would call a house party.

The University of Virginia is only seventeen miles away—just the distance to cover on horseback, reaching Mirador in time for tea or to spend the night, or it might be several nights when there was "special company." At that time, when some of the belles and beaux of that day were guests in this charming home, there would be dancing each evening, and the negro fiddlers would call the figures as the young people would turn their partners and swing corners in the picturesque dances and the popular Sir Roger de Coverly.

Prominent among the guests in the early days at Mirador was Colonel Crozet, the distinguished French engineer in charge of the extension of the Virginia Central Railroad, which at that time only ran to the foot of the Blue Ridge Mountains, but which, under Colonel Crozet, after eight years of hard work, crossed the mountains and opened up the great Valley of Virginia, and the greater West, to modern transportation. During these years (1850-58) the distinguished engineer spent much time at Mirador.

With all its air of stability and gracious dignity the real charm of Mirador lay in its grounds. The lawn, or yard, to use the less pretentious term of that day, was terraced, making a "falling garden." Stone steps led from terrace to terrace, and brick walks, flanked by low-growing box, made a background for the lovely monthly roses—the roses of Provence—that filled these and the two long borders that ran from the hospitable front door to the lower terrace. Under the windows there were lilacs, crepe myrtles, and jasmines, where the robins found their first resting places in the spring and where later on they made their nests. The trees on the terraces are one of the chief beauties of the place. There are splendid oaks, and old hemlocks, yews that came from a far country, maples, holly and mimosa.

The garden proper was behind the house and was enclosed by a white paling fence over which grew jasmines and climbing roses in great profusion, filling the air with their sweetness in the season of bloom.

Like the gardens of that day, there were vegetable squares edged with flowers, broad grass walks hedged by box and old-fashioned perennials of every kind, where jonquils, tulips, violets and hyacinths welcomed the spring, and peonies, roses and sweet-scented lilies held sway later on. There were masses of shrubbery and tall growing box, as well as jasmines and lilacs. Further on were the grape arbors, currant and gooseberry bushes.

It would be hard to say when Mirador was at its loveliest—whether in the June sunshine when the air was filled with the odor of all the blooming things and the shadows on the lawn were cool and beguiling, or in winter, when the first snows had fallen and turned the hemlocks, ivy and yews into a dream garden and the moon shone down on this peaceful valley with the mountains all white in the distance.

The old "Post Road" leading from Richmond and Washington to Staunton wound its way through this mountainous country in front of the Mirador lawn, and many noted travelers have stopped to rest a while at the old "Long House Tavern," just a short distance east of the place, before continuing their journey over the tortuous rocky road which led across the Blue Ridge Mountains and on into the Valley of Virginia.

Mirador, at the death of Colonel Bowen passed to his daughter, Mary, who had married Colonel O. R. Funsten, of Clarke County, and it was held by the Funsten family until 1890, when it was sold to C. D. Langhorne, and is now the home of his granddaughter, Mrs. Ronald Tree.

Bessie Carter Funsten.

Red Hill, the Home of Patrick Henry—Original House on the Left

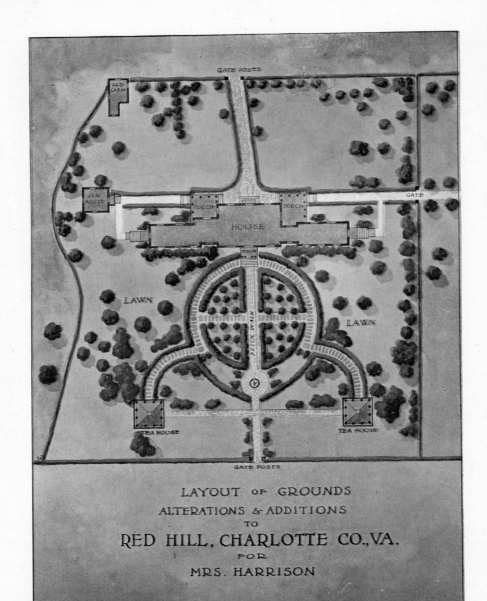

LAYOUT OF GROUNDS
ALTERATIONS & ADDITIONS
TO
RED HILL, CHARLOTTE CO., VA.
FOR
MRS. HARRISON

Charles Barton Keene

RED HILL

SEVERAL places in Virginia can claim the honor of having been at one time the residence of Patrick Henry but it was at Red Hill, in Charlotte County, that he spent the latter years of his life and which is his last resting place.

There are two approaches to Red Hill, one over the highlands, the other through the lowgrounds. The road over the ridge, through the woods, leads to what appears to be the front entrance, as the lawn on the north side is shady and inviting, being rather densely planted with a row of cedars along the fence, groups of spreading osage orange trees, several locusts, and hedges of tree-box. But the red clay road, like a deep gash in the hill from which the place was named, continues to the right and follows the contour of the lawn, outlined by a hedge of Japan quince, as far as the front gate, which faces south.

The grounds are not extensive and vehicles stop outside the gates. The front yard is as open to the sunlight as the rear is shaded and secluded.

Leaving the road, one passes between two stone capped brick posts set in the boxwood hedge which borders the lawn, to uphold a wrought-iron gate. A few feet from this gate stands a sun dial from which extends direct to the house a most remarkable maze of box.

In front of the house, towards the east, in one of the circles formed by the tree-box hedge, is a large, scraggly, old locust tree. There was once another on the west under which it is said Patrick Henry sat, on a summer day, with a can of water from a "cool spring" and a gourd, playing his fiddle and enjoying the view of the valley to the south. A large cedar and a pear tree are the only other trees on the front lawn.

[287]

A beautiful and luxuriant hedge of tree-box, about four feet high, pungent and aromatic in the sun, spreads across the front lawn in an unusual design and walls in the grass walks that lead to the house. An interesting feature about the hedges at Red Hill is that they are of tree-box, clipped and kept short, instead of the dwarf-box generally used for this purpose.

The house, which was frame and painted white, consisted of a two-story dwelling with an east wing. On the front porch every one stopped, involuntarily, to admire the extensive view, the long, gradual slope of the ridge, planted with tobacco and wheat, the wide lowgrounds of waving green corn on the Staunton River, and the dark green wooded hills of Halifax County across the stream.

As one entered the front door, the charming wainscoted Colonial hall in the two-story addition built by Patrick Henry's son, John Henry, extended straight through the house. The north door gave a delightful view of the cool and shaded rear lawn, while the south door seemed to be a frame for the distant landscape dazzling in the brilliant sunshine.

On the side lawn, to the west of the house, screened off from the rear by a high box-hedge and a tremendous holly tree, is the kitchen—one of those proverbial Virginia country kitchens that were so far away that hot battercakes had to be brought to the house on horseback! When the west wing was built by Mrs. M. B. Harrison, great-granddaughter of Patrick Henry, and the present owner, a kitchen was added to the house as well as other modern conveniences.

The east wing, a story-and-a-half Colonial structure, was the original house. It had high white mantels and a crooked, narrow, boxed-in stairway, and the massive brass locks on the doors were given Patrick Henry as a fee in a lawsuit. It was in one of the rooms of this wing that Patrick Henry died, sitting in his three-cornered mahogany chair, facing death with Christian fortitude.

At the end of this wing, through the shed that Patrick Henry added because "he wished to hear the patter of the raindrops on

Boxwood at Red Hill

The Tomb of Patrick Henry at Red Hill

its roof," lies the way to the garden which extended all along the east side of the lawn.

At the time that the west wing was added, the two offices— Patrick Henry's from the shady seclusion of the back yard, and William Wirt Henry's from the sunshiny front yard—were moved into the spacious garden and placed together to form a cottage. Since the house was burned in February, 1919, this cottage has served as the residence.

Along the fence, between yard and garden, jonquils are planted, and to the right of the garden gate once stood a handsome pecan tree which has long since blown down.

A bit to the east is the old garden where box-hedges separate colors and varieties of flowers and shrubs, some of which were brought originally from Mount Vernon. The situation and treatment of the garden which leads its well-clipped hedges down the slope of the hill in terrace form, were selected by Mistress Elvira Henry and prove her to have been an artist in this line. And the pride of her garden was a Martha Washington rose.

At the entrance of the garden, on either side of the walk, stand four large box-trees that meet at the top and form a leafy, green bower. An unique feature of this arbor is a yellow jessamine that blooms unseen in the tops of the box-trees and gives forth a delightful fragrance whose source is difficult to locate. There is a row of fig bushes to the left of the garden gate and a bed of white violets on the right. All along the garden walk, which leads to the graveyard, and the one bisecting it are planted tea and hardy roses, calycanthus, spiraea, snowballs and other old-fashioned flowering shrubs. The remainder of the ample garden is given over to vegetables.

The graveyard, at the extreme east side of the garden, is enclosed by a boxwood hedge. The ground around the tombs of Patrick Henry and his wife, Dorothea Dandridge, is covered with an ever green carpet of periwinkle, which in the spring is dotted with hundreds of little blue blossoms.

The slave quarters, which always prove of interest to visitors, lie some distance from the house, and the stories told of the old darkies who have dwelt in them would fill a volume of eighteenth century lore. To the right may be seen a spring-house sheltering a small pond of bubbling water, and farther on, racing merrily towards the river, runs the old Cool Spring from which Patrick Henry lifted many a gourd filled with fresh, cool water.

Walking about the grounds in the sunshine and in the shadows of the trees, one can almost visualize the scenes of former days, when the patriot, with his family and friends, trod these same box-bordered paths.

ELISE THOMSON CLARK.

THE OAKS

AMONG the large estates on the Staunton River in Charlotte County are Red Hill, the home and burial place of Patrick Henry; Staunton Hill, of the Bruces, whose noble mansion was for many years the most costly in Virginia, and is still one of the most beautiful; Ridgeway, of the Carringtons, and The Oaks, of the Rices—to name only a few of many, noted for their spacious homes and lovely surroundings.

The Oaks was for years known as South Isle, but the changing course of the river having left the distinctive island in its low-grounds high and dry save in times of freshet, the name had become a case of *"lucus a non lucendo,"* and was accordingly changed about two decades ago to one made obvious by a surrounding grove. We hear, however, that the present owner has returned to the earlier title.

Every old house was noted for its garden. In ante-bellum Virginia her garden was the pride, almost the passion, of the mistress of the plantation; it was as much outside the masculine province as was the cut of her gown. All that was required of the master was the loan of "hands" in times of emergency. The garden was designed by the Lady of the Manor and planted under her supervision. It was the expression of herself: a landscape gardener would have been an impertinent intruder.

The garden of The Oaks, as it now exists, was the creation, before mid-Victorian days, of Mrs. Izard Bacon Rice, a woman with the latent powers of an artist. Its ample acreage was divided by broad, turf-edged walks into plots of varying size and shape. The central walk was bordered by alternating shrubs of box and of "pink perpetual" roses. The roses have now become lost in a continuous wall of box more than six feet in height. Midway its

[291]

length the walk divides and embraces a large flower square, so placed that its point faces the walk, giving it a diamond-shaped effect. In the middle is a circular bed, the rest of the square being subdivided into symmetrical beds of diverse form, each bordered with dwarf box never allowed to exceed a foot, or even less, in height. The center of the circle was marked by a white crepe myrtle.

The beds were filled with flowering plants—tea-roses, Canterbury bells, hyacinths, peonies, tulips, iris, violets, pansies, lilies (including that empress of the garden, the lilium auratum), and annuals of many varieties. Self-sown cypress vines often flung over the box edgings their white and crimson stars, and heliotrope, brought from its winter pots, made the air fragrant from frost to frost.

But the flower garden proper is a small part of the floral beauty of the garden. Every vegetable square has its materialistic quality hidden by a broad border devoted especially to the taller flowers, such as delphiniums and cosmos—hollyhocks had not then come into their own and were over the fence in an adjacent lot—and to flowering shrubs, with every now and then a huge, pyramidal tree of box. At the intersections of the walks are trees of pink and of purple crepe myrtle, the glories of the garden during their long blossoming season. The dear old-fashioned shrubs abound: lilacs, purple and white; spiraea, calycanthus, Japan quince, snowballs, mock orange, syringa, flowering almond, white jasmine, and others. Frames held the yellow jasmine and microphylla roses.

Upon some of the borders the flower square seems to have spilled over its contents, for iris, peonies, hyacinths, tulips, crocuses, etc., are to be found, with phlox, verbenas, mourning bride, love-in-a-mist, nasturtiums, great beds of zinnias, and a profusion of snow-on-the-mountain. Many of these came up year after year at their own sweet will, often in most unexpected places.

When this garden was at its best, there were beds of pinks wafting their spicy incense to a distance of many hundreds of

Old Box Garden of The Oaks

The Oaks, Charlotte County

yards. There were long rows of Madonna lilies gleaming like altar candles and making the warm dusk of early summer heavy with fragrance. At one of the side gates was a large bed of

> "The naiad-like lily of the vale
> Which youth makes so pure and passion so pale."

Each spring saw a row of "sweet peas on tiptoe for a flight." Clumps of yucca looked down upon the asparagus, while the taller roses were everywhere; the yellow Harrison, beloved by the master, and the musk-cluster by the mistress of the house, predominating.

To repeat the names of the flowers is to have a thrill of "sweetness and light" beyond that of the catalogue of celestial handmaidens in "The Blessed Damozel."

Three cherry trees, a row of incomparable figs, others of raspberries, great beds of strawberries, a far-flung Scuppernong vine, a long walk bordered with grapes, each in its season made generous contributions to the tables of neighbours, as well as to that of the owners. For all fruits possession must needs be disputed with the birds, for surely that garden was "the most bird-haunted spot" in the world. The mocking birds were so tame that they made pecking assaults upon the hats of intrusive humans who ventured into the grape walk when the fragrant clusters were ripening.

To walk in such a garden in the cool of the day, or, better still, in the dewy morning, was to dream dreams and to see visions. To paraphrase old Izaak Walton, it was to say: "Lord, what joys hast Thou prepared for Thy saints in Heaven since Thou givest sinful man such delights upon earth?"

The adjoining plantation of Ridgeway had a fine garden of unusual size and of great age, but the frail health of its owner, Mrs. Paul Carrington, had caused it to fall into some decay before the plantation passed into other hands. The enormous growth of its shrubbery, the box having become trees, gave it distinction. These and its pleached walk converted it into a pleasaunce, with abundant, but subordinate, flowering plants.

[293]

The most imposing garden of that region was the garden of Mrs. Winston Henry. It covered several acres, and was surrounded by a faultlessly trimmed osage orange hedge. It descended to the lowgrounds in a series of turfed terraces, and displayed in a variety of evergreens many specimens of topiary art—the only examples of that art in the neighborhood. It was filled not only with hardy flowers, but with rare exotics, housed during the cold season in a conservatory extending from the ground to the third story of the mansion. It was no uncommon thing for Mrs. Henry to commandeer from the plantation thirty men at a time for her garden, while every drop of water for the conservatory had to be "toted" from a distant spring upon the heads of negroes. Demanding the labor which does not now exist, this, the most ambitious of the Charlotte County gardens, has wholly vanished, save for a few scraggly evergreens and straggling plants. The conservatory is only a heap of shattered glass.

It is well that these ladies of the century past, feeling themselves in the creation of beauty "workers together with God," had no prophetic vision.

When a cedar hedge at Ridgeway, having fallen into decay, was destroyed, an ancient "mammy" mournfully remarked: "I hates to see dat hedge cut down. Ole Miss scuffled and baffled over it so."

Unless a new generation of owners is inspired to carry on the work of their predecessors, it will not be long before "Scuffled and Baffled" is written over many of these gardens that hold the very heart of the old Virginia.

It is well, therefore, to gather what we may of the loveliness and perfume of the day that is dead.

MARIE GORDON PRYOR RICE.

Part of the Garden at Red Hill

The Ailanthus Avenue at Berry Hill

BERRY HILL

HALIFAX COUNTY

BERRY HILL, the home of Malcolm Graeme Bruce, in Halifax County, is one of the historical places in Virginia. It first came into possession of the family about 1769, as shown in the following deed:

This indenture made on the —— day of November in the year of our Lord one thousand seven hundred and sixty nine between Benjamin Harrison of Berkley in the county of Charles City on the one part and Isaac Coles of the county of Halifax on the other part witnesseth that the said Benjamin, in consideration of eight hundred pounds current money of Virginia to him in hand paid, doth grant bargain and sell to the s'd Isaac and his heirs one tract or parcel of land in the county of Halifax containing one thousand and twenty acres lying on Dan river and bounded by the several lines and boundaries mentioned in a plot and survey thereof made by one Thomas Jones of the county of Prince George; the said one thousand and twenty acres being parcel of a larger tract formerly the property of the honorable William Byrd and by him sold and conveyed to Richard Bland Esqr. by indenture bearing date the sixteenth day of April one thousand seven hundred and fifty one; to have and to hold the said tract of one thousand and twenty acres with all the appurtenances thereunto belonging to the s'd Isaac and his heirs forever, and the s'd Benjamin for himself and his heirs doth covenant with the s'd Isaac and his heirs that the s'd Benjamin and his heirs the s'd tract or parcel of land to the s'd Isaac and his heirs shall and will forever warrant and defend. In witness whereof the s'd Benjamin hath hereto subscribed his name and affixed his seal on the day and year first above written.

BENJ. HARRISON. (Red Seal)

Signed, sealed and delivered in presence of:
RO. C. NICHOLAS
EDM'D PENDLETON
J. S. MERCER

[Endorsement]

Harrison
to   } Deed
Coles

Proved by 2 Witnesses
Fully proved & to be Reco'd
Recorded & Exe'd

Virginia Jct's
At a General Court held at the Capital the 5th day of May 1770—
This Indenture was proved by the Oaths of Edmund Pendleton and James Mercer witnesses thereto and on the seventh day of the same month the said Indenture was proved by the Oath of Robert Carter Nicholas Esq. another witness thereto and ordered to be Recorded.

Teste   BEN WALLER, Cl. Cor't.

The several hands through which the estate passed from Colonel William Byrd, of Westover, were Richard Bland, Benjamin Harrison, Isaac Coles, the Bruce ancestor; General Edward Carrington, and to his first cousin, James Coles Bruce.

The original house of red brick was built by Isaac Coles and had a garden enclosed by a brick wall. These were replaced by James C. Bruce in 1839, but the original box hedges, thirty feet high, oaks and other trees remain. The grounds consisted of twenty acres, surrounded by a stone wall, with a lilac hedge on the inside. The garden of ten acres required a trained gardener, and sometimes forty men were brought in to keep it in order.

Mrs. James Coles Bruce, grandmother of the owner, was a great lover of flowers, and she collected foreign as well as native flowers and shrubs for her garden.

Gravel walks sixteen feet wide led through the garden and separated from each other grass plots sixty feet square. These were bordered with flowers to a width of six feet. A large, round bed marked the center of the garden and roses bloomed all through it—the moss and the cluster, Giant of Battles, Shamrock, microphylla, the Harrison and the Blush.

Leading to the grounds was an Ailanthus avenue one-half mile long. This Ailanthus, or Tree of Heaven as it was then called, was an imported tree, not indigenous to the United States, and was considered very rare.

The pictures give a better idea of the house than I can, and show the beauty of proportion, lines, and extreme simplicity. One wonders at the result from a home architect. I think my grandparents had a great deal to do with the building and no doubt received help from an intimate friend of theirs, John E. Johnson, who was noted for his good taste.

The names of many faithful servants were associated with Berry Hill. "Uncle" Aleck, the butler, was noted for his honesty and strength, and never told an untruth. During the War Between the States, he asked not to be told where the silver was buried, as he could not be unfaithful to his master, nor could he lie. And when one of the enemy stole his master's watch, this faithful servant took it from him. There were three generations of butlers and three of cooks at this house. The cook during my father's life was very black and claimed his ancestor was a king.

My grandfather, though a Union man at the beginning, had four sons in the Confederate service, losing two of them, so he felt

[297]

the war very keenly. When he heard the enemy was approaching, he left his home and ordered the butler to fire the house rather than have it fall into their hands. My father, Alexander Bruce, who was trained at the Virginia Military Institute under Thomas J. Jackson, afterwards General Stonewall Jackson, collected all the men at home on leave or unfit for service and held Staunton Bridge, which prevented the enemy from coming through. Needless to say, when my mother used to tell me about it when I was a child, I felt it was the most important battle of the war, just as I thought the Presbyterian Church in Lexington, Virginia, the largest in the world. My grandfather, James C. Bruce, died the day Lee surrendered, and said he took a grim satisfaction in leaving the world on the day that meant the death of his class. General Merritt, one of the youngest Federal generals, was stationed at Berry Hill after the surrender.

After the war, my father, Alexander Bruce, felt it would be impossible to keep the garden as it should be kept, so he had it removed, and trees set out matching the rest of the grounds, leaving only the box, crepe myrtle and other shrubs, removing all the walks and flower beds, though my mother and sister were in tears at the thought of having to give it up. But there still remain quantities of jonquils, hedges of box, and interesting flowering trees and shrubs. Many think the place was improved by removing the garden and the cedar hedges, which divided the flowers from the vegetables; these hedges also separated the vegetables from the park, and the park from the orchard. The pictures will give some idea of the place as it now is, with the house in the center of the park. In the old garden were peonies, snowballs, smoke trees, magnolias, Japan apples, flowering apples, crab apples, jasmines, honeysuckles on frames, crepe myrtles, dogwoods, Roses of Sharon, fringe trees, red buds and many mimosas. Every tree had something planted beneath to come up in the spring, such as double and single jonquils, hyacinths, snowdrops, peonies, or narcissi.

ELLEN BRUCE CRANE.

The Pillared House at Berry Hill, Home of the Bruces

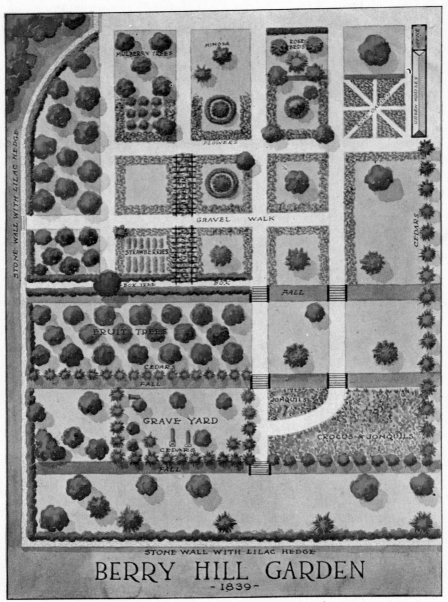

BERRY HILL GARDEN
-1839-

Metropolitan Engraving Company

BELLEVUE

HE Bellevue estate in Halifax County, about five miles southeast of the Courthouse, originally contained something more than one thousand acres. It was purchased about 1825 by John B. Carrington, a great-grandson of George Carrington who came to this country from the Island of Barbadoes. He was also a grandson of Judge Paul Carrington of Mulberry Hill, member of the House of Burgesses, and the Committee of Safety. Judge Carrington was later a member of the Virginia Convention of 1776 which adopted the State Constitution and the Bill of Rights and directed the Virginia members of Congress to move for independence from Great Britain. In 1788 he became Judge of the Virginia Court of Appeals.

The dwelling at Bellevue, which was built by a former owner, is a commodious one of brick, fifty-six feet long and forty feet deep. The rooms were about eighteen feet square and there was an upper and a lower hall sixteen feet wide running through the house from front to back. The interior division walls were of brick. The front porch was an impressive one, two stories high with double columns extending to the roof on each side of the entrance steps. On the second floor was a balcony. There were two back porches, one at the end of the hall and the other at the corner of the house. In the room entered from the latter was a large cabinet in which were kept medicines, bandages, etc., for the farm hands.

The house was situated in a grove of several acres containing handsome oak, original pine, sycamore, cedar, holly, boxwood and mimosa trees. The yard was filled with shrubs and vines of various kinds. Back of the "big house" and about one hundred feet away was the kitchen with its big open fireplace. A brick walk led from it to the dwelling and, if the biscuits were not "piping hot" when they reached the dining-room, there was trouble in store for the cook. Between the kitchen and the vegetable garden were three important little buildings—the smokehouse, from the rafters of which hung a goodly supply of old hams and bacon, the dairy and the weaving-house with a potato cellar under it. In this house was also a room in which were kept surplus supplies for the store-room, garden tools, a work bench and carpenter's tools.

The icehouse was about one hundred feet back of the kitchen. This was a log house built almost entirely underground and covered with shingles. The inside was lined with oak boards and the building was drained at the bottom to carry off the water from melting ice.

No well-appointed plantation was complete without its office where all business was transacted. The office at Bellevue was a white two-story dormer-windowed little building with dark green outside blinds. It had three rooms, one, and sometimes two of which were used as overflow guest rooms for young men.

The entrance to the farm was a hundred yards or more down the road from that to the dwelling. This led to the overseer's house and on to the stable, granary, hay barn and other such buildings. There were also barns for curing tobacco, and log cabins for farm hands were situated on little knolls here and there over the farm.

On the right of the dwelling was an old-fashioned flower garden which deserves special mention. It was square in shape and enclosed on two sides by a thick hedge of tall box-trees; on another side by a row of fig trees planted close together and on a third side by a white picket fence. In the corner where the box and fig trees came together there was an outdoor room made by box-trees planted in a circle meeting overhead and trimmed out on the inside. This made a delightful place to read on a summer morning and enjoy the flowers and figs. In the center was a circle of box four feet high, within which were old-fashioned roses, and in the beds around this perennials and other flowers were attractively arranged.

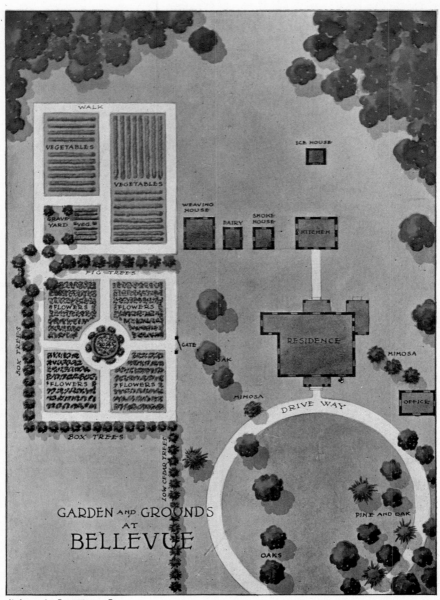

Robert A. Lancaster, Jr.

Bellevue, Halifax County

A glance at the spot where for years the roses bloomed so blithely reminds one of Father Tabb's lines in his "Child's Verse":

"There was laughter 'mid the roses,,
  For it was their natal day
And the children in the garden were
  As light of heart as they.

"There were sighs amid the roses
  For the night was coming on
And the children—weary now of play—
  Were ready to be gone.

"There are tears amid the roses
  For the children are asleep
And the silence in the garden makes
  The lonely blossoms weep."

Around the ring of box was a circle of snowball bushes with the box showing between. There were grass walks around the garden and from each side to and around the inner circle.

Beyond the fig trees was the vegetable garden, in one corner of which was the family burying-ground. The walk to this passed along the hedge of fig trees. The orchard of apple, pear and peach trees was on the other side of the house.

This garden made a more lasting impression upon the writer than did some of the larger and more elaborate ones visited by him. The fact that the trees were laden with ripe fruit may have accounted for this.

The property remained in the Carrington family for about seventy-five years, but has since changed hands several times.

ROBERT A. LANCASTER, JR.

BANISTER LODGE

THE situation of its three-thousand-acre plantation on the Banister River, in Halifax County, gave to this fine brick mansion—built in 1830—its name of Banister Lodge.

The plan of the house was simple and commodious. An English basement underneath the entire building, and above, the usual four large rooms, two on each side of the broad hallway that led to the twenty by twenty-five-foot dining-room in the wing at the rear. Rooms and hall on the second floor corresponded in size and design with those of the main floor.

The folding doors between the parlor and library were a novelty in that part of the State, and people came for miles around to see them. On the walls of these rooms hung pictures, by famous artists, of members of the family and connections of William H. Clark, the owner and builder of Banister Lodge. Amongst the notable portraits was one of Patrick Henry, who was the grandfather of Mrs. Clark (nee Elvira Henry). She herself is represented by a Sully portrait, showing her standing at her harp—a handsome instrument imported from London in 1820.

Mrs. Clark was an unusually brilliant and talented woman. At the age of sixteen, while visiting in Washington at the home of her cousin, William Wirt, Secretary of State under Monroe, she, by special request, played on her harp at several of the President's levees. Besides performing on harp and piano, she also composed music for both of these instruments. Her artistic accomplishments, however, did not interfere with her duties towards home and family, as she was a famous hostess and an exemplary wife and mother.

Her husband, William H. Clark, was a man of great intellectual force and profound learning, and noted for his active and progressive spirit. After attending colleges in Virginia, he completed his education at Harvard University. His library at Banister Lodge, to which he was constantly adding whatever was good amongst new publications, numbered more than three thousand volumes.

Mr. Clark gave his children every educational advantage, sending the boys first to the Virginia Military Institute, thence to the University of Virginia, and after that to Paris for a two years' finishing course.

His wine cellar, stocked with spirits of many rare vintages, was quite famous throughout the country. All of its contents that had not been removed and securely hidden, fell into the hands of the Federal troops who raided this section in 1865. As a climax to the revelries following their visits to this cellar, the soldiers repaired to the front of the house, and demanded the presence of the young daughters of the family.

Mr. Clark, then a white-haired old man, stood in the front doorway, with outspread arms and flashing eyes, as he exclaimed, "You will enter only over my dead body!"

What the outcome would have been, we can only surmise, as response to his challenge was averted by the quick wit of Matilda, one of the loyal negro maids, and herself a "likely gal." Stepping forward, she addressed the foremost soldiers in these words:

"Young mahsters, y'all hug me, an' let de young ladies alone!" This they proceeded to do in perfect good humor, but were interrupted by the appearance of one of their officers, who berated them soundly and ordered them off.

The garden at Banister Lodge was designed by Mrs. Clark from her own ideas. It was divided into nine sections, each of which was about one hundred feet square. Only one of these— that of the flower garden—is diagramed here. The other eight were devoted to vegetables and small fruits, but bordered by hedges of white and purple lilac. The entire garden, except at the front, was hedged in by rows of fruit trees.

The grounds, including the garden, comprised about one hundred acres. In the fourteen flower beds in this old garden there were, at the various seasons, snowdrops, blue bells and violets; hyacinths, tulips and jonquils, with narcissus poeticus for spring. Then came larkspurs, columbines, lilies, "old maid pinks," iris, primroses, lilies of the valley, and "Fair Maids of February."

The shrub list included all the old-fashioned ones—snowballs, forsythia, pomegranate, pyrus japonica, spiraea, syringa, crepe myrtle, honeysuckle, althea, wistaria, yellow jessamine, and the old favorite, white "Confederate" jessamine.

The list of roses at Banister Lodge is both comprehensive and interesting. There were, first of all, moss roses, so rarely seen now. The Maiden's Blush grew along garden walks and beautified more than one bed, while Giant of Battles, Marechal Neil and delicate tea roses followed on the heels of the prodigal Harrisonia. One whole bed was covered with an arbor covered with running roses.

The front yard, which was laid off with formality, was separated from the rear by a hedge of tree-box, probably thirty feet in height. On either side of the front porch, stood trees of arbor vitae and boxwood. Of the two driveways, one led straight away (after rounding the large circular center of the lawn) through a grove of magnificent oaks, to the main highway; while the other, approaching from the stableyard at the right, swept around towards the left and back, through the plantation, to the river.

On the opposite side of the house from the garden, and in a corner of the lawn, was a flower bed in the form of a large five-pointed star. On the rear lawn stands one of the largest oak trees to be found in Virginia.

ETHEL CLARK WILLIAMS.

Banister Lodge, the Clark Homestead, in Halifax County

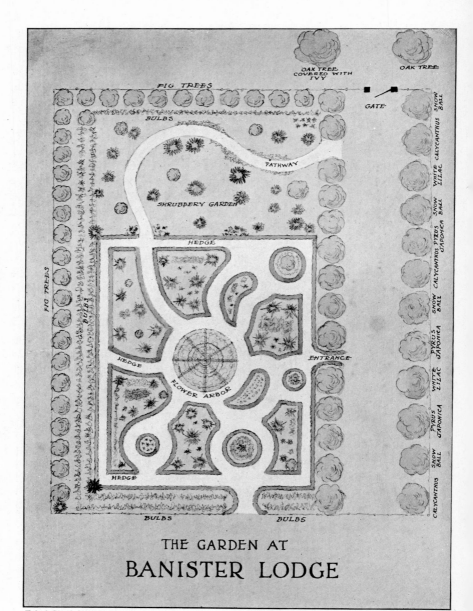

THE GARDEN AT
BANISTER LODGE

Ethel Clark Williams

STAUNTON HILL

TAUNTON HILL is situated in Charlotte County, about forty miles southeast of Lynchburg, on the Staunton, really the Roanoke River, for the latter, as John Randolph of Roanoke once said, passes for a considerable distance *incog.,* under the name of the Staunton.

The tract of some six hundred acres, on which the Staunton Hill mansion stands, was acquired by James Bruce, in 1803, and was afterwards enlarged by purchases of adjoining lands, made from time to time, by James Bruce and his son, Charles. The former resided at Woodburn, in Halifax County, and it was not until 1848 that the house at Staunton Hill was erected by Charles Bruce, on the six-hundred-acre tract just mentioned. This, with the additions made to it by James and Charles Bruce, in 1896, the year of the latter's death, amounted to five thousand and fifty-two acres.

The mansion is built in the Gothic style of architecture of stuccoed brick with towers and battlements. The front porch is constructed of marble, which was imported from Italy to Philadelphia. After being reduced to the proper shapes there, it was conveyed by sea to Albemarle Sound, and thence by bateaux up the Roanoke River to the Staunton Hill estate.

One of the most striking features of the house is the well-nigh perfect proportion of its external details. Extending back from the rear there is a colonnade about two hundred feet long. The roof of this is supported by iron pillars painted white, and the floor is flagged with large granite blocks. Along it are ranged the kitchen, laundry and service quarters. From the west side of the house projects a conservatory, and a short distance to the southwest of this is a Gothic outbuilding of five rooms. This is known as the office, where the business of the plantation, which was worked in three shifts by a large force of hands under three overseers, was usually transacted.

The mansion contains twenty-five rooms, three of which—the front drawing-room, the center drawing-room and the library—constitute a suite of rooms which in point of design, finish and space would compare favorably, if not more than favorably, with any similar suite in any of the conspicuous homes of the Virginia past. The library, which is a truly beautiful Gothic room, is furnished with a fine collection of standard books, mainly purchased by Charles Bruce in London in or about the year 1848. One of the most attractive features of the house is its vestibule, with a floor of black and white marble, and supplied with niches filled with classic figures.

The grounds and flower gardens are about eight acres in area and were laid out by a Mr. Kirk, a Scotch landscape gardener, at or about the time the residence was built. Under his supervision, the grounds were adorned with many varieties of trees, native and exotic, such as the ash, the beech, the deodar, the cedar of Lebanon, and other species of domestic and foreign trees too numerous to mention. Scattered among these are clumps of shrubbery. As the original plantings have succumbed to the ravages of time, they have been renewed with the same painstaking care that marked their origin.

Equal skill and good judgment were shown by Mr. Kirk in his scheme of grass plots, roadways and walks, which are fully worthy of the extensive space over which they are spread. The flower garden is broken up by a system of judiciously designed grass walks into many beds of varied shapes. In form, it is semi-circular, and environing the semi-circle is a dense background of noble oaks and other forest trees. In this garden a perpetual succession of roses of different varieties has always been maintained throughout the summer months, to say nothing of many kinds of flowers. In few, if in any, of the old gardens of Virginia can be found such

Staunton Hill

A Bit of the Park at Staunton Hill

a profuse and brilliant mass of crepe myrtle as this garden displays in midsummer.

Outside of the house grounds proper are stretches of park-like woods enclosed by a stone wall between a mile and a half and two miles long. This wall was constructed to a great extent by slave laborers, as were the mansion and office themselves. A road from the house, shaded on one side by a dense woods, carpeted with periwinkle, and on the other by elms and mimosa trees, leads over to a peaceful little graveyard surrounded by a stone wall covered with English ivy. In another direction a shaded path strikes off from the grounds to a swimming pool. Opposite this, there is a picturesque walk known as the "Lovers' Walk." This begins in the park, winds in and out through the forest bounded by the stone wall and, after many detours, returns to its starting point.

The mansion and some two thousand two hundred and thirty acres of the original Staunton Hill plantation are now owned by William Cabell Bruce, of Baltimore, the son of Charles Bruce.

Louise Este Bruce.

PRESTWOULD

TO those of us who spend our working hours fighting to make our glorious country "safe for Democracy" and our leisure in studying the annals of the Court of St. James, it may be of interest to trace the lineage of the Skipwith family in Virginia, from Sir Grey, who emigrated to America during the usurpation of Cromwell, to Sir Peyton, founder of the Virginia Prestwould, which he named for the ancestral home in Leicestershire County, England. And, in passing, it may not be amiss to call attention to this oft misspelled and mispronounced name, "Prest-w-o-u-l-d," not "wold" nor "wood," though with the sound of the latter.

Sir Grey Skipwith was succeeded by his only son, Sir William, who married Sarah, daughter of John Peyton. His first-born dying, he was succeeded by his second son, Sir William, from whom the title passed eventually to Sir Peyton. Sir Peyton Skipwith was married twice; first to Anne, daughter of Hugh Miller; and second to her sister, Jean—which brings us to the designer and presiding genius of the Prestwould Garden.

But, first, a few words in regard to Prestwould itself. A little-known bit of history, which might have been lost to us but for the watchful eye of the Honorable H. F. Hutcheson, Clerk of the Court of Mecklenburg County, Virginia, follows:

A part of the Prestwould estate (including the three islands, "Saponi," "Occaneeche" and "Totero"), was originally the Bluestone Castle plantation owned by Colonel William Byrd II, founder of the cities of Richmond and Petersburg, Virginia. Indeed, it was probably while visiting this plantation that he conceived the idea of those cities, as he writes in his famous diary, on September 19, 1733: "After returning to 'Bluestone Castle' from a trip to the

[308]

Prestwould, Mecklenburg County, built by Sir Peyton Skipwith about 1756

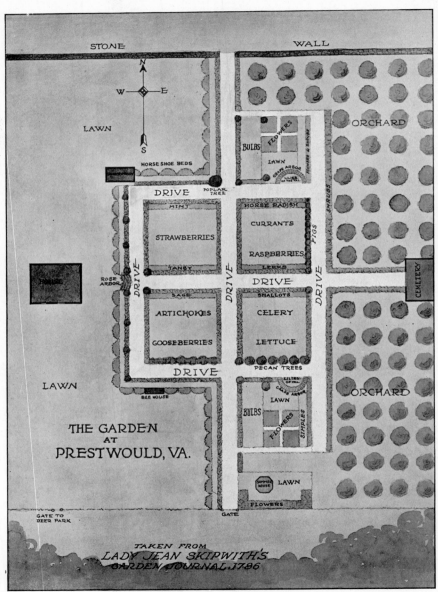

THE GARDEN
AT
PRESTWOULD, VA.

TAKEN FROM
LADY JEAN SKIPWITH'S
GARDEN JOURNAL 1786

From Garden Journal of Lady Jean Skipwith

islands, we laid the foundations of two large cities. One at Shaccoes, to be called 'Richmond,' and the other at the point of the Appomattox, to be called 'Petersburgh.' "

According to family tradition, Colonel William Byrd III and Sir Peyton Skipwith were together in Norfolk during a downpour of rain, which continued steadily for several days. Being congenial spirits and well supplied with the finest of wines, the two gentlemen whiled away the time agreeably, drinking and card playing, with the result that when the skies finally cleared, Sir Peyton had won from his opponent the deed to Bluestone Castle. In his will, Sir Peyton makes mention of "that portion of my landed estate known as 'Prestwould,' which I acquired of the Honourable William Byrd and others."

On a commanding hill overlooking the surrounding country for miles, stands the massive "four-square" house of Prestwould, built of stone quarried on the place by the family slaves, and from whose river front there is an entrancing view of the Dan and Staunton rivers at their confluence with the Roanoke. Between the first-named rivers lie the three islands, the center one of which, Occaneeche, was the stronghold of a tribe of Indians of that name, whom Nathaniel Bacon practically exterminated in a desperate battle.

Approaching the house from what is termed the land front, one drives through a roadway between stone walls and leading to the large wrought-iron gate opening upon the lawn, whose most noticeable feature—barring the house itself—is the gigantic oak tree, measuring twenty-seven feet in circumference, which stands near the northwest corner of the mansion. This tree is said to have served as a landmark for the Indians, who held powwows and smoked pipes of peace beneath its shadows nearly two hundred years ago.

Impressive and inviting as is the mansion—furnished now, as in Sir Peyton's day, with probably the handsomest and most complete collection of original furniture to be found in any home in Virginia—had the question been asked of a visitor, even within the present century, "What is the outstanding feature of Prestwould?" the answer would have been, unhesitatingly, "The garden!"

As may be seen from the accompanying plat, drawn from the original in Lady Jean's Garden Journal, the garden comprised five acres of ground enclosed by stone walls. Note the six beds, each one hundred feet square, formed by the intersection of the drive-ways which are eighteen feet in width. Four of these beds were devoted to vegetables, herbs and "simples," as follows:

Beginning with those on the right of the central drive as one enters through the rose arbored gateway: (1) Gooseberries, arti-chokes, sage. (2) Lettuce, celery, shallots. On the left: (3) Tansy, strawberries, mint. (4) Leeks, raspberries, currants, horseradish.

Of the two beds containing only flowers and herbs, with insets of grass, bulbs predominated, though there was abundant space at the other side of each bed given to simples. The semicircles repre-sent the Scuppernong grape arbors, underneath which the lily of the valley flourished.

But, whether planted in choicest flowers or in prosaic vegetables, each bed was encompassed by a five-foot border of roses and shrubs, and, on the further sides, by rows of fig and pecan trees.

The scallops on the plat represent horseshoe beds, but whether planted in bulbs, annuals, or wild flowers, is now a matter of guess-work. Lady Jean's Garden Journal contains a list of thirty or forty different wild flowers, but no mention of their location.

At the northwest corner of the garden, the line of horseshoe beds was broken by a conservatory, twenty-four feet in length, and, near the southwest corner, by a fifteen-foot bee house. Between these same beds and the driveways were the graveled walks and the continuous borders of roses, shrubs and flowers of all varieties, while at each corner of bed or border, was planted a boxwood, which, in course of time, and where not kept in check, grew to such proportions as to merge completely with its neighbor across the eighteen-foot driveway—the appearance presented being that of one

Orchard Hillside at Prestwould

Old Stone Wall and Gateway at Prestwould

Dan's Hill, Pittsylvania County

immense tree instead of two, whose glossy leaves hid the secret of the trunkless interior. Upon parting the branches, one entered a spacious vaulted chamber, with walls and cathedral-arched roof of living green, and provided with garden seats for prolonged enjoyment of the sensation of having found a new world!

By this time, however, Sir Peyton had been lying in the cemetery, at the back of the garden, for more than eighty years, and Lady Jean for only twenty years less; the War of the Confederacy had been fought and lost and the slaves freed more than two decades before, so there were no equipages to traverse the driveways and be halted by the boxwood trees and other overgrown shrubbery—but we are getting ahead of the story.

A list of Lady Jean's flowers would prove tedious reading, as it differs so little from our own lists of today. She gives both the botanical and the common names, sometimes followed by a note as to where a specimen was obtained, and usually by comments on the color, habits or best mode of culture, as

"Limodorus Tuberosum—from South Carolina—by Jim."

"Bermudiana (see Sisyranchium), the blue flowers with grass looking stalks and leaves—plenty in the orchard."

"Erythronium, Dog's Tooth Violet—from Royster's low grounds and the Island."

"Sessile Trillium, Liver coloured flower from the Point of the Island."

"Shrubs to be got when I can:
Widow-Wail (see Cueorum), a low evergreen shrub with a small yellow flower easily raised from seed sown in the fall.
Early Shrub Anonis (see Ononis) raised from seeds in the open ground, very beautiful, and when once established gives no trouble; the seeds should be sown in Sep. Commonly called Kest Yarrow. Purple Shrubby Kest Yarrow grows naturally on the Alps."

"Bulbous roots to get when in my power:
Meadow Saffron (see Colchium) a bulbous root about
the size of a Tulip, flowers in Autumn, and the leaves
continue green all the winter; called by the common
people, Naked Ladies. Great varieties may be obtained from seed."
"Purple cupped Statices or Thrift; dried, it retains its
colour, which renders it ornamental for a Mantelpiece
in winter. A Biennial, yet often increased by parting its
roots, but more advantageously from Seeds."

Of the Iris she lists at least nine varieties: "Bulbous Flag Iris,
red flower; Dwarf Flag; Large Flag, or Flower de Luce; Evergreen Purple; Common Blue; Persian; Florentine White, and
Corn Flag."

Amongst the Wild Flowers she mentions eight varieties of
"Solomon's Seal, or Convollaria Polygonatum." Also, "Clay-
tonia, little narrow leafed Black rooted flower from the foot of the
garden"; "Ixia Bermudiana, with an Iris Leaf, perhaps the Blackberry Lily in the garden"; "Hibiscus, American Retmic, what was
sent me by the name of Holy Oak, 4th sort. 6th sort, Indian
Retmic, I expect is the flower Helen found at the Spring. Medeota
Lily, or Little Martagon, perhaps what we got by the branch at
Elm Hill, with the Whorled leaves."

Orange, lemon, lime, oleander and dwarf myrtle are listed with
others under the head of "House Plants."

A "Memo: respecting raising Trees" gives methods of propaga-
tion, from seeds and from scions, of the poplar, mulberry, cedar
and holly. The directions for the latter, when raised from seeds,
ends with the patient announcement "They will be large enough to
plant out in four years"!

Of Fruit Trees, there is a lengthy and most tempting list, each
item of which, where a gift is followed by the name of the donor:

"Bary or Roi Pear, the finest Pear in the world, from St.
   G. Tucker.
Newington Peach, from Mr. Seawell.
Pound Pear, from Mrs. Anderson.
Cluster Cherry, ripe in May, from Mr. Eppes.
Mr. Kennon's Pear."

Under "List of Grafted Fruit Trees of different kinds Grafted
or planted at Prestwould 16th March 1792," are many kinds of
cherries, with "plumbs," nectarines, quinces, peaches, and an
"Esopus Spitzemburg, a very large red apple, reckoned the finest
eating apple in America, next to the Newtown Pippin. From
St. G. T."

Dated 1807 is Lady Jean's "Memo: of the Seasons when the
different Fruits at Prestwould are ripe, or fit to gather," and from
it we may judge whether or not the seasons of the present time are
different from those of her day:

"May Cherries, Duke Cherries, and Strawberries of different kinds, from early in May to the middle of June.
Black, White and English Raspberries, from the beginning
   of June to the middle of July.
Red and Black Currants, and Morello Cherries, from the
   middle of June to the middle of July.
Red, White and Blue Plumbs, from the 1st of July to the
   1st of August.
Honey Pear, from the Island, about the middle of July.
Catherine Pear, from the Kitchen Garden, between the
   middle of July and 1st of August."

Besides the vegetables in the flower garden, there were many
in the kitchen garden, and more grown on one of the islands, so
that, as shown by old invoices, seeds and plants were ordered in
great quantities. On one, if not on all of the three islands, there
were orchards of peach, pear and apple trees, as well as other

[313]

fruits. These were worked by the slaves, numbers of whom lived on the islands.

Sir Peyton himself seems to have superintended some of the seed planting, as we find, written in his hand and signed "P. Skipwith," the following:

> "Memo. of Seeds sown in plant-patch next to the Prize-Barn, beginning with the two short beds nearest to said Barn."

One sighs for the vanished patience of those days, of which the following heading to a formidable list is evidence: "Peach Stones buried at Prestwould, October 1791." Amongst the stones enumerated we find "Sir Peyton's, Mostly August Plumb; Mrs. Blackbourn's soft peach, ripe in September," and many others. Nectarines and cherries were included in the list, as were "Plumb Stones from General Parsons."

Many more subjects connected with the fragrant realm of Lady Jean's creating might be mentioned; the solace she sought in its quiet depths during the trial of Sir Peyton on a charge of treason, and the receipt of the joyful news of his honorable acquittal; the octagonal summer-house with its tinkling spinet and romantic associations; the hopes and aspirations that budded and reached fruition, as well as those that succumbed to biting frosts; of lilacs that blossomed in the open on the twenty-seventh day of October of a certain year as a bouquet for the first bride ever wedded at Prestwould; and of the golden-haired Helen, Queen of Hearts, who led her lovers a merry dance through the sunlit pathways of her "Court of Love and Beauty" and flowery fragrance.

Therefore, what has been written will be regarded by the many who have threaded its alluring mazes in the company of Cupid, as merely a preliminary to the real story of the Prestwould Garden.

MARTHA FEILD BLAIR.

Prestwould is now the property of Mr. and Mrs. William T. Hughes, who are restoring both house and garden to their original beauty.

The Dan River
Near this spot General Greene crossed when he retreated before Cornwallis
during the Revolution

The Box Hedged Walk to the Summer House at Dan's Hill

DAN'S HILL

AN'S HILL, situated in Pittsylvania County, Virginia, about five miles from Danville, on the Dan River, covering an area of about sixteen hundred acres, is the ancestral home of the Wilson family, the present owner, Robert Wilson James, being the fifth generation in direct descent to have lived here.

The first member of the family, John Wilson, settled here during the Revolutionary period, and the present house, with the numerous outbuildings, consisting of stables, carriage-house, in which the old four-horse coach was kept, the weaving-house, where expert weavers in former days made the homespun worn by the house servants and farm hands, a laundry room, dairy, smoke-house, icehouses, kitchen with huge fireplace in which a person could easily stand, and the several log cabins for servants' quarters were built by Robert Wilson. These were in course of construction about eight years and were completed in 1833. All of the bricks used in these buildings were made on the estate and the lumber was cut from the native forest; both are still in a good state of preservation.

The residence is a spacious three-story brick structure of the Colonial type, containing twenty rooms, and furnished with the original mahogany furniture placed there years ago. The present owners, Robert Wilson James and his wife, who was Miss Irene Dwyer, of Ohio, have recently installed in this home all the modern conveniences, consisting of heat, electric lights, bathrooms, and an up-to-date refrigerating plant, making it, in addition to its traditional charms and general beauty, one of the most comfortable homes possible.

A fireside grouping in the drawing-room shows the beautiful old imported marble mantel and the brass fender and andirons. The oil painting above the fireplace is a portrait of Robert Wilson, the builder of the present home, and it is interesting to know that this portrait was painted in the very room in which it hangs. The antique porcelain jars on either end of the mantel complete the picture.

The house is surrounded by extensive lawns and terraced gardens, covering about three acres, which extend to the river. The walks are bordered by wonderful old boxwood hedges which were planted when the house was built. In the gardens are some very rare old bulbs, put there when the gardens were originally laid out, and which the Department of Agriculture at Washington listed some time ago as practically extinct.

At the intersection of four walks stands an octagonal summer-house, with massive brick columns, in a perfect state of preservation, having already withstood the storms of nearly a hundred years— a delightful spot, overlooking the river, to sit and muse on the romances of the crinoline days. Near the summer-house is the old flower-house, known in former days as the greenhouse, where rare and beautiful flowers bloomed the entire winter.

On the hills and fields surrounding the house is a beautiful growth known as Scotch broom, which in the late spring is covered with a golden bloom. There is an interesting old legend about this plant. It is said that the seed were brought to this country by the English during the Revolutionary War in the feed for their horses, and that wherever they camped, this Scotch broom sprung up after they moved on.

On this estate is also a very fine mineral spring—the water having been analyzed some years ago and found to contain medicinal qualities rivaling some of the springs of the most famous health resorts.

All in all, Dan's Hill is a charming home, combining the dignity of Colonial days with every comfort of the most modern establishment, and where true Southern hospitality is graciously dispensed by Robert Wilson James and his lovely wife.

Mrs. Rorer James.

A Corner of the Formal Garden at Chatmoss, Henry County

Boxwood Planted at Chatmoss in 1845

Garden at Brierfield Near Danville

Berry Hill, the Seat of the Hairstons, in Henry County

THE VALLEY OF THE DAN

OAK RIDGE

AK RIDGE, Pittsylvania County, Virginia, about ten miles from Danville, is owned and occupied by Mrs. Jessie Wilson Word and Mrs. Lizzie Wilson Hall. The house was built between the years 1840 and 1850, by their maternal grandfather, Mr. John Adams, and Justina, his wife. Oak Ridge is splendidly kept and retains to a remarkable degree its pristine beauty. The only occupants are the two widowed sisters, who manage personally and successfully their large estate—tobacco being the money crop.

The approach to the house from the gate is through a wide driveway of smooth, white sand, on either side of which tower huge oaks, maples, holly and other varieties of our native trees, many of which are entwined with ivy and some with wistaria. The house, which is delightfully spacious, is filled with rare and exquisite furnishings, having the home charm about them. The gardens, enclosed by a hedge of cedars, lie to the right of the house and must be seen to be appreciated. The cedars seem to protect the endless variety of beautiful flowers, vines, shrubs and evergreens which here reach a degree of perfection and loveliness rarely ever seen. Nut and fruit trees also abound.

BRIARFIELD

Briarfield plantation, which is owned and conducted by Mr. Harden Hairston, is situated in Pittsylvania County, about fifteen miles from Danville, Virginia. The plantation is a very old one, having belonged to this branch of the Hairston family for four

[317]

generations, but no residence was ever on same until the present house was built in 1902.

The development of the Briarfield Plantation has been very unique. Driveways were cut through the primeval forests to the site of Briarfield House, which stands on a very high hill. This hill, purposely, has never been cleared. In the very early days, some small houses were built by "redemptioners," who figured so largely as a sure source of labor for our ancestors. These were the planters of early colonization—the indentured immigrants who sold their time for passage across the Atlantic to the new world. On either side of Briarfield House wide borders have been planted, care being exercised to obtain the effect of bulbs, shrubs, perennials and vines just coming each season as do the wild flowers. Thus, thousands of flowers of many varieties bloom happily together, creating a delightful departure from the usual formal gardens of lawn and hedges, with designed flower beds. Every effort has been put forth to conserve all wild growth, and one can enjoy here dwarf iris, bluettes, partridge clutch, white and yellow orchids, also trees of "Dogwood," "Sourwood" and "Fringe Tree." From the southwest gallery of Briarfield House a view for sixty miles of the Dan River Valley is a source of endless joy, whether by moonlight, sunlight, or in shade or shadow. The fertile lowgrounds sweep out of sight to the foot of the Blue Ridge Mountains, and even when extensive freshets cover miles in width the scene is one of great beauty. The money crop of this plantation is tobacco, and at Briarfield and Chatmoss, together, about a million tobacco plants are usually set out.

CHATMOSS

Chatmoss, built in 1850 by Samuel Harden Hairston and his wife, Ailsy, parents of present owner, is six miles from Martinsville, in Henry County, on the National Highway.

The twenty-acre lawn has a wonderful collection of native trees. The garden, which is quite large, contains a wealth of dwarf box.

Oak Ridge, Pittsylvania County, the Wilson Home

The Broad Garden Walk of Oak Ridge

River View from the Briarfield Garden

Thornfield, the Home of Joseph H. Scales

It is said that there are thirty-six thousand linear feet of this hedge in the formal garden with tree box outside. Some of the tree box is over thirty feet high. Clipping the formal garden hedges each spring is three weeks' work for six men.

THORNFIELD

Thornfield, the ancestral home of the Scales family, is about twenty miles from Danville. The land was granted to the first owner by George III of England, and the original grant, signed by the English king, is still in the possession of the family.

The brick house, beautifully situated upon an elevation that overlooks a wide expanse of fertile country, reminds one of an English country home. Handsome trees, boxwood and shrubs abound. Mr. Joseph H. Scales now owns the place.

WINDSOR

Windsor, which is owned and occupied by Mr. Samuel H. Wilson and family, is eighteen miles from Danville. The house, built about 1860 by Samuel Pannill Wilson, and the servants' quarters, are of brick made on the place.

This estate has never changed hands, and as there are several sons, there is no doubt that the name of Wilson will forever be associated with this attractive place.

The gardens, which were designed by a Prussian landscape gardener, are exclusive, and many varieties of roses, bulbs, perennials, shrubs and evergreens still abound.

One can see flower beds of the earlier days, edged with brick, and a heart-shaped bed tells its tale of love and romance. Noticeable for their wonderful size and stateliness are the many boxwood trees, sentinels of the passing years.

ELLEN WILSON JAMES.

OAK HILL

F one wants to have a suggestion of "days befo' de wah," then he must see Oak Hill, the home of Mr. Samuel Hairston. This solid, imposing residence, in its decided colonial outlines, invites to the mind those happy reminiscences of festive evenings, when the old-time "square dance" was a delight, on ample and mirror-like floors; when there were big crowds, big dinners, big suppers, with company, not just for a few hours, but overnight and all next day, for the fox hunt often followed the dance, and the bay of dogs and the silvery ring of the horn was the recessional music of the fiddle and the banjo. Yes, these memories are revived when, as might be said, one stands in the presence of one of these old homes, built in the early eighteens.

Such a residence, then, is this Oak Hill, built in 1825 by Mr. Samuel Hairston, and now owned by a descendant of the same name of the third generation. Situated right on the crest of a high hill, around which the Danville and Western Railroad makes a graceful curve, and has its trains to stop conveniently for the back-door entrance; with a wide extent of level land at the foot of the hill to relieve or bring out the boldness of its situation, there is for Oak Hill a landscape setting rarely seen. The magnificent oaks that measure birthdays by centuries are no minor ornaments from nature's hand, for they flourish on all sides of the house and furnish a dense grove. The work that nature has done for Oak Hill is not all, for architectural beauty is brought out in simplicity in the construction of the house. It is a brick structure of straight lines and plain proportions, with colonial windows and porches with a rock-laid walk from the front gate to the porch, with its accompanying boxwood borders. Inside the colonial appearance is carried out in the high wainscotings, heavy doors, wide halls, winding stairways

Oak Hill, Pittsylvania County

A Garden Walk at Oak Hill

Box Hedges at Oak Hill

and spacious rooms. Antique furnishings and oil paintings of one Hairston generation after another further impress the idea of the length of days that is a heritage of this mansion.

Other than its situation and the appearance of the residence, there is another charm to Oak Hill. This is its old, old-time flower garden. Here Wordsworth would have been at a loss to have worked into metre the names of such a host of flowers. The winding walks, with their neatly trimmed boxwood borders, are a striking feature, but at every turn and on every side there are shrubs of every name, and in passing the blossoms our grandmothers used to love and care for peep out here and there; evergreen trees towering above all furnish shaded retreats, and a dreaminess and rest steals over one as this contact is made with so much beauty and fragrance in flora's bower. A cedar house is one attraction; a mammoth magnolia tree, raised from seed brought from Florida seventy or eighty years ago, holds attention to another point, but the grove of wild olive trees outrivals all else in interest, for it has a tradition in the supposition of having been brought from the East by a tourist in the Hairston family. The trunks of the trees and the manner of growth are similar to those of Palestine, but this resemblance is not the only thing to make them worthy of cultivation. Its resplendent lustre of fern-like foliage throughout the year and its lily of the valley-like flowers and beautiful winter berries make it a prized evergreen, as pretty and effective as any for decoration.

This olive grove, magnolia tree and winding walks and oval and square and rectangular flower beds are not all. The view from any of its terraces of the low ground stretching away right to the bank of the Dan, flowing on so slowly as if loath to leave so inviting a spot, makes for this garden an enchantment equal to its own charms. Visitors often state that its situation and arrangement make it so beautiful that it must be like the old castle gardens described or painted by novel writers.

The present Mrs. Hairston, nee Miss Jopling, of Danville, an adept in the art of entertaining, utilizes its adaptability for "garden parties" and teas in the cedar house, thus affording functions of quaint and rare appointments. As a matter of interest, if not beauty, is a pile of brick in one corner of this garden that marks the site of an old schoolhouse. Here, with the father of the present owner of Oak Hill, "went to school" William A. Stuart and General J. E. B. Stuart, the father and uncle of Honorable H. C. Stuart.

A connection with men of public life is also given to Oak Hill in being the birthplace of the mother of Honorable S. H. Wilson. Oak Hill is now an up-to-date farm, with the house supplied with all modern conveniences, a side annex having been built and hot and cold water supplied. Arrangements are being made for an electric plant to be put in to light the whole place. The outhouses and servants' quarters are well kept up, and a large, perfectly equipped dairy has been created, for Oak Hill is known as a stock farm. Its milch cows and Angus cattle, Shropshire sheep and Berkshire hogs claim attention, as well as its thoroughbred saddle horses. This live stock is well supported, for the 2,000 acres attached are in splendid cultivation. Corn yields from thirty to forty bushels per acre, while wheat figures out from ten to fifteen bushels. Large quantities of hay are also raised. The American field wire fencing gives the plantation a cared-for appearance, and in every detail about the farm Mr. Hairston, the proprietor of the place, and one of the largest landowners in Virginia, is characterized as a progressive and successful man in his line of business.

Trinity Episcopal Church, erected mostly by donations from the Hairston family, is a worthy addition to this Oak Hill estate. Regular services are held once a month, as is the custom of country churches, and a large Sunday school, composed mostly of tenants' children, meets every Sunday, with Mr. Hairston as its superintendent.

Near Oak Hill is Berry Hill, the ancestral home of the Hairstons, and is one of the most interesting of the several estates owned by various members of that family, so prominent as landholders and slave-owners before the war. Mr. Hairston, of Oak Hill, has in his possession a grant from George III.

The obsolete appearance of Berry Hill gives it distinction. It is used as a tenant's dwelling, being typically colonial in size and arrangement, and brings up the household plans of other centuries, so inadequate for modern conveniences. Berry Hill is noted as being one of the oldest places in the Garden of Eden. The Hairston burying-ground is at Berry Hill, and the graves of many generations are marked at that place.

BERRY HILL

ERRY HILL, Pittsylvania County, is one of the Colonial places of Virginia, probably the oldest place equally far inland. It was the home of the Hairston family, who originally inherited it from the Perkins', into which family the Hairstons' ancestors married. It has never been sold, but has passed down from the original grant from the King of England only by successive wills for about three hundred years, and is now the property of Mrs. Ruth Hairston Sims, who inherited it from her great-grandmother. It is located on Dan River, in Pittsylvania County, Virginia, and Rockingham County, North Carolina, and happens to be at the point where the Colonial army, under General Greene, crossed this river in his famous strategic retreat before the army of General Cornwallis after the battle of Guilford Courthouse.

After effecting the crossing of Dan River under great difficulty, General Greene camped his army on the river bank, where he prepared to, and did, offer resistance to his pursuers. The heavy rains under which this crossing was effected caused the river to rise abnormally and cover the extensive bottom lands, forcing General Greene's army to move back on the flat land. Cornwallis' forces drew up on the bluff on the right, or south, bank of Dan River, from where his artillery opened fire. The Berry Hill house, in which General Greene had taken up his headquarters, overlooked this crossing and battlefield, and in the cannonading the old outside chimney that served General Greene's room was struck but not wholly destroyed, and was later successfully repaired.

There has been some controversy as to the exact spot on Dan River at which General Greene's crossing was effected, but this was finally settled in 1896 when the unprecedented severe freshet covered the entire bottom, washing the land and exposing not only the smoked stones that had been used around the campfires of General Greene's soldiers, but the remains of some of the old revolutionary muskets, as well as bullets, bullet-moulds and lead. Incidentally, the fact that these pieces of equipment were left, would indicate that the retreat of General Greene's men to the higher flatland adjoining the bottoms was due to fire from across the river as well as to the rising water. The high water that occurred at this time evidently buried these articles, and succeeding freshets covered them deeper and deeper, until they were between three and four feet under ground. The successive layers of this covering were clearly discernible when the freshet of 1896 scoured the land away down to the original level of the date of General Greene's crossing.

It may be of interest to remark that at the time of General Greene's crossing the land on which he camped was a clover field. This fact was evidenced from the circumstance that after this three to four feet of earth was washed away the land soon became covered with clover, sprouted from the seed that had lain buried for over a century—incidentally proving that the seeds of some plants retain their vitality indefinitely if sufficiently far under the surface of the soil.

The original house was made entirely of hewed lumber, even the flooring having been made of puncheons split out of logs from the original forest. Some of these puncheons are still in place. The oldest part of the house was added to some time before the Revolutionary War. The laths were rived, and the nails used to fasten them were made one by one, by hand, in a blacksmith shop. Grass was used as a binder for the plaster. In about 1806 the so-called "new part" was added. The gable end of this part, with the outside chimney, is shown in one of the views of the north side of the house. The last addition, which is shown with the porch extending around it, was made by the present owner in 1911.

On the west side of the house is the garden, which is still surrounded by its ivy-covered stone wall. The eight beds composing this garden are each surrounded with the dwarf variety of boxwood, much of which is now over six feet high. Of this boxwood hedge there is almost a half mile. To the west of the garden adjoining it is the old Hairston family cemetery.

The summer-house is built of hewed locust and, though small, yet picturesque, is one of the older structures, though its exact age is not known. It is known, however, that about 1840 the then older members of the Hairston family were at that time speculating as to what previous ancestor had built it.

ALFRED VARLEY SIMS.

The Valley of Virginia

Serpentine Garden Wall at Folly

Folly, One of the Notable Homes in the Valley of Virginia

A Corner of the Garden at Folly

Carter Hall, the Home of the Burwells

FOLLY

OLLY, in Augusta County, is the residence of Joseph Smith Cochran. The house, now in its second century, was built by Joseph Smith, the great-grandfather of the present owner, and has been occupied by four successive generations. Following the architectural style of its day, the dwelling is of red brick with large white pillars on the front and side porches. At that time there were no railroads in the Valley, so the farm wagon was sent to Philadelphia—300 miles away—to get the finishing touches for it. The marble mantelpieces in the drawing-room and the dining-room were the first to come into the Shenandoah Valley.

Coming down to the western side of the garden and overflowing onto the lawn is the forest primeval. This piece of woods, extending for a mile, resembles a park; with its handsome oaks, hickory, chestnut, and walnut trees, free from undergrowth, it affords shady and interesting walks and drives in the summer-time, reminding one of an English estate with its extensive grounds.

Facing the house, and at the end of the avenue, is a rocky, wooded slope. In olden times this was enclosed by a high fence, and was known as the deer park. In it roamed and bounded from rock to rock twenty-odd deer. They were so gentle that they would come up to their mistress to be fed, and would lick out of her hand. Sometimes she would let down the bars and they would follow her up to the house, playing about the lawn. This deer park extended for a quarter of a mile along the Staunton and Lexington turnpike, and travelers passing by in stage-coaches and private vehicles would stop to admire the deer and watch the little fawns play on the soft moss. Finally, thoughtless people would put their dogs over the fence to watch them chase the deer, and many a beautiful animal lost its life. This so grieved their young mistress, that she begged to have the fence pulled down and let them return to their mountains.

An unique feature of the garden is a red-brick serpentine wall, extending around three sides of it. There is said to be only one other of its kind in the State, and that is the one at the University of Virginia, another English idea brought here, as if the flowers needed the protection of a brick wall to keep off cold winds. Tradition says that after a time our great-grandfather realized the folly of so much brick wall and said the place was to be called "Folly."

In this old garden roses have always flourished. Beginning with the burr rose or pink microphylla, which grew in a huge bush, the cinnamon rose, the hundred-leaf rose, the seven sisters (a climbing rose), the Persian yellow, the red Giant of Battles, the Pink daily, the Hermosa, and the Souvenir de Malmaison. On one side of the front porch, and trained up on the banisters, grew a white microphylla; on the other side a Maiden's Blush rose; and on the corner of the house climbing to the very eaves was a vigorous single pink cluster rose, called by us the Kentucky rose. We must not forget the pink damask rose, so deliciously sweet that its petals are used for pot-pourri or sprinkled in the linen closet. It is from this rose that the attar of rose perfume is made in Eastern countries. These old-time roses are now supplemented by the ramblers, which luxuriantly cover the pergola with their profusion of bloom.

The lilac and snow-ball bushes—especially one white lilac— have grown so large, they can no longer be called anything but trees, which are about fifteen feet high. Once the glory of the garden was a Persian lilac; when in bloom it was a feathery mass of rosy lavender blossoms with the most fascinating fragrance, a sight never to be forgotten! The flower border follows the graceful curves of the serpentine wall, making charming, wavy masses and sweeps of colour the entire extent of the wall. Driving up to the front gate, hollyhocks, peeping over the wall, greet one in every variety of colour. Later on in the season golden-glow extends a welcome—sunflowers, hardy asters, and cosmos following in succession.

The present chatelaine of Folly keeps up the old family traditions and finds the same joy in her garden as her predecessors; it grows and flourishes under her loving care.

We come in from the restless world to the quiet retreat of this old garden, and, as we sit beneath its grand old trees, we dream of the days of old.

Memory brings to mind many a fair young girl and brave young man wandering out in the land of romance and learning, with the birds, the first love-twitterings. They have all scattered far and near, many of them making the history of this fair land; but the enjoyment of this flower garden forever remains impressed upon their minds.

Another picture—a sad one—comes down the years. It is of the turbulent days of 1864. General Sheridan had made his terrible raid up the Shenandoah Valley and had sent General Hunter on to Lexington to burn the Military Institute. As his army passed by Folly, on a bright summer's day, the ladies were seated out under the shade of the trees, anxiously watching. A horseman was seen dashing up the avenue; he hitched his horse at the front gate and walked in. He was an officer from the Federal army, and asked for some refreshment. Mrs. Cochran sent her servant for the meagre supply on hand and, as they were sitting with their backs to the forest, they were startled by a ringing command, "Surrender!" Looking around, at the back gate, they saw mounted on his horse, a young Confederate scout. "Hold up your hands," he said to the officer, and aside to a young lady, a sister of Mrs. Cochran, he bade her lead out the officer's horse. She bravely went, but it was an ordeal, for the horse was large and spirited, and she a tiny frail little body. But through main force of will she brought the steed to the back gate. The officer mounted, and with all haste they disappeared in the woods. This daring and reckless scout was John Opie, afterwards Captain Opie. He succeeded in concealing himself and his prisoner in some cedar thickets and remained there all night, having tied the officer to his arm, lest he should drop off to sleep and his prisoner escape. The next day when the Federal army had passed on, he took him across to Waynesboro and delivered him to the Confederate Army.

In the meantime the capture had been witnessed by the passing troops and in a few minutes the lawn swarmed with soldiers. A number of them went in hot pursuit of their officer, but in vain. The soldiers said that if it were Colonel Cochran who had taken the prisoner they would burn the house and destroy everything on the place. The frightened women were called out and testified most earnestly that Colonel Cochran was away with the Gray Army, and knew nothing of the capture. No! The men would not believe them until the family Bible was brought out and all, including the servants, were made to place their hands on it and swear that it was not Colonel Cochran. One stalwart young slave, Grandison Ware, by name—he was a mulatto but looked more like an Indian warrior—stepped behind his young mistress and whispered low, "Don't you be skeered, Miss Lizzie, I done brung my axe and I'm gwine use it, too, if these Yankees do any harm." And he stood with his axe in his hand until the last blue-coat had disappeared.

The next morning as John Opie was taking his prisoner to the Confederate camp, he passed by Woodland, an adjoining estate, and seeing the young daughter of the house seated on the porch, he called, "Here, Bettie, take this officer's sword and keep it for me. If I am killed it is yours, but surviving I will return for it when the war is over." Bettie Eskridge took the sword and carried it up into the garret; she prized a plank from the floor and put the sword underneath, then carefully nailed the board back in place. There it lay undisturbed until the war was over. Captain Opie returned, got the sword and sent it North, to Captain Johnson, the captured officer, who had been on General Crook's staff. The handsome sword was engraved with his name, and "Presented by the Ladies of Philadelphia."

[332]

The old cedar tree standing by the fence could have told a tale; for in its closely clipped branches were a lot of dried beef tongues. At the very last minute they were discovered in the smokehouse, the army was in sight, and they were hurriedly pitched into the cedar tree for safe keeping. To a casual observer, they were only brown leaves drifted down from the oak tree.

When the news came that the Northern Army would pass Folly the next day, Mrs. Cochran got up in the wee sma' hours of the night, and waked her housekeeper. The two silently collected all the silver, including the service, basket and spoons, brought over from England, put it all into a wooden box and between them carried it down into the garden. They dug a hole in the soft earth of the asparagus bed and buried it. What was their joy the next morning to find it pouring down rain, thus obliterating all trace of freshly-dug earth.

These and many other old tales are brought to light only for the sake of history and to tell to our children and grandchildren. Time has so mellowed the recollections that they seem a part of a dream, but enhance the human interest of this old garden.

ANNIE COCHRAN RAWLINSON.

CARTER HALL

THERE was a time when our place-names in this country were either pure Dutch, pure French, pure Spanish or pure English, and we had not yet to tack on a German *burg* or a French *ville* to a simple English word. The little village of Millwood was named at that time, and quite properly named, as it grew up about two stone-built water-power mills set in a great wood. The land upon which the village stood (with the exception of a few freehold lots) and all the surrounding land was owned by Colonel Nathaniel Burwell, a young man from the Lower Country, as it was then called. Though he still lived at Carter's Grove, the Burwell seat on the James River, he usually brought his family to spend the summer in the cooler and more healthful climate of the Shenandoah Valley. At such times he occupied a house which still stands in Millwood today.

But in 1790 Colonel Burwell began to build a permanent home upon this large land—a holding of his in what is now the County of Clarke. The situation chosen, like that of each of the old houses hereabouts, was of necessity near a good spring, and hundreds of oaks had to be cut away for the building site and to open vistas over the surrounding country; that to the south offering a view of the Blue Ridge from each of the principal rooms of the house, and that to the east showing the mountains still nearer, and allowing one to trace the course of the Shenandoah by the white trunks of the sycamores along its banks. This cutting still left a fine body of oak and walnut timber extending from the north, through west, to the southwest of the house. Sad to say, the trees are much fewer in number today, though there are still enough to form the western border of the park.

It was under these oaks that General Pickett camped just after

Gettysburg. Under a very large black walnut tree General Jackson had his headquarters in the fall of 1862, and here his meals were brought to him by a son of Carter Hall, who still remembers seeing the General seated at a pine table reading his Bible. He also remembers the gallant Stuart as he dashed up and dismounted for a consultation with his senior officer. General Jackson had declined an invitation to make his headquarters in the house at Carter Hall upon the ground that the tramp of soldiers' boots and the constant arrival and departure of couriers would disturb the ladies.

And it was in a room that looks out on these old trees that there had died many years earlier—in 1813—a friend of Colonel Burwell's, Edmund Randolph, Aide-de-Camp to General Washington, and later Governor of Virginia, first Attorney-General of the United States and Secretary of State.

To the southeast of the house lies another little wood, left perched upon that bluff from the foot of which the great spring gushes; these trees, except for the scythe of Time, are as they have been for longer than the short century and a quarter since the house was built. It is in another part of this same bluff that there is a cave about which many legends cluster, as they do about the whole place. But there is only space to mention the fact that this cave is the real home of the ghost.

Unlike most ghosts, this one has a scientific reason for being. Often enough, even to this day, a coach may be heard to rumble up to the portico of the house and the old-fashioned folding steps may be heard bumping down as they are unfolded. It is, of course, very probable that the cave extends under the house and on to the west until it passes beneath the highway. Certain it is, that the road sounds queerly hollow at a certain point, and the unbelieving maintain that the sound of the coach is only that of a truck or a wagon passing over "the hollow place" in the highroad, and that the sound is carried by the cave to the earth under the house a quarter of a mile away.

This house that Colonel Burwell built extends, east and west, for a hundred and ninety feet—an arrangement that allows the winter sun to pour in and the summer breeze to sweep through from south to north. To the east and to the west of the main building are the offices; that on the west, besides having extra bedrooms, was also used "befo' de war" as a school-house. Here the tutor to the children of the Burwell family instructed, in addition, the young people from the neighboring estates, all of whom were cousins of one degree or another. One of the boys was William Meade, afterwards Bishop of Virginia. The building to the east of the main house afforded rooms for those servants who did not live, as the others did, at the quarters; it also contained the laundry with its flagged floor and ten-foot fireplace, its brick ovens and its crane.

Though these offices are two stories in height, the east wing of the main building has only one story, over which is a very low gable. It was in this pitch-black little space above the ceiling that the family silver was successfully hidden throughout the War Between the States—successfully hidden in spite of the fact that the place was not only near that center of fighting, the town of Winchester, but also directly on the highway between Winchester and Manassas. Time and again, it was used as the headquarters of one army or the other, General Merritt, during his stay, having slept on a sofa now standing in the hall.

Another occupancy by Union troops was more uncomfortable. This was the visit paid the house by "Blenker's Dutch." It is believed that they were not Dutch, but Germans. At any rate, they could speak no English and maintained, truly or not, that they could understand none. Unfortunately, soon after their arrival they broke into the wine cellar, got very drunk and made things unpleasant, if not actually dangerous, for members of the family, who then included Mr. George H. Burwell, first, well advanced in years and almost entirely blind, his little son, and various ladies. The harm went no further, as it happened, than frightening the

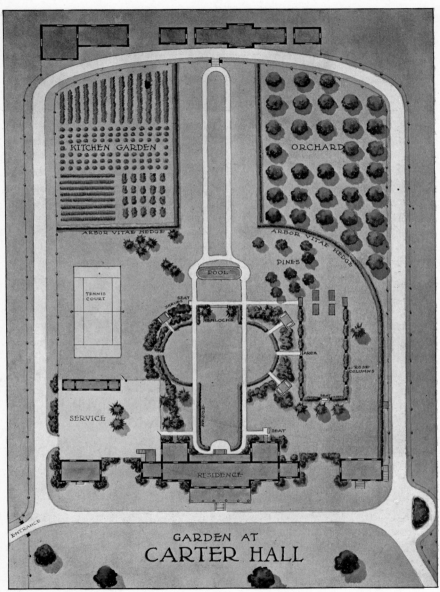

GARDEN AT
CARTER HALL

Warren H. Manning

Carter Hall—From an Old Print

ladies by much yelling, the smashing of glass and china upon the floor, and the parading through the house with certain articles of feminine apparel waving at the end of rifle and sabre. The timely arrival of a Union officer of American birth stopped all this, and a guard was stationed by him about the house to protect the family.

One other occupancy of the house by Union troops must be mentioned, because it has to do with the garden. There stands under one of the southern windows of what was then "the chamber" a very large bush, and near it grows a trumpet vine. When the soldiers arrived this time, Mrs. Burwell, from the window above, dropped into this bush a sword that had belonged to her elder son, Nat, who had been killed at the Second Battle of Manassas. Her other son, then a boy, owned some bantam hens and, as all the large poultry had been killed or carried off, the soldiers turned their attention to the bantams. Some of these little fowls ran under the bush to escape capture and the soldiers after them. Sad to say, when the pursuers emerged they had not only the bantams, but the sword, which, of course, they carried away.

This bush is one of a great many old shrubs, principally lilac and mock-orange, that are still hale and hearty. Scattered about under them and through the grass of the garden are hundreds, perhaps thousands, of daffodils, as well as a few poet's narcissus and grape hyacinths. The ancestors of these bulbs were planted long ago—no one knows just when—and, together with the shrubs and some interesting old trees, constitute what is left of the old planting, though, of course, the terracing and general outline of the garden is still the same. And it is upon this foundation that the garden is being rebuilt, little by little, the location controlling the character; for it lies north of the house and between it and a line of old stone stables. These, in the days before the railroads came, housed the particular wagons and horses used for hauling farm products to Alexandria, sixty-five miles away, and bringing back necessary supplies for the house.

Parts of the garden are much shaded by houses and trees and,

[337]

sloping as it does to the north, the tone of the design must be cool and peaceful, tending more to grass and evergreens and massing of shrubbery, than to brilliance and bloom.

It is probable that there was a flower garden here from the first occupancy of the house. But it is certain that, in 1830, Mr. Spence, a Scottish landscape gardener, was employed to embellish the existing grounds. This he did in the garden proper by grading and terracing the land into three levels, though they are no longer level today. The lowest of these, that farthest from the house and next the stone stables, is the kitchen garden. Upon the intermediate terrace is a pool and some fine old white pines which form a pleasant little grove of seven. The principal part of the flower garden lay then, as it does now, upon the highest of the three levels, and was entered through gates set in a picket fence that divided it from a little lawn next the house. In this part of the garden were most of the shrubs and all of the flowers, and here Mr. Spence set out a number of hemlocks, probably as ornamental bushes. They are now large trees, and two of them frame a small vista down the center of the garden to the pool. A number of other evergreens must have perished, though they can be remembered by persons still living and are described as having been of considerable size. Only the pines and hemlocks survive at the age of about ninety-three, which is youth itself compared to the oaks in the park.

Some work of additional improvement was done upon the garden about 1855. But then came the war and destruction. Indeed, so far as the garden was concerned, the tragic years that followed were worse than the war itself. In the seventies, Mr. George H. Burwell, first, died; his family moved away, and the place was rented. No doubt, the garden was allowed to grow as it pleased and, being on fertile ground, it grew into a jungle.

When the present owner came into possession of the property, in 1908, there were only single foot-paths through great tangled masses of shrubbery and scrub. But the trees were still there, particularly the hemlocks. The terraces, the pool, and the general out-line were also there. But wild-cherry trees, a foot in diameter, had grown up in the flower beds, and weeds and scrub were more than head-high. For some years efforts at restoration were made without professional advice. A great deal of clearing and renovating was done, but the results were not very satisfactory because of the lack of knowledge of *garden design*. Much moving was done and some planting, but the sum total was without effectiveness, because it was without a closely-knit composition. The essence of art lies in composition.

What was desired was to restore, as nearly as possible, the old general plan of the garden; to remove the picket fence and throw into the garden the little lawn next the house. It was felt that the garden plan should be symmetrical as to the north and south axis of the house, but it was in the close interrelation of its parts that difficulty was encountered. No home-made plan seemed satisfactory, so there followed much study of Humphry Repton's "The Art of Landscape Gardening," of Robinson's various fine books, of the work of Charles Eliot, and much reading of the Garden Magazine. But, at length, the conclusion was reached that professional advice must be had, both for purposes of economy and to obtain a workable, livable and beautiful result.

Very fortunately, the services of the well-known landscape designer, Mr. Warren H. Manning, of Boston, were secured. The plan that Mr. Manning made has proved most satisfactory and, though it is still far from being carried out completely, it is being built up, little by little, year by year. The problem was to utilize the basis of the old garden, bring it into closer association with the house, link up all the utilitarian parts of the place, screen out the unattractive and, in short, to combine the useful and the beautiful. In addition, the plan was to be direct and simple and permanent, as well as economical in upkeep. A difficult problem it seemed, and it is, to the untrained, but not beyond easy accomplishment by the professional. That the result is free from

[339]

labored effect may be understood from the following comment, recently heard: "I don't see any design. Just looks like two walks and a lot of bushes."

A ripening friendship with the garden and the needs of the family have determined a few modifications. It is doubtful whether the rose garden will ever be made—certainly not in the place shown in the plan. More probably the space will be thoroughly leveled for bowls, croquet and clock golf, and the west and south boundaries, formed by low retaining walls of field stone, planted with sedum, wall-flowers, and rock-cress. Probably the seats in the shrubbery will never be placed, as it has been found most pleasant to have garden chairs and tables under the pines near the lily pool. Again, it was found that the arbor vitae hedge on the second terrace did not do well under the large trees, so this part of it has been replaced by a border of cornels, viburnums and shrub roses, to which holly is being added from time to time.

Up to the present, the design has been carried out only on the first and second terraces, and some little idea of the material used must be given. In the corners, against the north side of the house, are American holly and American and Japanese mahonia, under which are ferns. Bordering the west walk, and screening the service yard, is a forsythia bank about thirty yards long, planted with viridissima and intermedia edged down with suspensa. This is now about eight feet high, and behind it are a few small flowering trees. The shrubbery backing the herbaceous border to the west is almost entirely of lilac and mock-orange, with a few red buds to break the skyline. This shrubbery is not much seen from the house in winter, and the unattractiveness of such bushes during the dormant period is not conspicuous. The shrubbery backing the other border is composed of viburnums, cornels and barberries, with some edging of stephanandra. On the terrace bank, under the pines and near the pool, are summer hydrangea, sorbaria Aitchisonii, aralia and ferns. These are interesting throughout the fall and

Winter at Carpet Hill, Washington County

winter, as is also a neighboring American Pillar rose with its red hips on an ancient cedar tree.

That part of the terrace bank lying under the hemlocks is covered with periwinkle, both giant and small. Through this, stone steps go down to the level of the pool. And in the pool, grow pink and white nymphaeas and a few aquatics especially placed there for the goldfish. Around the edges of the pool are several clumps of iris.

In bringing to life this old garden, and keeping it simple and unpretentious, an effort has been made to regain its old-time air of restfulness, livableness and charm; to make it possible for it to become more and more beautiful as time goes on.

J. T. BURWELL.

SARATOGA

I N 1772, General Daniel Morgan purchased land in what is now Clarke County, Virginia, and five years later built the house upon this estate, naming it Saratoga in honor of the second battle of Saratoga, October 19, 1777, in which he had so honorably served.

At the second battle of Saratoga a large number of Hessian prisoners had been captured by the Continental Army, and these prisoners had been sent to Winchester, not many miles distant. Among them were many skilled workmen, especially stone masons, so he employed a large number of them to build for him a house of stone, which stands today in excellent preservation.

The estate of Saratoga came into the possession of the family which now owns it through Nathaniel Burwell, who purchased it in 1809. He married Elizabeth Nelson, known as "Pretty Betsy" Nelson, of Yorktown. The place was bequeathed to Mrs. Robert Powell Page, of "The Briars," and from her passed to her son, R. Powell Page, who still owns it.

From the porch one looks down on a bold spring, the over-flow of which forms a pond sufficiently enticing to bring the ducks from far and near. Fine oaks formerly covered the slope, and a row stood in front of the house, but the last of these were de-stroyed in the storm of 1922, and now one looks across the grassy slopes where the sheep are grazing, to the Blue Ridge Mountains, which stretch as far as the eye can see.

Flowers have always bloomed here, but not in a formal garden. There were roses and shrubs in the vegetable garden at the back of the house. I can remember the servants bringing in baskets of rose leaves to scatter among the linen. The greenhouse was eighteen by twenty-five feet, heated by a brick flue which encircled

From an Old Print

Saratoga, built by General Daniel Morgan about 1777

The Garden at Saratoga

The Old Mill Pond at Saratoga

it. The blossoms, together with the tropical plants in large tubs, were very attractive. We refugeed the winter of 1862, and when the family returned the flowers were all dead and the glass broken. Since then it has been turned into the dining-room.

The flower garden was and is on the left front of the house, with two little, gnarled arbor vitae trees still keeping watch as they have for generations past.

General Lee, in June, 1863, on his march to Gettysburg, camped at the edge of the woods which stretch to the county road about a quarter of a mile away, and General Stonewall Jackson, before this time, in October, 1862, had made his camp in the glen.

R. POWELL PAGE.

ANNEFIELD

I N 1790, Matthew Page, Esq., of Broadneck, Hanover County, Virginia, came to Clarke County and took possession of a tract of twenty-two hundred and eighty acres inherited by him. He began the erection of a beautiful stone house that year, which he named Annefield, after his wife, a sister of Bishop Meade. Mrs. Page was a lover of flowers and a garden was laid out for her in the rear of the residence.

Part of the estate, with the house, was purchased by Thomas Nelson Carter, of Pampatike, in 1840, and his wife, "Sweet Anne Page," who was also a great lover of flowers, made many additions to the garden.

The central part was reserved for flowers only. Surrounding this on three sides and separated by a lilac walk formed by a double row of lilacs twelve feet in height, plantings of box-bushes, that are now fifteen feet high, were made. Syringa and mock-orange were also set out, as well as arbor vitae. One of these, near the entrance to the garden, was pronounced by Professor Charles S. Sargeant, of the Boston Arboretum, as the finest specimen he had ever seen.

After Mr. Carter's death in 1866, the estate was bought by his son-in-law, Robert H. Renshaw, and again a flower lover wielded the fortunes of the Annefield gardens. Mrs. Renshaw was Annie Wickham, of Hickory Hill. In speaking of her second home, she said:

"I have rarely seen such lilac bushes or such blooms. The big clumps of syringa, mock-orange and snowball had taken entire possession, and I fear I slashed too heavily. The syringa by the main walk as you enter was the most wonderful I ever saw. It climbed up into the evergreens and seemed dazzlingly white when in bloom. Its stamens and pistils were pure white. I carried many things to Annefield—cowslips, violets, snowdrops, daffodils, and dwarf iris—from Hickory Hill, and such growth I never imagined." Mrs. Renshaw planted the box-hedge on the front of the garden. She introduced many perennials and the old hundred-leaf rose.

In 1900, the estate passed into the hands of Edward G. Butler, and, as good fortune would have it, Mrs. Butler was an enthusiastic garden lover, so the work of development and improvement was carried on. At the end of the main walk, a hedge of white lilacs, extending back to an orchard of small fruits, was planted on both sides. This hedge is now bordered by purple iris. The main walks she edged with boxwood and to the already fine collection she added numerous bulbs, peonies, and Japanese anemones. A small fountain, surrounded by native ferns, a bird bath, and an old sun-dial were next placed in the garden.

The rose reigned as Queen of Annefield and many new beds were laid out under the direction of Mrs. Butler. Records of the first bloom in her garden in 1909 show that the Gruss an Teplitz was the earliest; May 22nd, old hundred-leaf; May 29th, Paul Neyron; May 29th, Frau Karl Druschki, and May 30th, Mrs. John Lang.

The approaches to the garden were developed by Mrs. Butler and many new shrubs planted. On one side, the hardy hydrangea bloomed at the same time as the crimson rambler, which was trained over the end of the old laundry and presented a beautiful effect. On the opposite side, bridal wreath spirea was massed against the kitchen most charmingly.

In 1921, William Bell Watkins became the owner of Annefield, and Mrs. Watkins is taking a keen interest in maintaining the old garden.

We often think we are planting flowers and roses for our own enjoyment, but how true are the sentiments in the poem:

[345]

MY NEIGHBOR'S ROSES

"The rose is red upon my neighbor's vine
Are owned by him, but they are also mine.
His was the cost and his the labor, too,
But mine, as well as his, the joy their loveliness to view.

"They bloom for me and are for me as fair
As for the man who gives them all his care,
Thus I am rich, because a good man grew
A rose-clad vine for all his neighbors' view.

"I know from this that others plant for me,
And what they own, my joy may also be;
So why be selfish, when so much that's fine
Is grown for you upon your neighbor's vine."

EDWARD G. BUTLER.

Annefield, Clarke County

Flowers and Hedges in the Annefield Garden

Beyond the Mountains

PLAN OF GARDEN AT "THE MEADOWS"

Gay Robertson Blackford

The Meadows, Washington County

THE MEADOWS

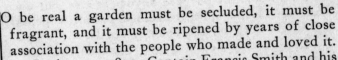

O be real a garden must be secluded, it must be fragrant, and it must be ripened by years of close association with the people who made and loved it.

In the year 1817, Captain Francis Smith and his wife bought an estate of three thousand acres near the town of Abingdon, Virginia, and named it Mary's Meadows in honor of their only child, Mary, who was then only five years old. The Bloor Crown Derby china made for them at this time has an S, with "Mary's Meadows" in gold, ornamenting each piece. The name of the place was changed later to "The Meadows."

When Mary Smith married Wyndham Robertson, at one time Governor of Virginia, the family lived in Richmond, only returning to their place in the mountains for part of the year. After the War Between the States, however, the Robertsons made The Meadows their permanent home.

The grandson of Francis Smith, Captain Frank S. Robertson, inherited "The Meadows." As a student at the University in 1861 he was one of the "Sons of Liberty" that aided in the capture of Harper's Ferry after the John Brown raid. After Virginia seceded he was lieutenant of engineers on General J. E. B. Stuart's staff until General Stuart was killed. Then he served as engineer officer on the staff of General W. H. F. Lee until the close of the war in 1865. Since that time he has made "The Meadows" his home.

The Meadows is far from Tidewater Virginia; twenty-three hundred feet above sea level, and in the midst of the Alleghany Mountains. It was almost on the frontier in the year 1819, when the big garden, covering two acres, was planned and most of its trees and shrubs planted. This garden was surrounded by a paling fence, seven or eight feet high, with each paling sharpened like an arrowhead. The entire fence was whitewashed every spring, when the walks were freshly filled with tan-bark. I have never seen tan-bark used for this purpose anywhere else, but even months later it made an elastic, quickly-drained path for pedestrians when mud was ankle deep on the country roads.

The garden sloped gently towards the east and towards the house. The upper half was laid out in formal beds with a broad walk dividing it in equal parts. Down the center of this walk were apple trees, whose branches spread out on either side forming a long, shady aisle in the heat of summer. This was broken only in the center by an arbor of seven sister roses—red, pink, and white roses borne on the same cluster. From this arbor four other walks radiated to the corner beds of turf which seemed to rivet the plan together. Groups of cedar trees, whose branches swept the grass, were planted diagonally opposite in these corner beds. To balance them was a gigantic blackheart cherry tree, and a service berry tree.

Besides these corner beds there were eight larger beds, formed by the intersection of the walks, each one grass-edged and bordered by flowers. The flower borders were not supposed to interfere with the good, homely vegetables for which the beds were designed, and which were laboriously spaded and raked every spring.

Perhaps in the days before 1861, when the trees and shrubs were pruned carefully and when the servants were sufficient in number to furnish competent gardeners, the vegetables were able to hold their own against the encroachment of the flowers which bordered their domain. But since that time lilies of the valley have spread in many thick mats; lilacs and snowballs have waved their plumes far over the potatoes; tulips and jonquils have associated freely with the onions, while white violets have spread under the cedar trees, over the grass and among the currant bushes, until they appear, when in full bloom, like a light fall of snow, and the passing breeze comes laden with their perfume. In the seventies pink hyacinths grew thickly along the borders, and often in the grass in the corner beds. One of the servants, "Uncle Stephen," an autocratic white-haired old negro butler, announced as an undisputed fact that Easter eggs boiled with a kettle full of pink hyacinths would absorb the lovely colour of the latter. The children of that day were only too ready to believe him and gathered masses of the fragrant blossoms for the purpose. When the eggs remained hopelessly white "Uncle Stephen" was not in the least embarrassed, but turned upon the old fat cook "Aunt Esther" and accused her bitterly of conjuring them.

The lower half of the garden was divided into rectangular beds, and most of the small fruits, damsons, plums, currants, and gooseberries, bordered them, while Indian peaches, wax-heart cherries, Siberian crab-apples and golden-yellow pears were planted in the long beds nearer the eastern fence.

On the slope of the hill, and covering the space of two beds, variety was given by a circle of cedar trees with low-growing branches, that completely surrounded a large, octagonal summerhouse. The old variety of sweet pea—a hardy vine bearing clusters of magenta-colored blossoms, struggled to keep a place with the climbing roses tangled in the lattice. Sidney Lanier's lines always seemed to express the feeling given by entering this covert sweet-scented with cedar and violets:

> "O, braided dusk of the trees and woven shades of the vine,
> While the riotous noonday sun of the June-day long did shine;
> Ye held me fast in your heart and I held you fast in mine."

For five generations the children of The Meadows have played in the old garden. In summer, hiding in the thick shrubbery, pulling the flowers with a lavish hand and eating the fruit, ripe and unripe. In winter, when the shrubs were half-buried by snow and all paths obliterated, they have felt the spell of the garden even more, perhaps. The exquisite stillness, the flash of a redbird and the scurry of a little molly-cottontail seeking shelter, are apt to sink deep into a child's memory.

As grown women many of these children have lingered long at the summer-house, when the moon was full, and there was one spot in the pleached walk, where a young woman of the first generation reared at The Meadows told her granddaughter that "love had first been whispered in her ears." And she was barely sixteen, but read early Victorian literature: Scott, Miss Austen and Mrs. Sherwood!

The little garden at The Meadows is to the left of the house, as the old garden is to the right, and was planned a few years later. It was laid out in four square beds, with beds at either end shaped to conform to the road which curved here to the stables. The box-hedge to the east was a screen for the woodyard, very thick and over eight feet in height. The other box-hedges, which outlined the beds, were trimmed severely every spring; but, in spite of this, they reached a height of thirty or thirty-three inches and a breadth of twenty-five, encroaching far over the space left for the walks. The sun-dial, with the name "F. Smith" and the date, 1821, cut sharply into the slate, was placed where the paths intersected.

It is this garden that later generations have filled with old-fashioned pinks, daily roses, geraniums, heliotropes, and hardy annuals. The bleeding heart and deep-red peonies were crowded in with phlox and mignonette; but, on a sultry afternoon in August, the smell of the box mingles with and dominates them all.

GAY ROBERTSON BLACKFORD.

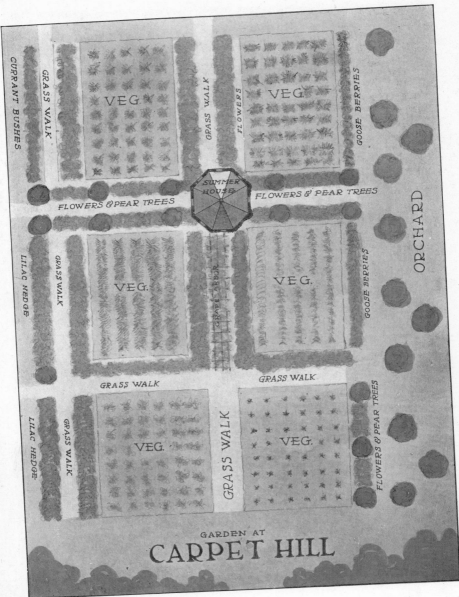

GARDEN AT
CARPET HILL

CARPET HILL

SITUATED in the southwest corner of Virginia, in Washington County, is the quaint old town of Abingdon, headquarters of the first pioneers west of the Appalachian Range. It was founded in 1788, and is said to be the first town incorporated west of the Alleghanies. Here Daniel Boone spent many months, and Parson Cummings lived most of his life as a forceful and fearless exponent of the Presbyterian Church Militant. He used to preach with his loaded rifle in the pulpit by him in case of an attack from Indians.

One of the most notable places in this section was Carpet Hill, the White homestead and the center of the gatherings of that family for more than a hundred years. The name originated from the mantle of blue grass that covered the slope and was heavily carpeted with violets in the spring. The first owner of this estate was William Young Conn, who bequeathed it in turn to his nephew, William Young Conn White. The latter married Margaret Jane Greenway and the two left many descendants, a few of whom still live in Abingdon.

From the house, situated on the top of a gentle rise, could be seen nearly thirty miles distant, Mount Rogers and White Top Mountain, the two highest points in Virginia, White Top with an altitude of five thousand six hundred and seventy-eight feet above the sea level.

The driveway leading up to the residence was bordered on either side with stately Norway pines, which in the spring became the home of countless blackbirds, robins and orioles. The walks beneath these trees were covered with tan bark, the color of which was effective against the dark green of the pines. The turfed circle

[353]

directly in front of the house had a walk through the center and large elm trees on either side of the driveway around it.

The dwelling, a large rambling frame structure, seemed to have been designed for comfort rather than architectural beauty. It was surrounded with wonderful old trees—elm, maple and walnut. Most conspicuous of all, however, at Carpet Hill, were the beautiful grounds which comprise four acres, including lawns and flower garden, in addition to a large acreage in vegetable garden, orchards and meadow land. On two sides of the lawn was a hedge of purple lilac, which was beautiful and fragrant when covered with its countless spring blossoms, but decorative for two seasons with its compact foliage. The flower garden to the right of the house was outlined with boxwood about thirty inches high. The borders were filled with hyacinths, pinks, snapdragons, hollyhocks, a wealth of yellow day lilies, and many other old-fashioned flowers. Outside the large circle were beds of lilies of the valley, and two smaller circles of roses. Sweet violets formed a carpet underneath the trees near the garden, and many spring bulbs bloomed under still other trees.

Some distance to the left were the orchards and the vegetable garden. The squares for the latter, each of which comprised one-third of an acre, were outlined by flower borders which showed a profusion of bloom. Conspicuous among the flowers were hollyhocks, peonies and Harrison roses. Here, during the War Between the States, the family silver service was buried for safe keeping. Three crops of potatoes were raised over it before any one dared unearth it!

The vegetable garden was oblong in shape and had grass walks throughout. In the center was a large summer-house covered with wistaria and trumpet vine, and some of the borders outlining the squares were wide enough to have dwarf pear trees planted among the peonies. The orderly rows of currant and gooseberry bushes were also here, as well as a huge strawberry bed and picturesque grape arbor. The orchard proper was very large and contained many varieties of fruit, though apple and peach trees were in the majority.

Recently Carpet Hill was sold to the Presbyterian Church as the site for Stonewall Jackson College.

MARGARET WHITE WILMER.

Date Due